Sovietology, Rationality, Nationality

SOVIETOLOGY, RATIONALITY, NATIONALITY

Coming to Grips with Nationalism in the USSR

ALEXANDER J. MOTYL

COLUMBIA UNIVERSITY PRESS
New York

Columbia University Press
New York   Oxford
Copyright © 1990 Columbia University Press
All rights reserved

Library of Congress Cataloging-in-Publication Data
Motyl, Alexander J.
Sovietology, rationality, nationality :
coming to grips with nationalism in the USSR
Alexander J. Motyl.
p.   cm.
Includes bibliographical references (p.   ) and index.
ISBN 0-231-07326-7
1. Nationalism—Soviet Union.
2. Soviet Union—Politics and government—1945–
3. Soviet Union—Ethnic relations.
4. Soviet Union—Politics and government—1917–
5. Sovietologists.
I. Title.
DK288.M68   1990
947.684—dc20
90-2032
CIP

To Irene and Katya

Contents

Contents

II. WITH NATIONALISM IN THE USSR

Preface

It's moving behind me! Under me! Hollow. Lis-
ten! It's all hollow down there!
— Georg Buchner, *Woyzeck*

This book is the product of nagging doubts about the intellectual legitimacy of Sovietology, a firm belief that only theory can transform
Sovietology into a stimulating vocation, and the no less firm suspicion that even theory cannot resolve the epistemological dilemmas
of the social sciences. This book, then, is as much about studying the
Soviet Union as it is about the Soviet Union. Indeed, I am persuaded
that there is no substantive difference between these two pursuits: as
it is impossible to gain unmediated access to the reality of the Soviet
Union, Sovietologists can never escape the intellectual webs of their
own profession. In a very real sense, therefore, to study the Soviet
Union is to study the study of the Soviet Union.

As the last sentence suggests, this book is self-reflective, perhaps
to a degree that some readers will find alienating. It also rests on
doubt, admittedly uncertain ground on which to build a scholarly
edifice, but there is, I submit, no alternative to such self-reflection
and doubt—except for an unwarranted and even more alienating

dogmatism—especially if one consciously embarks on the theoretical quest that this manuscript represents. It is impossible to produce a piece of theoretical Sovietology without enquiring into the nature both of theory and of Sovietology as well as into the relationship—or, more precisely, the lack thereof—between the two. But there is a problem here. As thoroughly as I believe that theory is indispensable and Sovietology is salutary, I cannot rid myself of the gnawing feeling of unease—of ambivalence, of hesitancy, of hollowness—regarding the ultimate validity of both theory and Sovietology. To abandon these pursuits is impossible; to engage in them, however, appears only slightly less so. *Die Sache*, to quote the Viennese, *ist hoffnungslos, aber nicht ernst*. My sentiments exactly.

This book offers no answers. Least of all does it offer the definitive answer to the questions it raises. All it does, or can claim to have done, is to suggest how answers might be sought. The answers I seek concern the phenomenon of nationalism in the USSR. There are several excellent reasons for using this issue to marry Sovietology with theory. First, as the quintessence of the Soviet nationality question, nationalism forces Sovietology to abandon its traditional Russocentrism, to venture beyond the Kremlin's thick walls, and to compare republics and ethnic groups. In a word, nationalism forces Sovietology to be comparative and thus willy-nilly to flirt with theory.[1] Second, nationalism provides a conceptually rich and politically significant lens for viewing the Soviet political system in general and the vicissitudes of the Soviet state in particular. Finally, by being—as Gail Stokes rightly puts it—undeveloped theoretically, the study of nationalism forces Sovietology to grapple with just those theoretical and conceptual issues that, I believe, it must confront in order to remain a viable intellectual pursuit.[2]

This is, then, a study not just of nationalism, but of the way in which a critical investigation of nationalism can enrich our theoretical understanding of the Soviet Union. To facilitate the reader's confrontation with the text, I have divided it into two parts: the first deals largely with questions of theory, the second provides an interpretation of nationalism in the USSR in light of theory. Inevitably, I begin in the introduction with a discussion of Sovietology, of its achievements, but especially of its failings, the most serious of which is, I suggest, its excessively atheoretical nature. A call to theory necessitates a discussion of theory in general and of its pitfalls, the task of chapter 1. Thereupon, I proceed in chapter 2 to a particular theory, that of rational choice, which, despite its many inherent faults, I find to be of use in understanding nationalist collective action. Chapter 3 follows this train of thought by defining nationalism—as a political ideal that associates nations with their own states—and suggesting how nationalist collective action may be understood in light of collective choice theory. Chapter 4 examines how collective action can emerge, persist, and achieve its goals under maximally constraining conditions that are radically different from those on which rational choice theory is based. Chapters 5 and 6 complete the theoretical discussion of part I by investigating both why the "imperfectly totalitarian" Soviet state is prone to nationalist assaults and also how such assaults might take place in particular circumstances of systemic change.

Part II hopes to alleviate the impatience of empirically inquisitive readers. Chapters 7 through 10 examine the nationalist activity of incipient states in 1917–1921 (chapter 7), of the guerrilla struggles of the Basmachi, Daghestanis, Ukrainians, and Balts (chapter 8), of Émigrés (chapter 9), and of dissidents (chapter 10). Chapter 11 investigates the topic that is currently so much in vogue within Sovietology—Russian nationalism—and concludes that there is little substance, but much significance, to the myth. Gorbachev's nationality problems and the manner in which his policies have directly contributed to the emergence of an unprecedented phenomenon in Soviet history, nationalist mass movements, in the Baltic republics, Armenia, and elsewhere, receive treatment in chapter 12. The book closes the circle with a speculative discussion of another possible breakdown—this time, not of Sovietology, but of the Soviet state.

There is only one more thing to say. The last line of Dick Howard's introduction to a recent work puts it nicely: "It remains to acknowledge my debts, and to begin again."[3] Beginning again is difficult; acknowledging debts is not. A topical issue and a lifelong interest for me, nationalism was also the subject matter of a class I taught in 1987 on the lectures and discussions of which the first draft of this book was based. A later draft was subjected to the critical comments of another class in 1989. Needless to say, students are especially adept at seeing through intellectual facades and mine, fortunately, were no exception. To all of them I am grateful. In addition, I thank Donna Bahry, John Battle, Seweryn Bialer, Douglas Chalmers, Charles Furtado, Robert Jervis, Rebecca Kook, Andrew Nathan, Myroslaw Prokop, Dennis Quinn, Joseph Rothschild, Laurie Salitan, Jonathan Sanders, Irwin Selnick, Thomas Sherlock, Jack Snyder, Mark von Hagen, Edward Walker, Kate Wittenberg, and several anonymous reviewers for their invaluable comments, insightful criticisms, and heartfelt encouragement. Finally, my thanks to the International Research and Exchanges Board and the W. Averell Harriman Institute for Advanced Study of the Soviet Union for the financial assistance that enabled me to travel to the Soviet Union in 1988 and 1989. It goes without saying that all inaccuracies, flights of fancy, ambiguities, and the like are my responsibility. Readers are welcome to judge such inadequacies severely. I trust, however, that they will view more kindly the inability of the book, the final draft of which was completed in early 1990, to anticipate all the momentous changes that are sure to have occurred in the months that followed.

As I suggested above, this book is about many things—about Sovietology, about theory, about nationalism, and about the USSR. Some scholars are sure to find my approach infuriating. To them I commend Mao Zedong's slogan: "Let a hundred flowers bloom! Let a hundred schools of thought contend!" Other scholars will, I hope, find my approach compelling. To them: *Na zdorov'e!*

A.J.M.
February 1990
New York City

Sovietology, Rationality, Nationality

Introduction: The Dilemmas of Sovietology

Water, water everywhere, Nor any drop to drink.
— Samuel Taylor Coleridge

Ironically, although most contemporary Sovietologists are political scientists, most of the Sovietology they practice is not contemporary political science.[1] Instead, contemporary Sovietology represents an awkward amalgam of data collection, policy analysis, and journalism that is as divorced from scholarship as sense impressions are from theory. The reasons for Sovietology's underdevelopment involve far more than some ingrained incapacity to make a great leap forward to comparative communist studies or, even, to comparative politics.[2] Although the profession's proud refusal to acknowledge theory—and thereby to appreciate that its continued viability as a scholarly pursuit depends on its reintegration into political science—is a large part of the problem, no less important are the outside pressures that force Sovietology onto a Procrustean bed of their own making. As I shall argue, it is the influence of the university, the state, and the media that confronts Sovietology with dilemmas that it is, alas, unequipped to resolve in its own favor.

1

Introduction

A brief excursion into the past reveals that things were not always this way. A theoretical gap between the study of the Soviet political system and political science emerged only in the aftermath of World War II. In the interwar years, the two fields occupied different conceptual worlds, rarely intersected, and were therefore incommensurable. While students of government were comparing legislatures, executives, judiciaries, and constitutions, most students of Russia remained devoted to their primary vocations—history, language, and literature. For a variety of reasons, many of which were associated with the postwar rise to superpower status of both the United States and the Soviet Union and the attendant need for policy-relevant information about various parts of the contested world, Sovietology and political science experienced both a takeoff and a rapprochement in the 1940s and 1950s. As soon as their trajectories approached each other, however, a theoretical time lag became evident. The first inclination of postwar Sovietology was to appropriate the formal-legal baggage of prewar political science and fill it with totalitarian content. Then, in the 1960s and 1970s, as totalitarianism went into eclipse, Sovietologists belatedly discovered the concepts that political scientists had utilized in the 1950s, among them systems, interest groups, modernization, and political culture.[3]

More recently, just as many of their colleagues in political science were choosing postbehavioral approaches, students of Soviet domestic politics have embraced behavioralism. At present, tragically, this process of playing catch-up has largely ceased. Joseph LaPalombara summed up the problem succinctly in 1975: "It is instructive, I believe, that so few of the textbooks on the Soviet Union or Eastern Europe are self-consciously theoretical or represent even modest efforts at theoretical innovation . . . Soviet and East European textbooks do not advance our theoretical understanding very far. Moreover, they are obviously time-lagged in the sense of not reflecting some of the methodologically and conceptually richer work on these political systems which has emerged in recent years."[4]

Not only, as Lawrence C. Mayer suggests, has behavioral and postbehavioral political science continued to develop conceptually and theoretically, while Sovietology has not, but also, with the notable exception of the best work of the best Sovietologists, the outstanding feature of the current "era of stagnation" is that Sovietology's version of behavioralism has become a routinized pursuit of numbers.[5] After all, when Roger E. Kanet defined behavioralism in 1971 as a "concentration on both the observable political actions of individuals and groups and the psychological processes which influence these actions," with the expectation that the "result will be the identification of uniformities in political behavior that can be expressed in generalizations or theories with explanatory or predictive power," his goal was not merely to collect data but to generate theory.[6] In contrast, the ossified behavioralism that has come to replace the original behavioralist vision has halted Sovietology's admirable effort to keep pace with theory; by largely abandoning the quest for theory, it has also deprived its practitioners of the capacity to explain what they purport to describe. At its worst, this deification of data, or what I call routine behavioralism, has reduced much of Sovietology to a form of political journalism.

The essence of routine behavioralism is what Jacques Barzun perhaps too caustically refers to as "doing research"—the vigorous pursuit of data on the faulty rationale that, as only data can generate knowledge, more data must translate into more knowledge.[7] Doing research thus has the advantage of being its own justification: where there is a gap in the data—and there is always some gap waiting to be filled, say, the development of working-class protest songs in Orel in 1910—doing research is always ready to spring in. Clearly, an approach such as this is a boundless enterprise. Because the number of Soviet oblasts, raions, cities, towns, villages, status groups, nationalities, and classes runs into the thousands, and because each of these has a long and colorful history, the permutations and combinations for doing research verge on the infinite.

Unlike its routinization of behavioralism, which, as I argue below, is largely the result of factors external to it, Sovietology's halting theoretical development stems from its own professional and intellectual history. An important part of that history is pedagogical. Frederic J. Fleron, Jr. noted long ago that the vast majority of Sovietologists have never had—and, it seems, still lack—an adequate grounding in political science theories, concepts, and methods.[8] For the most part, Sovietologists are trained as area specialists with only minimal exposure to the larger intellectual universe they inhabit. Such pedagogical inclinations are understandable, both historically, in view of Sovietology's roots in Russian studies, and academically, in view of the peculiar intellectual challenges that the magnitude and complexity of the USSR represent. Given these limitations, it makes some practical sense for Sovietologists to eschew cosmic questions and focus their energies on the mystery that is wrapped in an enigma. To be sure, the mystery no longer appears so mysterious nor the enigma

3

so enigmatic as Sovietologists once thought them to be; nonetheless, students of the Soviet Union continue to confront the kinds of empirical obstacles that have long since been surmounted in other fields.

The theoretical distance between Sovietology and political science is also a function of the dissimilar intellectual development of the two fields. Contemporary political science has its origins in the self-styled scientific study of more or less mundane American and West European political institutions and legal documents.[9] Sovietology, on the other hand, has traversed a politically divisive path beginning with the impassioned debates surrounding the establishment, consolidation, and growth of the USSR's brand of socialism in the 1920s and 1930s. The Russian Revolution and Stalinism opened vistas of liberation for some—especially the "political pilgrims" described by Paul Hollander[10]—and confirmed the worst fears of others. In so ideologically polarized an atmosphere, early students of the Soviet Union often were political activists, journalists, and exiles: people directly involved or concerned with Russia, such as Sidney and Beatrice Webb, Malcolm Muggeridge, W. H. Chamberlin, Louis Fischer, Leon Trotsky, and Boris Nicolaevsky. Of course, the degree to which nonscholars dominated the field in the interwar period was also symptomatic of the adolescent state of Russian studies. Scholars, journals, and research programs were few, to a large extent concentrated in Germany, while their understanding of the USSR was often woefully inadequate. Walter Laqueur conveys nicely the then prevailing intellectual environment:

> The Russian experts, almost without exception, under-rated the importance of the revolutionary movement. After the revolution their difficulties increased; they had now to deal with a country that in many essential respects had undergone radical change. Little had been known in the West about Russian socialism and communism; the comments on this subject published by German and British experts during the first world war must be read to be believed; one of them translated "Trudoviki" as "The Weary Ones" (this was not intended as a joke); another introduced Trotsky as a Ukrainian nationalist. In Germany, Staehlin, the leading historian of modern Russia, interpreted the Bolshevik revolution and subsequent events in terms of religious philosophy; Pares, after prolonged and bitter opposition to Lenin's Russia, came to display as much enthusiasm for Stalin's Russia as he had for Nikolai II's; in America Samuel Harper, the only

4

American scholar to deal with contemporary Russian affairs, began by declaring the Sisson papers, that crudest of anti-Bolshevik forgeries, authentic, and twenty years later described the big purge as a necessary stage on Russia's road to constitutional government.[11]

We may smile at Laqueur's list of foibles, but we can also sympathize with early scholars, who confronted the young Soviet state's frightening newness and awesome impenetrability. Even the Stalinist apologetics of the Webbs appear comprehensible, though no less reprehensible,[12] in view of capitalism's seeming collapse, fascism's seeming triumph, and the GPU's demonstrated ability to manipulate even its sworn enemies.[13]

Pedagogical imperatives and historical origins may account for Sovietology's perpetual lagging behind political science, but they do little to explain its current obsession with facts. To be sure, the radical rejection of totalitarianism as a conceptual mode pushed Sovietology away from theory; to a certain degree it may be argued that, in ridding themselves of the bath water, Sovietologists also threw out the baby. That is, in rejecting the so-called totalitarian model, Sovietologists also rejected its healthy theoretical pretensions, indeed, theory as a whole.[14] But this argument cannot make sense either of the routinization of behavioralism or of its tenacity. Understanding so intellectually counterproductive a turn in Sovietology's theoretical development requires that we look outside of Sovietology at three thoroughly familiar institutions, the university, the state, and the media. As we shall see, changes within these institutions combined with changes in Sovietology's theoretical inclinations to produce a confluence of powerful forces that encouraged the routinization by Sovietologists of behavioralism.

To its credit, the university's influence has been least pernicious. Nevertheless, although it aspires to promote genuine scholarship, the manner in which the university did so in the 1970s and 1980s became increasingly conducive to routine behavioralism. Unfortunately, market dynamics explain this trend best. With too many academics bidding for too few openings—the result of rapid educational expansion in the 1950s and 1960s and steady decline in the years thereafter—universities responded by raising the price of tenured slots. Simply put, the number of publications required for tenure rose dramatically.[15] Fearful that quantity might prove to be incompatible with quality, scholars resolved to overcome the pitfalls of the "publish or

5

perish" syndrome by adopting the logic described below by David Ricci:

> Thus political scientists who aspire to advance professionally try to make scholarly contributions that can quickly earn them recognition. And within large organizations, one way of getting ahead is to invent something not yet being provided by any other member of the organization. It follows, in scholarly communities, that one tends to develop research projects which break ground that others have not tilled before, to stake out small areas of inquiry that other scholars have not yet invaded and conquered for their own. There is, therefore, a propensity constantly to refashion the scope of political science into smaller and smaller realms of expertise, so that some scholars can quickly stand forth as patently competent with regard to subjects that other scholars have somehow overlooked.[16]

Not only does a strategy such as this not sacrifice scholarly integrity to the pressures of the academic marketplace, but it is also interesting to the scholar engaged in unearthing past or present intrigues or collating statistics, very publishable, and—no small consideration—virtually above criticism. The structure of incentives is such that rational scholars are hardpressed not to subordinate their theoretical inclinations, if such there be, to the environmental constraints that encourage and reward routine behavioralism.

While the university's disequilibrated relationship with scholars is slated to improve in the 1990s, as the supply of academic positions more closely approaches the demand for them, no such favorable forecast can be made for the state's willful exploitation of Sovietology. Unfortunately, if unavoidably, all states have traditionally drawn on the advice, information, and expertise of patriotically inclined students of Russia who, for a variety of reasons, have been more than willing to provide it. Writes Laqueur of Sovietology's early years: "It is no exaggeration to say that all leading students of Russia at the time advised their governments in an official or unofficial capacity, though not all rose as high in rank as their erstwhile colleague Thomas Garrigue Masaryk."[17] After World War II, the relationship between Sovietologists and the state changed dramatically. The transformation of the United States and the Soviet Union into superpowers, together with Stalin's expansion into Eastern Europe, placed the USSR at the top of Western political agendas. Moreover, the growth of extensive intelligence apparatuses translated into a permanent demand for data on and analysis of the Soviet Union.[18] Understandably, the demand for Sovietologists grew apace, and vast sums of government money were poured into universities in the 1950s and 1960s. After slackening during the detente years, investments picked up in the 1980s, promising once again to convert Sovietology into a growth industry.[19]

The state's growing interest in Sovietology has encouraged routine behavioralism in two ways. First and most obviously, the state attempts to set Sovietology's research agenda. Thus, the bourgeoning need for policy-relevant data and the availability of funds for pursuing it have created strong incentives for Sovietologists to roll up their theoretical sleeves and just do research. More pernicious perhaps is the state's encouragement of policy analysis. Notwithstanding its importance for democratic government, policy analysis inclines Sovietologists to eschew the very stuff of theory—big questions with no simple answers. Stephen F. Cohen goes even further, arguing that "policy-oriented scholarship, which is designed for political consumption, can impose serious intellectual constraints. Complex political history must be rummaged for present-day relevance; 'lessons' and predictions become primary objectives. Such scholarship thus tends to grow narrow in focus and politically palatable in findings."[20] In a word, such scholarship is driven toward routine behavioralism.

The second way in which the state encourages routine behavioralism is far more subtle. The state confronts Sovietologists with a moral dilemma that is most easily resolved by flight into routine behavioralism. The state politicizes Sovietology, thus compelling it to consider what its attitude toward the Soviet Union should be: approbation or condemnation. A choice would have to be made in any circumstances, but state affiliation forces the issue. Although outward neutrality is generally the visage most scholars prefer to assume, it is unavailable to Sovietologists because of the nature of the beast they study. Naturally, one can love the peoples, languages, and cultures of the USSR, but it is difficult not to experience a sense of tragedy, if not shame or revulsion, with respect to the Soviet authorities.[21] Sovietologists cannot avoid confronting and living with the fact of the Soviet state's long-lasting involvement in terroristic practices and crimes against humanity. For most of their history, as even official Soviets increasingly admit, the "empire" was indeed "evil."[22] Tengiz Abuladze's film, *Repentance,* like the independent social organization *Memorial*, should persuade us that morality is an unavoidable question for everyone connected with the USSR.[23]

Introduction

For all its excesses, the totalitarian "model" provided solid moral ground on which to stand: all totalitarian dictatorships were alike— be they Hitler's or Stalin's—and all deserved moral condemnation. The demise of totalitarianism left a moral vacuum at precisely the time that the state's interest in Sovietology assumed increasingly institutionalized forms. A moral response was imperative, yet exceedingly difficult, because behavioralism was premised on presumed scientific objectivity and *Wertfreiheit*. Not surprisingly, behaviorally inclined Sovietologists have sought refuge from this moral dilemma in routine behavioralism: when facts can speak for themselves, scholars are absolved from speaking out.

A less distressing Soviet system—a realistic possibility if *perestroika* proves successful—will help resolve part of the moral dilemma, but it will not dispel the state's interest in the Soviet Union and therefore in Sovietology. As long as the United States continues to share a world with a nuclear-armed Soviet Union, intelligence and policy analysis will be necessary, regardless of the condition of Soviet-American relations: indeed, the end of the Cold War may only increase the state's reliance on Sovietology for the data and policy advice it needs to steer in wholly uncharted waters. As the state's drafting of Sovietologists is unlikely to diminish anytime in the foreseeable future, the incentive to engage in routine behavioralism will remain strong.

The third source of Sovietology's infatuation with routine behavioralism is the media. The pervasiveness, influence, and prominence of the media—the result of the Vietnam War and the Watergate scandal—their fascination with impressions and images, and their disdain for history, complexity, and depth impress themselves on Sovietology, encouraging scholars to describe bits and pieces of events or processes, to seek out the unusual and exotic, and to avoid systematization, historical perspective, and comparison. Sovietology is especially prone to succumb to the media's blandishments as a result of its politicization by and close relationship with the state: just as the modern media tend to set much of the political agenda for the state, so, too, a politicized Sovietology is forced to draw on the media for much of its own agenda. Consequently, the media structure Sovietological perceptions of the Soviet Union as much as, if not more than, the profession's own attempts to penetrate the black box—and they are likely to continue to do so for some time. Recent events in the USSR and the way the media have brought them to our attention tend to confirm this interpretation. As any Soviet nationality expert can testify, there was always abundant evidence to suggest that the nationality question was critically important to the Soviet state.[24] And yet, it was only after the media discovered the non-Russians in 1987–1989 that mainstream Sovietology finally acknowledged that there was something to see in what its own subfield had been looking at for so many years.

In sum, Sovietology's prospects for escaping routine behavioralism's tentacles appear to be bleak. Besides the discipline's pedagogically and historically based theoretical underdevelopment, the state, the media, and, although decreasingly, the university will continue to reward doing research and to discourage, if not quite penalize, theory. Worse still, the information explosion brought about by *glasnost* is likely to impel Sovietologists to burrow even deeper into the mountains of data that Gorbachev, like the Prophet, has caused to come to them.[25] Because the system of environmental incentives and disincentives is unlikely to change dramatically, transcending routine behavioralism and reintegrating Sovietology into political science can be accomplished only by a collective act of will on the part of Sovietologists. As the pressure to publish or perish subsides, pedagogical reform—a field of endeavor wholly within Sovietologists' control—becomes imperative. Training in theory must come to supplement Soviet area studies: there is simply no other way to break routine behavioralism's stranglehold on the profession. Whether or not voluntarism will suffice to overcome the institutional sources of routine behavioralism and to restructure Sovietology is, of course, another question and one that I am inclined to answer negatively.

One thing, however, is quite clear. If Sovietology does *not* abandon routine behavioralism, it will eventually approach an intellectual dead end. In a word, Sovietology will face a "crisis"—a condition on the successful resolution of which Sovietology's survival as a scholarly discipline will depend.[26] The reason for so dire an outlook is that routine behavioralism is, quite simply, untenable. A nontheoretical Sovietology is not only impossible but also self-defeating. For better or for worse theory represents a form of intellectual endeavor that cannot be rejected, overcome, avoided, or ignored.

Whether we want it to or not, theory envelops Sovietology in two related ways. First and basically, theory suffuses the language and concepts we use, because no words exist independent of the variety of meanings attached to them. To use terms is to accept or to reject their connotations. To string terms together is to enmesh them in a connotational web that bears close resemblance to a theory. Indeed,

Introduction

Vernon Van Dyke defines a theory as nothing more complicated than a "series of concepts which are interrelated in a series of propositions."[27] To define a concept—to state what it is and what it is not—is to distinguish it from related concepts and thus to suggest how sets of concepts "hang together." As I argue in chapter 1, such hanging together of concepts is rudimentary theory.

Facts, to be sure, are as necessary for understanding as theory, but routine behavioralism has two of them quite wrong. Contrary to what routine behavioralism would have us believe, intelligent appraisals of events, personages, and developments cannot possibly demand possession of all the data on these subjects, as the quantity of data that impinge on anything or anybody is literally infinite. The problem of data is doubly difficult in Soviet studies because of the relative paucity and unreliability of pre–1987 sources. Except for the Smolensk materials and a smattering of other documents, until recently scholars had no direct and unimpeded access to Soviet archives. In addition, for most of the USSR's history, Soviet evidence, like reflections in Socrates' parable of the cave, was several times removed from the purportedly objective reality: it was filtered, screened, selected, and even misrepresented. Reliability of data is still a problem, and even Soviet scholars question the accuracy of their country's statistics. Scholarly techniques can help overcome these limitations, but they should not blind us to the fact that, by applying such techniques, we—like Heisenberg—are interpreting data as well as distorting them. Indeed, if we were to be as rigorous about evidence as routine behavioralists insist, we would have to throw up our hands in despair and abandon the profession.

Paucity and unreliablity of data, while severe limitations on behavioral Sovietology, are not really the central issue. More important is the second fact that routine behavioralism, like its more worthy predecessor, behavioralism, obscures: that understanding actually precedes the collection of data and the ordering of facts. Stephen Gaukroger's comments on this subject are worth quoting at some length:

> Observation is simply not possible without some kind of conceptualisation. When we observe something we observe it as being something of a certain kind. This identification is dependent on some conceptualisation, some classification. No demonstrative reference could be successful unless there were some shared principles of classification. For example, if I am asked to count

the number of items in a certain area, I must restrict myself to a single system of classification—if I am counting the number of things in a room I cannot include a chair, wood, legs, molecules and oblong shapes in the same total. Thus observation is necessarily a conceptual activity insofar as it involves a system of classification and criteria by which things of a certain class are identified as being such, and thereby differentiated from other things of that class and from things of other classes.[28]

If, then, we want to understand Soviet politics, where do we start? By carefully reading the New York City telephone directory? The Moscow directory? Of course not. Why? Because our theoretical inclinations tell us that these are nonfacts and that we should be looking for real facts in, say, *Pravda* or *Izvestiia*. How do we know that a speech by Gorbachev is a fact we should consider? Because we are already working on the assumption that general secretaries are important personalities in the Soviet political process.

Conceptualization not only precedes observation but also imparts meaning to the things observed. Indeed, data—or the jumbled and random impressions that our senses are exposed to—become meaningful facts only after they have been interpreted; that is, raw data acquire meaning only if a theoretical or conceptual framework assigns meaning and "factness" to them. Contrary to Francis Bacon and the inductivists, data do not generate understanding; indeed, on their own, sense impressions are quite meaningless. As Sir Karl Popper has persuasively argued, we cannot logically make the jump from individual observations or from individual pieces of data to some generalization. No matter how many white swans we see, we cannot conclude that all swans are white. As generalizations, therefore, theories cannot be derived from data, even if we were to assume—incorrectly, I believe—that data can be apprehended without the mediation of human perception.[29]

Consider Alexander Rabinowitch's excellent book, *The Bolsheviks Come to Power*, which wants "to let the facts speak for themselves."[30] In violation of Popper's injunction, Rabinowitch jumps to the conclusion that Lenin's supporters were not the unified, disciplined Leninist party of traditional studies, because the existence of many disorganized Bolsheviks must mean that the Bolsheviks were disorganized. Even if this conclusion, which is a classic example of the composition fallacy, were justified, critics could rightfully reply that the Bolsheviks were still better unified, better disciplined, and more Leninist

11

than any other party, and that that fact made the difference.[31] At the root of the disagreement is not the data—after all, both Rabinowitch and his critics "know" what happened in 1917—or the methodological error Rabinowitch commits, but the interpretive framework used by both sides of the debate. Revisionists, such as Rabinowitch, implicitly prefer to think that elites play an incidental role in revolutions; traditionalists hold that elites are indispensable. Which perspective is correct is beside the point for my argument: namely, that only a perspective *of some kind* can give meaning to data.

The following example may also be illustrative. Generally speaking, if we want to show that some local phenomenon, X, is systemically significant, we do one of two things. Either we claim that some other phenomenon, which is demonstrably significant, is somehow a measure of X, or we claim that localized evidence for X is generalizable. As an example of the first technique, we might argue—as Sheila Fitzpatrick does—that widespread social mobility in the USSR during the 1930s, which is demonstrable, is evidence of regime support, which is harder to get at.[32] As an example of the second technique, we might argue, as J. Arch Getty does, that data from the Smolensk Archive are meaningful for other oblasts as well.[33] Strictly speaking, both conclusions are insupportable. Evidence of social mobility is evidence of social mobility and nothing else; Smolensk data may tell us a lot about Smolensk, but not, *ipso facto*, about Tashkent or Kiev oblasts. Here again the jump from specific evidence to generalizations requires some preexisting theoretical perspective on why social mobility translates into systemic support and why Smolensk is just a typical Soviet oblast. In the latter case, of course, even a persuasive conceptual connection cannot establish an unbreakable empirical tie between Smolensk data and the entire USSR. Clifford Geertz's judgement is even harsher:

> The Jonesville-is-America writ small (or America-is-Jonesville writ large) fallacy is so obviously one that the only thing that needs explanation is how people have managed to believe it and expected others to believe it. The notion that one can find the essence of national societies, civilizations, great religions, or whatever summed up and simplified in so-called "typical" small towns and villages is palpable nonsense. What one finds in small towns and villages is (alas) small-town or village life.[34]

Routine behavioralism is, therefore, manifestly counterproductive. It may dovetail nicely with the research inclinations of Sovietologists, but it decidedly does not contribute to or enhance our understanding of the Soviet Union, and it will do so even less as Soviet data increase in number and reliability. Instead, routine behavioralism drives Sovietology into a self-delusionary and self-destructive position. On the one hand, Sovietology's infatuation with trees can never help it apprehend the forest; on the other hand, its rejection of theory pushes it relentlessly into the role of servant of the state or, heaven forbid, of the media. To be incapable of grasping the USSR is bad enough; to lose one's scholarly soul to a wholly unworthy temptor is, I suggest, intolerable. If so, there is no alternative to marrying Sovietology to theory, to reintegrating it into political science.

— I —

COMING TO GRIPS

— 1 —

The Labyrinth of Theory

Difficilis facilis, iucundus acerbus es idem
Nec tecum possum vivere, nec sine te.
— Catullus

Were the quest for theory like the ascent to a Platonic source of light, all political scientists long since would have become theorists. Alas, finding a philosopher king may be impossible, not because there are no candidates for the role, but because there are too many, and all of them have equally good credentials. The conundrum is all too familiar: theoretically curious political scientists turn to their colleagues in philosophy for the answers, only to discover that they, too, disagree violently. And if the forms elude even those who claim to know them best, then what are mere political scientists to do? Far too many scholars fall into despondence, abandon their theoretical ambitions, and immerse themselves in area studies. There is another, somewhat more hopeful, response. If the multiplicity of philosopher kings is regarded as an inevitable epistemological condition of the social sciences, then it permits us to seek guidance from all quarters and undertake the upward journey on our own, as completely auton-

17

omous—though, admittedly, thoroughly terrified—agents. It is a condition of which Immanuel Kant would have been proud.

What, then, does theoretical enlightenment entail? Let us start our ascent by considering three definitions of theory.[1] Giovanni Sartori defines it as a "body of systematically related generalizations of explanatory value."[2] George Caspar Homans says that a "theory consists of a cluster of deductive systems."[3] Johan Galtung's definition is the most formal: "A *theory*, T, is a structure (H, I) where H is a set of hypotheses and I is a relation in H called 'implication' or 'deducibility' so that H is weakly connected by I."[4] The terminology is different, but all three definitions suggest that theories are coherent sets of logically related statements that purport to explain something. Grand, middle-range, and low-level theories differ not in their degree of logical coherence or explanatory structure, but in the level of generalization at which their explanations aim. Thus, to take an example, although theories of mass movements are grander than theories of particular kinds of mass movements, which in turn are grander than low-level theories of particular mass movements—all are theories.

How, then, are theories structured and how do they explain what they claim to explain? Stephen Gaukroger dissects theories—or "explanatory structures," as he calls them—into four intimately related, mutually dependent, and equally important parts. Explanatory structures, according to Gaukroger, consist of an ontology, "that primary structured set of kinds of entity in terms of which explanations can be given in that discourse," or what other scholars call axioms, principles, or assumptions; a "domain of evidence," which is the "set of those phenomena which could confirm, establish or refute purported explanations"; a system of concepts that link "the ontology of a discourse to its evidential domain" and which are "peculiar to that discourse"; and a "proof structure which circumscribes the class of valid and invalid consequences and derivation relations which may hold between any statements in the discourse."[5]

Ontologies are intuitively derived premises that form what Imre Lakatos calls the "hard core" of a theory.[6] They cannot be proven; they are neither right nor wrong, correct or incorrect: they simply are taken for granted.[7] The parallel postulate in geometry, which asserts that only one line going through some point can be parallel to another line, is a typical example of such an unprovable assumption. A similar assumption in political science might be that human beings are selfish, altruistic, rational, irrational, and so on. Naturally, the assumptions that constitute an ontology should not be an arbitrarily arranged hodge-podge. Instead, as Sir Karl Popper notes, the "system of axioms must be free from contradiction, . . . independent, i.e., it must not contain any axiom deducible from the remaining axioms," and sufficient and necessary for the "deduction of all statements belonging to the theory which is to be axiomatized."[8]

The second and third parts of theories consist of concepts and the evidential domain within which we expect the theory to hold. Sartori defines *concept* as "the basic unit of thinking. It can be said that we have a concept of A (or of A-ness) when we are able to distinguish A from whatever is not-A."[9] Walter Carlsnaes agrees: concepts "are not linguistic expressions or classifications but abstract constructions pointed to or symbolized by terms or expressions." A concept conveys an "abstract property shared by some substances and not by others."[10] It follows from both definitions that poorly defined concepts can but result in unfocused thinking. But poorly defined concepts have this unfortunate consequence only because lack of definitional precision precludes binding concepts to the ontological foundations of the theory. As definitional precision is possible only on the basis of the axioms, assumptions, and premises underlying a theory, lack of precision necessarily results in a thoroughly disjointed, indeed an incoherent, theory. No less important, however, evidential domains are to concepts as concepts are to ontologies. The conceptual framework underpinning a theory generates those facts that the theory will count as relevant evidence and eliminates problematic data from consideration as evidence by treating them as nonfacts. As I argued in the introduction, theory chooses the facts it wants, and it does so by means of the exclusionary power of its concepts. Gaukroger's claim, that "a physical phenomenon is such if and only if it is the referent of a concept specifying what 'physical phenomena' are,"[11] gets to the heart of the incestuous relationship between concepts and evidence.

Finally, proof structures combine the elements of a theory into a coherent and meaningful whole by providing them with internal logical consistency and by determining, in Gaukroger's words, "what kinds of inference are valid and under what conditions." Such a structure "provides the constraints on the formal relations between the concepts of a discourse, and hence on the statements produced in that discourse."[12] Most important for our purposes, proof structures detail the "initial conditions"—x, y, z—that must be present for a theory—

If A, then B—to hold.[13] Without specification of these conditions, theories will always hover above the empirical domains they claim to
address.

What should strike us immediately in considering these four elements is that they are not slapped together in a haphazard way. Quite
the contrary, if a theory is well crafted, its elements will fit tightly
because they will have been chosen, modified, and adjusted to fit
tightly. But if well-crafted theories are human constructs that can
explain only what they purport to explain, then it is impossible to
tell whether or not social scientists paint bull's-eyes around gun shots
or actually shoot at the targets. Galtung's proposition—"*If the hypothesis fits, then it fits;* and if the degree of confirmation is maxi-
mum, then so much the better"[14]—goes still further, even suggesting
that, contrary to our expectations, the better a theory, the *less* susceptible it is to refutation. Thomas Spragens takes the argument to
its logical conclusion, by speaking of the "inescapable ultimate circularity of all human thought—a circularity which can be repressed
only by confining inquiry to proximate questions and denying the
dependence of these proximate questions upon irreducible presup-
positions . . . " Indeed, Spragens finds that "because epistemology
is inherently reflexive—that is, it is thought about thought, to the
point of infinite regress—it can finally rest only upon self-confessed
circularity which will be 'paradoxical' or upon an affirmation of certainty which will be dogmatic. There are no other alternatives." Although Spragens suggests that the "choice between these two ultimate paradigms must itself be a matter of personal judgment," he
prefers the "former alternative, self-confessed paradox . . . because
it incorporates and accepts its own contingency. As Robert Merton
has suggested, this justification of knowledge resembles Munchhausen's feat of extricating himself from a swamp by pulling on his own
whiskers. But the alternative resembles standing on thin air, a tenuous basis for laughing at Munchhausen's efforts."[15]

To acknowledge the validity of Spragens' circularity thesis, or what
W. V. Quine calls "holism,"[16] is to accept several far-reaching epistemological positions. First, the truth value and meaning of theoretical statements have no sense outside of some theory. Because we
cannot apprehend the world in a manner that is unmediated by men-
tal processes, truth and meaning are immanent qualities of theoretical understanding and have no independent ontological reality of their
own.[17] Second, because the specific meaning of given concepts is contingent on the theoretical framework of which the concepts are an

organic part, concepts can never have only one divinely ordained meaning. Indeed, Quine and his interpreter Paul A. Roth go so far as to argue that there is "no objective basis that uniquely settles questions concerning what a given utterance means."[18] As translation is indeterminate, we can never quite fathom "what the native said." Third, despite our certainty that an objective world exists, there can be no philosophical certainty that what we purport to observe is, in fact, what is. Thus, the facts that we claim as evidence for or against a theory are facts and are therefore evidence only because the theory acknowledges them as such. Lest this seem to be a recipe for anarchy, it is important to keep in mind that the data that enter the pool of potentially usable evidence acquire factness as a result not of individual whim, but of an intersubjective consensus that is formed on the basis of a little understood interaction between commonly held theoretical frameworks and the objective world.[19] And fourth, because facts are inextricably bound to intuitively derived conceptual frameworks, the fact-value distinction necessarily breaks down and normative considerations automatically become an integral part of all social science theorizing.[20]

If we accept these positions—and I stress that there is no law telling us to do so—we may be inclined to draw additional theoretical consequences. The least controversial such consequence concerns the explanation-interpretation dispute. Adherents of explanation, whose work is variously referred to as empiricist, positivist, and scientistic, claim that the social sciences should utilize the methods of the natural sciences. Supporters of interpretation reject the natural sciences as their *Vorbild*. As an ideal type, explanation looks at many cases by comparing only certain salient variables largely without reference to the concrete environmental and historical conditions that molded those features or to the entities into which they are developing. Interpretation, on the other hand, focuses on specific units of analysis and attempts to understand the actors involved in terms of the entire concatenation of factors embedded in the life of some society or country. Galtung only slightly overdraws the difference between these two ideal types by suggesting that explanation deals with space and interpretation with time.[21]

Holism breaks down any hard and fast distinction between these two approaches. By bridging the distance between subjective perceptions and objective facts, holism undermines positivism's pretensions to the status of a hard science. And by emptying concepts of any one given meaning, circularity explodes interpretation's hopes of attaining a genuine *Verstehen* of foreign thought systems, one that would be untainted by our own perceptual inclinations. In this sense, Jack Snyder's effort at reconciling the two approaches, although admirable, can be criticized for being premised on the view that they are, after all, distinct.[22] Far more in line with Quine, Roth, and Spragens is Douglas Chalmers, who argues that explanation and interpretation are not only complementary, but actually two sides of one coin: "Theory in the social sciences is clearly not one or the other. It is not a pure model of the sort of theory found in the natural sciences, nor is it purely a matter of understanding or interpretation. The social sciences appear to be the arena in which explanation and interpretation come together."[23] Such "interpretive frameworks" combine elements of natural science with interpretive historical methods and values in a manner that, willy-nilly, appears to inform the theoretical perspectives of both those who insist on explanation and those who prefer interpretation.

The second, more disturbing consequence of circularity and holism is, as Chalmers suggests, that political science and politics, just like facts and values, definitely overlap.[24] At some level, political science agendas are political agendas, and it would be self-delusionary to pretend otherwise. Naturally, as Spragens points out, political science and politics are not identical: "The old disjunction between thought and action may have been overdrawn at times, but it remains true that a commitment to a theoretical paradigm in the service of truth is not the same as a commitment to a partisan program in the service of particular political goals." Although "political science obviously has bearing upon political action" and "men act upon the basis of what they believe reality to be," the point is that "no finite political act can legitimately claim the sanction of political science, first, because of the ineluctable element of contingency within scientific knowledge itself and, second, because of the equally inescapable slippage between the judgment that such-and-such is true and the judgment that thus-and-so should be done, even where the normative component of truth is recognized."[25] Although we cannot escape Mannheim's paradox, we can strive to construct our theories in a manner that, while inevitably ideological in his sense, continues to differentiate between politically inspired constructs and political programs.

Third, and most distressing perhaps, theoretical holism and conceptual contingency force us to the conclusion that theoretical pluralism, or "theoretical anarchism" in Paul Feyerabend's words, is an inescapable condition of the social sciences.[26] That is, it is perfectly normal—and not an aberration caused by the truculence of social scientists—that there should be many competing theories of reality. There is no one correct theory, and to think otherwise is to engage in what Chalmers calls totalitarian thinking.[27] Once we accept this proposition, however, we are forced to realize that, other things being equal, there can be no intrinsically theoretical reason for accepting or not accepting, developing or not developing any one well-crafted theoretical framework as opposed to another. The choice is ours, and making it appears to require a leap of faith—which is to say that our choice of theories, interpretive frameworks, theoretical discourses, and the like is contingent on ourselves: on our value orientations, political beliefs, research interests, and institutional affiliations.

Theoretical pluralism—or, for that matter, theoretical anarchism—is decidedly not the same as anarchy and rampant relativism. There are very sensible criteria for distinguishing better theories from worse ones, so that not every imaginable theoretical framework need be taken equally seriously by scholars. The first, most obvious, and probably most important such criterion, one that I intimated above, is that the parts of a theory must fit. We can judge axioms and concepts for internal consistency, clarity, and parsimony. We can also ask whether ontologies, concepts, and evidential domains cohere as they should for a theory to be well crafted. Of course, although such tests will separate the wheat from the chaff, they will not enable us to differentiate among several well-constructed theories.

A second criterion for evaluating theories is that they actually explain what they claim to be able to explain. It seems indisputable that theories that generally pass tests should be retained, while those that consistently fail should be discarded. But how are we to falsify theories? Many social scientists believe that they confront theories with objective facts: we may dismiss this approach for being at odds with the view of facts expressed above.[28] Far more relevant is the argument of Ernst Nagel and Popper, who believe that "basic statements" or "experimental laws" about reality, which are derived from other, commonly accepted theories and therefore serve as conventions, may be used as measuring rods.[29] There is much to be said for this view, but, as even the inductively inclined Galtung concludes, "it is difficult to falsify a theory; even if it looks easy according to *modus tollens*," which is the essence of Nagel and Popper's scheme.[30] The tight fit between ontology, concepts, domain of evidence, and proof structure will always make it possible to save a Popperian theory by going up or down its edifice and making internally consistent adjustments within any or all of its levels in a manner spelled out nicely by Quine:

> Any statement can be held true come what may, if we make drastic enough adjustments elsewhere in the system. Even a statement very close to the [experiential] periphery can be held true in the face of recalcitrant experience by pleading hallucination or by amending certain statements of the kind called logical laws. Conversely, by the same token, no statement is immune to revision. Revision even of the logical law of the excluded middle has been proposed as a means of simplifying quantum mechanics; and what difference is there in principle between such a shift and the shift whereby Kepler superseded Ptolemy, or Einstein, Newton, or Darwin, Aristotle?[31]

Although Quine may be right to suggest that all but the most incompetent kind of theories will resist the falsification Nagel and Popper envision, the process of saving a theory by absorbing recalcitrant evidence via changes in concepts, proof structure, axioms, or evidential domain may so complicate the theory as to undermine its fit— our first criterion for evaluating theories—and, thus, to make it vulnerable to attack by Occam's Razor. Lakatos makes just this point when he argues that research programs should be considered degenerative, and therefore worse, if changes in the "soft core" of concepts, hypotheses, and so on outweigh the additional empirical content that they—the changes—can account for.

In his own, non-Popperian approach to falsification, Lakatos insists that

> a scientific theory T [is] falsified if and only if another theory T' has been proposed with the following characteristics: (1) T' has excess empirical content over T: that is, it predicts *novel* facts, that is, facts improbable in the light of, or even forbidden by, T; (2) T' explains the previous success of T, that is, all the unrefuted content of T is contained (within the limits of observational error) in the content of T'; and (3) some of the excess content of T' is corroborated.[32]

Strictly speaking, according to Lakatos, theories are not so much tested as their empirical contents are compared. The procedure seems reasonable, but, as with Popper's version of falsification, the verdict on Lakatos' is mixed. It is easy to argue that, other things being equal, a theory the empirical content of which is greater than that of another theory ($n + 1$ as opposed to n) must be judged preferable. Difficulties arise when we drop the *ceteris paribus* clause and compare two theories with even slightly different ontologies, conceptual frameworks, and evidential domains: holism suggests that such theories are incommensurable. Although Lakatos' advice is helpful in eliminating contenders within larger theoretical families, it does not tell us how to resolve the competition among several well-crafted theories with different paradigmatic foundations.

Evidently, fit and falsification can only reduce the number of candidates for theoretical status, whereas those theories that fit tightly and resist falsification—and we know from Quine's underdetermination thesis that there always will be such theories[33]—must be judged equally sturdy and strong competitors. How, then, do we account for the fact that some theories rise, others fall, and still others are ignored? What accounts for the Kuhnian-like paradigm changes so characteristic of the social sciences in general and of political science in particular? As with Sovietology, contextual reasons, and not intratheoretical ones, appear to play a decisive role.[34] Most important perhaps, the value at any time of a theory seems to be a function of its acceptance or rejection by the community of scholars at large. "Theories," writes Chalmers, "and in particular, interpretive frameworks are tested in debate and not in the laboratory or through statistical analysis."[35] In a word, the popularity or unpopularity of good theories is determined by the value orientations of the scholars who judge them. For instance, it is difficult to explain the immense popularity of Theda Skocpol's theoretically vulnerable work, *States and Social Revolutions*, without reference to her skillful utilization of "the state" at a time when all political scientists appear to be "bringing the concept back in."[36]

Although a value-based procedure such as this obviously has certain safeguards built into it—the integrity of one's colleagues, their multitude, their different perspectives and values, and their competence, all of which militate against facile acceptance or rejection of some fashionable notion—it also opens a Pandora's box of potential, and sometimes very real, dangers. We need not accept Antonio Gramsci's notion of cultural hegemony to understand that scholarly consensus can often be a deadly thing. With regard to Sovietology, for example, both the totalitarian paradigm of the 1950s and the far more deeply entrenched totalitarianism-bashing of the 1970s and 1980s have stultified the field and prevented a multiplicity of views from arising—not because ideological hegemony necessarily suppresses alternative viewpoints in some quasi-coercive manner, but primarily because it excludes certain intellectual options from consideration by scholars and citizens alike.[37] Peter Bachrach and Morton Baratz's term, "nondecisions," refers to just that: the field of possible intellectual and political endeavor that is defined *a priori* as uninteresting or wrong.[38]

The above view suggests that the circulation of social science theories is probably a function of four factors. First is the way in which generational conflict and the tenure process interact. Junior scholars question given assumptions because they are junior and because the "publish or perish" syndrome demands a certain degree of originality; their perspectives become accepted as the conventional wisdom once they assume positions of influence in the academic world; in turn, their children question their hegemony, rediscover their grandparents, and so the cycle continues.[39]

Second, and no less important, the political, socioeconomic, and cultural environment—as mediated by the media—directly affects scholars' perceptions of the topicality, meaningfulness, and utility of theories. Marxism, for example, seems more compelling during times of intense group conflict, as in the 1960s; the pluralist framework appears to work better in times of social peace, as in the 1950s. The modernization approach foundered in the 1960s, when democracies were breaking down in all parts of the world, and seemed far more compelling in the 1980s, when numerous transitions to democracy occurred in rapidly modernizing countries.[40]

Third, political inclinations clearly do matter. Theories that address inconvenient questions and provide unpalatable answers tend to be ignored, while those that confirm political expectations tend to be accepted. When political pluralism is the norm within a scholarly community, such tendencies are not necessarily disturbing. They become so only if ideological hegemony maintains and theoretical challengers are discarded merely for being politically aberrant. The reasons for the emergence and persistence of ideological hegemony need not concern us here, but they appear to be related to generational change, perceptions of relevance, and, last but not least, the political environment in general and the academy's status position in it and relationship with it in particular.

Finally, I venture to suggest that the leading theories will tend to be the theories of the leading scholars. Just as Karl Marx argued that the "ruling ideas are the ideas of the ruling class,"[41] so, too, we may expect that the views, ideas, and theories of those scholars who occupy powerful or influential positions within the scholarly community and/or in the world at large will tend to be accorded greatest respectability and be subjected to the most gingerly of criticism. The obverse of this proposition is that the theories of less influential scholars will be most susceptible to exaggerated criticism by colleagues seeking to protect their academic flanks from possible rivals.

Our theoretical excursion is complete, and it has important methodological implications for Sovietology. The first is that Sovietologists should disabuse themselves of the totalitarian mentality they so decry in their object of study and accept the existence of a plurality of politically inspired perspectives on Soviet politics. Because all well-crafted theories are valid interpretations of Soviet reality, Sovietologists must understand that no one framework dare ever dominate the field. Just as the earlier hegemony of totalitarianism was counterproductive, so, too, the present aversion to anything that smacks of totalitarianism is surely misguided, especially when scholars of Anthony Giddens' calibre can write—in 1987 no less!—that they "consider Friedrich's concept of totalitarianism to be accurate and useful."[42]

A corollary of this conclusion is that policy advice is probably a self-defeating undertaking. Because no truth is true outside of some theoretical framework, theoretically sensitive scholars cannot provide policy makers with "objective" analysis of the sort that policy makers claim to want. The question of what states should do can be answered only provisionally: everything depends on the premises and concepts that one employs to provide an answer. We cannot suggest a line if all we can do is move in circles. And as there is no view the correctness of which is independent of the implicit or explicit theory one employs to find it, states and scholars and, for that matter, the media and scholars have little to say to each other—unless, of course, scholars have special political programs that they wish to pursue.

Although theoretical anarchism should be a liberating scholarly condition, it has the potential to create anarchy in Sovietology by reinforcing its atheoretical pretensions. To avoid this possibility, it is necessary that Sovietology adopt polemical restraint, conceptual self-discipline, and comparative vision—a tall order, if there ever was one. Fundamentally, accepting that theories, politics, and values are inextricably related means acknowledging the inevitability of passionate debate and, therefore, of the absolute necessity of civility. The ongoing controversy over the 1930s is a case in point. Revisionist social historians are not just proffering what they consider to be a more realistic view of the Soviet Union; they are also challenging the strongly felt values of generations of scholars and nonscholars. From the perspective of their detractors, the revisionists are doing nothing less than whitewashing Stalin and his crimes by declaring that no one was responsible for much that went on in the 1930s and 1940s and that these events, be they the famine of 1932–1933 or the Great Terror, were not so terrible as traditionalists and survivors insist they were. Revisionists may or may not be right, but they should understand that, from the traditionalist perspective, their arguments are the moral equivalent of attempts at denying the Holocaust. As a result, the traditionalist-revisionist controversy is inevitably passionate, because it is fundamentally moral. Because there is no escaping this dilemma, it behooves all scholars to refrain from mudslinging and to realize what issues are ultimately at stake.[43]

One way of acquiring greater civility is to pay closer attention to Sartori's insistence on conceptual clarity. Much confusion and infighting could be avoided if theoretically disinclined Sovietologists were to be more careful about the concepts they employ, wittingly or unwittingly. Indeed, I submit that most Sovietological debates only appear to involve differences of opinion: in reality, what is most often involved is radically different intensions and extensions of common terms. Conceptual clarity not only enhances intersubjectivity and understanding, but is also a precondition of intelligent debate. Sloppy concepts reflect sloppy thinking, and both are incompatible with intelligent theorizing, which, as I argued in the introduction, should be the ultimate object of Sovietology in the first place.[44]

Finally, comparison is critical as a control on flights of the Sovietological imagination. To quote C. Wright Mills: "Comparisons are required in order to understand what may be the essential conditions of whatever we are trying to understand, whether forms of slavery or specific meanings of crime, types of family or peasant communities or collective farms. We must observe whatever we are interested in under a variety of circumstances. Otherwise we are limited to flat description"—or, I would add, to undisciplined theorizing.[45] Comparison entails going outside the Soviet experience, thereby extending one's evidential domain and sharpening one's concepts. Without comparison, Sovietology will not only remain trapped in routine behavioralism, but it will be very difficult for it to accept and live with a theoretically plural world. Fortunately, unlike most other area specialists, Sovietologists can take a shortcut to comparison and, thus, to disciplined theory via the nationality question, the study of which represents comparative politics *par excellence*. Incorporating the non-Russians into Soviet studies would not only expand the field's empirical scope, but also transform what I have elsewhere termed "Sovietology in one country" into genuine political science.[46]

Naturally, my conclusions can resolve neither the theoretical dilemmas faced by the social sciences nor the existential dilemmas of Sovietology. All they can do is suggest what I believe to be a creative, challenging, and frightfully uncertain way of engaging in scholarship, while retaining one's sense of values and political commitments. That is, political science and Sovietology should draw on the Muses of art and science for inspiration, take a deep breath, and hope for the best. Catullus' predicament is inescapable.

— 2 —

Rationality, Resources, and the State

Cogito, ergo sum.
— René Descartes

For better or for worse, rational actor theory is currently sweeping the political science field. Its supporters hail it as the answer to the woes of the social sciences; its detractors decry it as the latest academic fashion. I agree with both: rational actor theory is, well, not bad. It is relatively well crafted, but, as its deconstruction suggests, like all theories it can pretend neither to have seized the entire world nor to be without serious internal problems.[1] Nevertheless, rational actor theory *is* useful, especially in the form of its *alter ego*, collective choice theory, as it provides us with a versatile theoretical instrument for dealing with collective action in general and nationalism, as a form of collective action or as individual choice, in particular.

The rational actor literature is enormous, and it would be foolhardy to suggest that the theories that have been spun and the definitions that have been proffered can easily be summarized. In general, however, the literature roughly may be divided into two camps, one opting for rigorous criteria, the other softening them considerably. All rational choice theorists agree that the crux of the problem is the relationship between means and ends. Given that individuals possess certain preferences (values, goals) that, to quote Robin M. Williams, do "make a difference" and are not "epiphenomenal,"[2] most scholars argue that rationality consists in choosing the means that satisfy them most efficiently: the greatest satisfaction at the least cost.[3] Theorists differ as to what this simple principle means in practice. Some insist on complete rationality. "Rationality," as Robert E. Goodin puts it, "does not consist solely in the *attempt* to tailor means to ends because, of course, one might get the means-ends calculation wrong. Someone who consistently does this would be said to be trying to be rational but failing. A rational man is, therefore, one who chooses means which not only seem to him but which also are in fact best suited to his ends."[4] Others weaken the requirement and suggest that what Herbert Simon calls "bounded rationality" suffices: that is, in view of, first, the human incapacity to absorb all available information, second, the theoretical and practical impossibility of attaining perfect knowledge, and, third, the unquestioned existence of a multiplicity of beliefs, values, and norms, it is pointless to insist on so stringent a requirement as complete rationality.[5] Rather, human beings should be considered as they presumably are, and not as some Platonic form of rationality would have us believe them to be.

Although there are problems with both perspectives—not the least of which is their misguided insistence that axioms approximate observable reality—the latter strikes me as being more consistent internally and more fruitful theoretically. Those who insist on a standard of rigorous rationality face two insurmountable problems. The first involves the fact that, if perfect knowledge truly is impossible for the rational actors being studied, then surely it is just as, if not more, impossible of attainment by those doing the studying. This objection is not new, of course, having been raised as a criticism of Utilitarianism and consequentialism a long time ago. If we cannot calculate all the possible effects of a particular action—and we cannot, even with computers (Soviet difficulties with planning millions of prices and millions of products are surely testimony to that)—then we can never be certain that some particular course of action truly was the very best. Searching for complete rationality is like searching for the first cause: the task is impossible.

Even more subversive of the rigorous rationality perspective, however, is the fact that it inescapably relegates the vast majority of human beings to a greater or lesser degree of irrationality, thus producing two consequences. The first is to undermine the central axiom of rational choice theory, that human beings are indeed rational. If some are, while most are not, then there is little reason to call it a theory of rational choice. *Irrational* choice might be a better word. The second consequence is that the requirement of stringent rationality ultimately reduces the theory to an exhortative tool and normative guide. The theory cannot explain or interpret what it purports to explain or interpret, but it can urge us to act in a certain, presumably appropriate, manner. Jon Elster states outright: "The theory of rational choice is, before it is anything else, a normative theory. It tell[s] us what we ought to do in order to achieve our aims as well as possible."[6] Now, if rational choice theory really could tell us what to do, its normative value would at least be assured. But if, as I suggested above, it is inherently incapable of doing so, then one can but conclude that insisting on rigorous rationality is bound to lead to theoretical, practical, and normative dead ends.

The less rigorous interpretation, that of bounded rationality, appears to be more persuasive. By insisting that all human beings are in fact rational in terms of the beliefs, values, and norms that they—and not supposedly disinterested outside observers—possess, the framework encourages scholars to relate means and ends to the actual persons involved and to understand human activity as a complex and densely packed matrix of actions, emotions, aspirations, and convictions. The work of Clifford Geertz—especially his impressive forays into "thick description"—unquestionably substantiates the value of such a perspective.[7] As we should expect, however, even this interpretation is not without problems.

One criticism of this view might resort to Occam's Razor: a bounded rationality interpretation does run the risk of either degenerating into mere description or accumulating so many additional assumptions, qualifications, and the like as to make the theory unmanageable. The criticism is valid, yet it pales in comparison to those that can be levied against the rigorous approach. Here, potential error and triviality are involved; there, actual irreconcilability and impossibility reign. The former, although hardly risk-free, seems the wiser—dare I say, more rational—choice.

A more substantive assault on bounded rationality might focus on the interaction between beliefs, values, and actions and on the rationality or consistency of each in light of that of the others. David Hume put his finger on the problem several hundred years ago:

It is only in two senses that any affection can be called unreasonable. First, when a passion, such as hope or fear, grief or joy, despair or security, is founded on the supposition of the existence of objects which really do not exist. Secondly, when, in exerting any passion in action, we choose means [in]sufficient for the designed end, and deceive ourselves in our judgment of causes and effects. Where a passion is neither founded on false suppositions, nor chooses means insufficient for the end, the understanding can neither justify nor condemn it. It is not contrary to reason to prefer the destruction of the whole world to the scratching of my finger. It is not contrary to reason for me to choose my total ruin to prevent the least uneasiness of an Indian, or person wholly unknown to me.[8]

Most rational choice theorists would agree with Hume that values, or what he calls passions, are impervious to judgments of rationality, of validation or invalidation. Passions are, if you will, analytic statements and cannot be refuted; they are true by definition. Beliefs, on the other hand, presumably can be subjected to criteria of rationality because, to be rational, they should not involve the "supposition of the existence of objects which really do not exist." Elster, using more formal language, insists on the following three criteria: "(1) The belief has a maximal degree of inductive plausibility, given the evidence. (2) The belief is caused by the available evidence. (3) The evidence causes the belief 'in the right way.' " According to Elster, "the first condition is an optimality condition; the others ensure that the person entertains the belief *because* it is rational, not by coincidence." In addition, Elster and others insist that both values and beliefs be internally consistent on the rationale that "if a desire is inconsistent, so that there is no way of realizing it, how could one choose the best means to realize it?"[9]

The bounded rationality interpretation, at least in its ideal form, can choose either to accommodate or to reject these objections. Accommodation can proceed along the following lines: the insistence that beliefs accord with all available evidence, while seemingly very rigorous, is really just a restatement of bounded rationality and the limitations of imperfect information. The evidence objectively available to people is usually quite limited, and the manner in which people subjectively determine what does or does not qualify as evidence is frequently a function of existing beliefs and values. We are, therefore, back to where we started.

33

Rejection can proceed along three lines. First, we could claim that too many criteria of rationality—and Elster's complete list, incidentally, is much longer than that quoted above—make research so narrowly focused as to be well-nigh impossible and probably fruitless. Second, we could object to the inductivist overtones of Elster's description of how beliefs are "caused." Finally, we could draw on anthropology for inspiration and insist that beliefs that strike us as irrational may in fact only *seem* that way. Indeed, they may simply be *non*rational.

Consider the following classificatory scheme contained in an ancient Chinese encyclopedia: "Animals are divided into: (a) belonging to the emperor, (b) embalmed, (c) tame, (d) sucking pigs, (e) sirens, (f) fabulous, (g) stray dogs, (h) included in the present classification, (i) frenzied, (j) innumerable, (k) drawn with a very fine camel hair brush, (l) *et cetera*, (m) having just broken the water pitcher, (n) that from a long way off look like flies." As Richard A. Schweder notes in reference to this outline, "equally rational and experienced observers need not be led by their experiences or by logic to the same classification of the world."[10] If this insight, which many wise anthropologists share, is valid, then there is no compelling reason to insist that all beliefs be based on suppositions of things that *we* claim objectively exist—a view that tallies nicely with Thomas Spragens' and W. V. Quine's interpretation of theoretical circularity or holism. Indeed, as Geertz has argued, the systems of meaning that humans construct *are* real, even if they seem not to have what we consider to be concrete referents in our version of the world.[11] Whether we like it or not, such beliefs, even religious ones, do have referents for the people who hold them, a position defended forcefully by Schweder and one that is illustrated persuasively by Thomas Merton, a thoroughly modern man—and Columbia College graduate no less!—who discovered a religious vocation and became a Trappist monk.[12] Leszek Kolakowski argues in a similar vein by insisting that myths underlie all human thought, including science.[13]

Such an argument verges on subverting rational choice theory, in any and all of its guises. If beliefs can be as seemingly irrational as the Chinese classificatory scheme cited above, then why make any assumptions of rationality at all? Why not abandon the entire project and, as Ernest Gellner recommends, search for some other theory?[14] The only answer we can give is: because our choice of core assumptions is, as Stephen Gaukroger and Imre Lakatos point out, ours. These assumptions may or may not be true to reality—something we cannot determine definitively anyway—and they may be as numerous or as few as we desire. About the only restriction placed upon them is that they be internally consistent—which bounded rationality interpretations certainly are—and helpful in constructing a theory that fits.

In view of these weighty caveats, it is comforting to know that there are some impeccable extratheoretical reasons for adopting rational choice as an "organizing idea."[15] The first and most important one is that many scholars, as well as policy makers, journalists, and data collectors, unwittingly use this perspective anyhow. (Economists use it wittingly, and to great effect.) In other words, rational choice theory is the analytical framework that many of us apply to our everyday lives, to our friends and enemies, to our problems. Deeper acquaintance with the motives, values, beliefs, and circumstances of individuals, groups, and states almost invariably impels us to admit, even if grudgingly, that their particular actions, however repulsive we may find them, do make sense in relation to those actors and their life histories. Rational choice theory only makes explicit what is implicitly assumed, systematizes these assumptions, and tries to be rigorous in the process.[16]

Not only does rational choice theory accord with current assumptions, it is strikingly visible in the work of classical political theorists—as good as any recommendation for adopting a certain framework. After all, the approbation we seek for our theories need not be found only among living scholars. Hobbes, Hume, Bentham, Mill, and Machiavelli explicitly search for rational means to given ends. Plato, Aristotle, St. Augustine, St. Thomas Aquinas, Descartes, and Kant, meanwhile, attempt to determine rational ends as well as means.[17]

A final extratheoretical reason for adopting rational choice theory is normative. To assign rationality to human beings is to infuse them with the capacity to make choices and to realize themselves as human beings. Rational choice theory, in other words, dovetails with standard democratic and humanistic assumptions, which, realistic or not, are laudable aspirations. Indeed, I venture to guess that supporters of democracy can but assume human rationality, because alternative assumptions—and associated images of the dark masses—tend to court authoritarian frameworks.[18]

The most compelling reason for adopting collective choice theory, however, is intrinsically theoretical, and fortunately so. Rational choice offers a simple and powerful tool for studying "collective action"— or the purposive activity of bounded groups. Obviously, not everything that involves many people is necessarily a collective action: clearly delineated groups have to be present and their activity must be oriented toward some goal. A collective action cannot be said to have occurred when many unconnected individuals engage in identical behavior simultaneously, such as watching the evening news on television, going to the beach on a weekend, commuting to work, or, for that matter, going to the ballot box. Voting, after all, is not the action of a collectivity: individuals vote, and not "the nation."[19] By the same token, no collective action transpires when a group, say, "the peasantry," pursues a goal without being conscious of doing so as a group. Even if all individual peasants attack landlords, we cannot be certain that "the peasantry" did so as well.

As with rational choice, the literature on collective action is enormous, but most of it revolves about the paradox stated first by Hume:

> Two neighbors may agree to drain a meadow which they possess in common, because it is easy for them to know each other's mind; and each must perceive that the immediate consequence of his failing in his part is the abandoning [of] the whole project. But it is very difficult, and indeed impossible, that a thousand persons should agree in any such action; it being difficult for them to concert so complicated a design, and still more difficult for them to execute it; while each seeks a pretext to free himself of the trouble and expense and would lay the whole burden on others.[20]

More recently, Mancur Olson has restated the paradox. Contrary to the popular belief that rational, self-interested individuals logically will join a group committed to pursuing desired "public goods"—goods that, if attained, cannot be denied to anybody—it will in fact be in their interest to take a "free ride":

> Since any gain goes to everyone in the group, those who contribute nothing to the effort will get just as much as those who made a contribution. It pays to "let George do it," but George has little or no incentive to do anything in the group interest either, so . . . there will be little, if any, group action. The paradox, then, is that (in the absence of special arrangements or circumstances . . .) large groups, at least if they are composed of rational individuals, will *not* act in their group interest.[21]

The likelihood that collective action in the pursuit of public goods will take place is, thus, inversely proportional to the number of potential participants. The smaller their relative contribution to the cause, the less noncontributors can affect the outcome significantly, the greater the incentive not to contribute. Note that while actions may be collective without involving public goods, it is only those actions that do involve such goods that are of interest to Olson's theory. Thus, the spontaneous worker demonstrations that preceded the overthrow of the Tsar do not, as Barbara Salert mistakenly argues, falsify Olson's theory, because, first, no purposive group was involved, and, second, the "public good" of overthrowing Tsardom was not on the minds of the demonstrators.[22] Under such inappropriate initial conditions, there can be no talk of rational individuals' weighing the costs and benefits of pursuing public goods collectively.

Why and how, then, does large-scale collective action, which is an intersubjectively accepted empirical reality, take place? Olson suggests that the most important intervening variables are positive and negative "selective sanctions": the application or withholding of coercive and material resources to those individuals "who do or do not contribute to the provision of the collective good."[23] Positive sanctions increase the benefits of contributing and therefore induce the rational actor to participate. Negative sanctions make it too costly not to contribute and thus coerce the rational actor to take part in some collective action. Taxation, compulsory dues, membership benefits and privileges, fines, imprisonment, and the like are typical examples of both kinds of sanctions.[24]

Olson's formulation and resolution of the paradox is compelling, yet, as a variety of theorists have noted, not quite satisfactory. The problem is not so much with the logic as with the fact that many large-scale collective actions do take place in the absence of substantial selective incentives. Indeed, as in the case of the Polish labor movement, Solidarity, the selective incentives that did exist in 1980–1981 were in the hands of the authorities. In light of the circularity of good theories and the unlikelihood of their falsification, such recalcitrant facts are not fatal, but they do necessitate some tinkering in the spirit of Ptolemy.

Adjustments to Olson's logic fall into three groups. The first category addresses rational actors' values. Some people may be altruistically inclined in the Kantian sense of willing good deeds, regardless of outcome; others may derive a peculiar thrill from participating in collective activity which compensates them for any expenditure of effort or for the uncertainty of achieving the public good. Still others value certain things so fanatically as to engage in any activity that furthers their ends. In other words, the *intensity* with which people hold values may be critical to understanding certain forms of collective action.

The second type of adjustment concerns beliefs. Edward N. Muller and Karl-Dieter Opp have argued persuasively that individuals may rationally believe that their contributions to large-scale rebellious collective actions *really* are indispensable:

> In contrast to the private interest theory, we assume that average citizens may adopt a collectivist conception of rationality because they recognize that what is individually rational is collectively irrational—that if people like themselves were individually rational free riders, the likelihood of the success of rebellious collective action would be very small, and that, therefore, it is collectively rational for all to participate, even though the objective probability of a single individual influencing the outcome is negligible.[25]

That the individuals who expressed such beliefs in the samples studied by Muller and Opp tended to be disproportionately well educated and therefore presumably most likely to be rational suggests that Muller and Opp's rejection of one of the central axioms of collective action theory may not be as unreasonable as their critics suggest.[26] Moreover, it bears repeating that to determine whether or not beliefs are rational, irrational, or nonrational is a complicated and risky undertaking, one that is not open to Solomonic resolutions. Inevitably and unavoidably, it seems, beliefs have to be viewed in the context of the *Lebenswelt* of the believers, that is, as part and parcel of human action, as suffusing and interpenetrating it at every step of the way.

Intensely held values and what may politely be termed *realitätsferne* beliefs are, I submit, nothing other than "ideals" or ideology.[27] We know from history and from experience that ideals and ideology can be a heady brew, that they can so inebriate individuals, even entire groups, as to induce them to partake in collective activities that averagely rational individuals might avoid. The history of fascism, Nazism, Bolshevism, and Maoism—not to mention nationalism—cannot be understood without reference to the all-consuming fanaticism that an ideational or ideological utopia can impart to its believers. Naturally, ideals and ideology, especially those of a particularly fanatical kind, are generally the preserve of a minority of some population. The majority may pay lip service to its tenets, but it is usually only an elite, a vanguard, that truly and sincerely believes what it professes and takes the initiative in translating these beliefs into action. Lenin, in this sense at least, was right.[28]

Clearly, these adjustments are another way of stating that most populations with certain belief and value orientations may be divided into progressively smaller categories: believers of convenience, true believers, fanatics, and martyrs. For believers of convenience, the structure of both positive and negative incentives will determine whether or not some form of behavior is a profitable path to pursue. For true believers the structure of negative sanctions alone will be decisive: they will pursue some behavioral form if and when it may be pursued. Fanatics will disregard both positive and negative sanctions. Finally, martyrs will willingly court death in order to make a point.[29]

The final adjustment to Olson's logic involves the emergence of conventions. According to Russell Hardin, the "tacit communication to cooperate" can arise if several conditions are met.[30] The first is the "sequential repetition" of a Prisoner's Dilemma situation regarding participation or nonparticipation in a collective action. The second is the incentive to cooperate, which is small in a single such game, but presumably increases with iteration:

> The prisoners in the story . . . face their dilemma only once, and they face it in isolation from other aspects of their relationship with one another. You and I, however, may repeatedly face a smaller version of their dilemma. We may therefore quickly realize that our self-interest now dictates that we cooperate rather than defect (which, in the case of the prisoners, would be not to confess rather than to confess). Since your cooperation tomorrow may depend on my cooperation today, I have incentive to cooperate today.[31]

The third condition is "knowledge of one another's preferences and comprehension of the situation." How do iteration, incentive, and knowledge emerge? The answer, writes Hardin, lies in the "overlapping nature of one's group-related activities, which may turn a sequence of one-time-only, apparently unrelated activities into the rough equivalent of an iterated Prisoner's Dilemma in which generally cooperative behavior may become rational."[32] A convention, defined in the following manner by David Lewis, may be said to exist if and only if it is true that, and it is common knowledge in [population] *P* that, in almost any instance of [a recurrent situation] *S* among members of *P*,

1. almost everyone conforms to [regularity in behavior] *R*;
2. almost everyone expects almost everyone else to conform to *R*;
3. almost everyone has approximately the same preferences regarding all combinations of actions;
4. almost everyone prefers that any one more [person] conform to *R*, on condition that almost everyone conform to *R*;
5. almost everyone would prefer that any one more [person] conform to *R'*, on condition that almost everyone conform to *R'*, where *R'* is some possible regularity in the behavior of members of *P* in *S*, such that almost no one in almost any instance of *S* among members of *P* could conform both to *R'* and to *R*.[33]

I suggest that the object of Hardin's abstruse reasoning and of Lewis's formal definition is reducible to one word—culture. Overlapping, group-related activities involving mutual knowledge and iteration are most likely to be found within populations that live in some region, interact intensively on a daily basis, and share certain assumptions and a system of meaning—that is, within cultural communities in general or ethnic and religious groups in particular. Whether we adopt the more traditional view of culture as sets of norms and ideas that guide behavior or as forms of behavior themselves, or the more sophisticated perspective of Geertz, who calls culture a "system of significant symbols" that have been, are, and always will be an "essential condition" of human existence,[34] culture provides its bearers with the knowledge, understanding, interaction, and iteration patterns critical to the emergence of collective action via convention—a point John Walton demonstrates with regard to national rebellions.[35]

All of these adjustments are more than just a bit commonsensical, as well as being implicit in rational choice theory. Rational actors, after all, possess values and beliefs, and they act on that basis. Certain combinations of values and beliefs may be termed ideals and ideology; others may be termed culture. It is unimportant for present purposes to distinguish between ideals, ideology, and culture more than superficially, because their meaning and significance are intuitively obvious as well as theoretically demonstrable. What *is* important is to realize that any sensible account of collective action will have to combine reason, ideas (which I shall use as a shorthand designation for ideals and ideology), and culture or else face irrelevance, and that ethnic groups generally are the carriers of culture. Indeed, cultural anthropologists claim to be engaged in *ethnography*. As there is a natural and evident connection between collective action and ethnicity, rational choice theory should be well suited to examining ethnically based collective action in general and nationalist collective action in particular, all the more so as the goal of nationalism, political independence, is so obviously a public good.[36]

Perhaps unexpectedly, although culture and ideas may be sufficient conditions of the emergence of collective actions, they can at best only facilitate their persistence or conversion into intended outcomes. Culture and ideas help us understand why certain activities are initiated—say, by fanatical believers or by homogeneous communities such as ethnocultural groups—but they only suggest why collective actions might continue or result in goal attainment. This distinction, between emergence, persistence, and consummation, which we shall encounter again in chapters 3 and 4, is crucial. Because they are quite different phenomena, we should not be surprised at their requiring different explanations.

As will shortly be evident, culture and ideas fail to account for persistence or success because they exist not in a vacuum, but in a world of constraints generated by power contenders who bid for popular support by means of positive and negative sanctions. The overall process is not unlike that described by Anthony Oberschall:

> Group conflict in its dynamic aspects can be conceptualized from the point of view of resource management. Mobilization refers to the processes by which a discontented group assembles and invests resources for the pursuit of group goals. Social control refers to the same processes, but from the point of view of the incumbents or the group that is being challenged. Groups locked in conflict are in competition for some of the same resources as each seeks to squeeze more resources from initially uncommitted third parties . . . In all this the individuals who are faced with resource management decisions make rational choices based on the pursuit of their selfish interests in an enlightened manner.[37]

The state is the most important actor in the competition for influence and support. The vast resources the state commands enable it to mold its subjects' values and beliefs, apply extensive sanctions, and generally dominate the tug-of-war it always and everywhere conducts with its adversaries. Douglass North's comparison of this tug-of-war to the relationship between a "monopolist" and "potential rivals" is suggestive.[38] As long as the state retains its monopoly position, it can influence consumer (i.e., citizen) preferences through socialization and to a large degree determine the behavior patterns of their consumption. The influence the monopolist-state exerts is so great because—as a "political organization whose rule is territorially ordered and which is able to mobilize the means of violence to sustain that rule"[39]—it alone effectively can determine society's life chances. By flooding society with coercive goods or depleting it of material ones (and vice versa, of course), the state can compel rational actors to calculate utility in relation to a preference that is generally taken for granted: survival. To prescribe or proscribe behavior in consistently monopolist fashion is nothing other than to include in the rational actor's calculations of costs and benefits a particularly high cost—life. Of course, most states, although monopolists of violence, do not act in a consistently monopolist fashion. They seek not to "corner" the entire market, but only to regulate and oversee its functioning. For reasons that are beyond the scope of our enquiry, most states apply only minimal constraints to populations; only a certain type of state—the totalitarian state—is maximally constraining, and its impact on rational choice and collective action will concern us in chapter 4.

Were contenders and states locked together in isolation, the cause of antistate oppositions in general and of nationalist oppositions in particular would be well-nigh hopeless, as it is hard to imagine how a challenger could outbid an entrenched state. After all, while nationalists are out to build a state, their opponents already have—or more precisely are—states. The deck, clearly, is stacked against challengers, because even nonconstraining, laissez-faire states mold the beliefs and values of their subjects and have police, army, courts, and bureaucracy to dispense the sanctions used to induce supporters and coerce nonsupporters to forgo free rides.

Fortunately for contenders, the resources nonconstraining states possess and the sanctions they impose on citizens and adversaries can diminish. Prolonged economic decline, rapid social change, political ossification, natural and man-made catastrophes, failed policies, succession crises, and the infirmity or incompetence of leaders can all reduce a state's capacity to acquire resources and to convert them into sanctions. In turn, population shifts, social and economic trends, coalition-building, and a variety of other commonly encountered developments can enhance the resources of contenders. How these two processes interact, how the resource endowments of states and challengers fluctuate, and how their political fortunes vary are all important issues that I shall not discuss: the work of Oberschall, Charles Tilly, and other scholars illustrates these dynamics more than adequately for our purposes.[40] Instead, it is sufficient for us to appreciate that the resource endowments of states and challengers do vary, and that antistate collective actions are, thus, "business as usual" for most nonconstraining states.

As states weaken, their opponents—relatively—grow stronger, and the collective actions they initiate will be able to persist: the benefits of remaining in collectivities are likely to be no smaller than those of dropping out. On their own, however, such internal permutations in resource endowments can only stimulate and maintain opposition, but, logically, they do not suffice for challengers to tip the balance against the state. After all, for our thought experiment to be persuasive, we dare not draw the all too facile conclusion that systemic problems affect only the nonconstraining state and automatically redound to the advantage of challengers. Instead, we should assume that the internal conditions that brought about these difficulties will affect contenders and *their* capacity to acquire resources as well. For the delicate imbalance between states and contenders to be decisively upset, therefore, an outside force is required, one that would either massively reduce the state's resource endowment or massively increase the resources of contenders.

Here, as will happen again later on in our investigations, a *deus ex machina* saves the day. This time it goes by the name of the world system. States, after all, are embedded in international systems; so, too, are antistate contenders. This is an obvious point, but one that we tend often to forget by looking for the mainsprings of revolutions or of national liberation struggles exclusively *within* countries: a reasonable approach to phenomena of over one or two hundred years ago, when societies were relatively self-contained, but one that is untenable today, when Eastonian political systems extend far beyond a nation-state's formal boundaries.[41] More concretely, even a superficial acquaintance with contemporary nationalist and revolutionary movements should persuade us that international support is frequently critical to their viability.[42] The success, persistence, or even existence of the Zionist movement, the Irish Republican Army, the

Basque ETA, the Croatian Ustaša, the Palestine Liberation Organization, the African National Congress, the Sandinistas, and the Nicaraguan contras have been in large measure due to the fact that many of their resources were externally acquired while the depletion of many of the state's resources was externally inspired. In evaluating the tug-of-war between states and contenders and its likely outcome, therefore, we must consider how external actors—states, international organizations, émigrés, and the like—supplement or detract from the arsenals of positive and negative sanctions that both sides possess.

These considerations lead to two important, if somewhat obvious, conclusions. First, if the state and its adversaries expect actors to partake in mutually exclusive collective actions, or zero-sum games (such as maintaining a state and subverting a state), and are willing and able to impose severe sanctions to force compliance, rational individuals are likely to heed sanctions and, over time, to downplay ideals, ideology, and culture. Where superior sanctions dovetail with values, all the better. Where they do not, the ideationally and culturally generated impulse for collective action is likely to dissipate. Under conditions of intergroup conflict and competition, therefore, values and sanctions should be inversely related in importance over time, as the more sustained a conflictual collective action is, the larger the number of sanctions that will come into play in order to maintain or quash it. But the stronger the sanctions, the higher the stakes and the lower the importance of ideas, culture, and values in general. Suicidally inclined martyrs and fanatics, who compulsively believe in an ideal or ideology, will be the exceptions to this rule.

If we pursue this logic to its end, we can but conclude that positive and negative sanctions of an extreme kind can suffice to involve culturally or ideologically disinclined individuals in some collective action. Neutrals can be induced to cooperate, while hostile persons can be forced to do so, at least for some period of time. Obviously, a resource-endowed monopolist-state is always in a position to elicit such participation. But so, too, is a contender who accumulates sufficient resources to outbid the monopolist.

Second, because even initially weak oppositions can attain their goals if outside assistance or obstruction is substantial enough, the likelihood of victory is, at best, only marginally related to the "internal" strength of contenders. If so, it should be—and obviously is—possible for external interference to produce victorious outcomes on its own, even in the absence of a strong contender or, for that matter, of widespread antistate sentiments or homogeneous cultures. "Revolutions from outside," which are instances of outside forces transforming a society without any significant assistance from the inside—such as the Nazi occupation of Eastern Europe or the Soviet occupation of the Baltic states and eastern Poland—are extreme, but enlightening, examples of this dynamic.[43]

In light of these conclusions, the connection between what I consider to be nationalist outcomes *par excellence*—independent states— and the popularity of nationalist ideas becomes tenuous at best. Indeed, nationalist outcomes should be able to take place irrespective of the nationalist fervor and cultural solidarity that a nationalist opposition does or does not enjoy—a proposition that the creation of the post-Habsburg Austrian republic persuasively supports. For a nationalist collective action to be sustainable, for it to succeed, the decisive question that its leaders will have to face is not Do the masses believe us? or Is the ideal persuasive?, but, Who is stronger, we or the state? Or, as Lenin put it quite rightly, *"Kto kogo?"*

— 3 —

Nations, States, and Nationalism

> Without Country you have neither name, token, voice, nor rights, no admission into the fellowship of the Peoples. You are the bastards of Humanity.
>
> — Guiseppe Mazzini

Although collective action may be a function of sanctions, culture, and ideas, it is not reducible to either sanctions, culture, or ideas.[1] The point seems obvious, yet the widespread tendency of scholars to overlook these conceptual boundaries is, I submit, largely responsible for the confusion that permeates the study of nationalism. Nationalism can be a type of only one of these phenomena; to argue otherwise is to confuse characteristics with causes (or effects) and to produce an unwieldy concept of little or no heuristic value. Which of these terms—collective action, culture, or ideas (I exclude sanctions, because no one reasonably would identify nationalism as such)—best applies to nationalism is a different question. Although there is no way of imposing a preference, a choice has to be made. That choice, as we shall see, is strongly determined by one's choice of other concepts as well as by one's personal values and theoretical inclinations. Naturally, the choice must be logical and most conducive to enhanc-

46

ing the tightness of the conceptual framework undergirding the logic, structure, and evidential domain of the theory being utilized.

According to Giovanni Sartori, there are two pitfalls to be avoided in delineating concepts: extensional indefiniteness, or vagueness, and intensional indefiniteness, or ambiguity.[2] While the former difficulty cannot, according to Sartori, be fully surmounted, as there will always be some lack of fit between "objective reality" and abstract "units of thinking," the latter problem, ambiguity, can—and must—be overcome. If there is lack of clarity at this, the basic, level of theorizing, the entire theoretical edifice will prove to be shaky and prone to collapse. The task facing scholars, therefore, is to define a concept in such a manner that we know both what it is and, far more important perhaps, what it is not. To repeat an earlier citation from Sartori: "It can be said that we have a concept of A (or of A-ness) when we are able to distinguish A from whatever is not-A."[3] But this seemingly straightforward procedure for defining concepts, which is not unlike that implied by Ferdinand de Saussure's theory of language, has its own pitfalls.[4] Most important, because the number of things that something is not can border on the infinite, Sartori's advice actually is tantamount to arguing that meaning can never be fully determinate. Indeed, conceptual clarity is always at best provisional: however much we try to be precise, some imprecision and some ambiguity will always be present.[5]

Conceptual clarity is especially daunting a problem because concepts generally fall into several "semantic fields."[6] That is, concepts always have a variety of different meanings, as they inevitably have different intensions. Friedrich Nietzsche recognized this fact long ago: "All concepts in which an entire process is semiotically concentrated elude definition; only that which has no history is definable."[7] Nietzsche's point is obvious, if perhaps a bit overdrawn, and it is evident in the everyday disputes that undermine communication in both the scholarly and nonscholarly worlds. (On the other hand, such ambiguity is the very stuff of diplomacy.) What makes the problem of competing semantic fields especially frustrating is that it is insurmountable. We cannot arrogantly dismiss competing intensions as irrelevant and claim that others are exclusively important; nor, for that matter, can we really follow Sartori's advice and reconstruct concepts on the basis of *all* their intensions. All that we can do is choose one semantic field and accept the consequences—mostly in the form of professional disapproval, a prospect that Paul Feyerabend might welcome and encourage, but one that is unlikely to appeal to scholars subject to the pressures described in the introduction and chapter 1.[8]

Naturally, a few intensions of some concept may be patently ridiculous and, if so, we may reject them out of hand. Generally, however, almost all of a concept's existing connotations will make some sense, and all, at least *a priori*, are of equal significance (but, as I suggest below, of unequal utility). Sartori's method of constructing definitions by drawing on all existing intensions is ultimately unacceptable, however, because it is premised on the view that concepts, like St. Augustine's notion of God, can be everywhere, that is, that they can occupy several semantic fields simultaneously. This proposition is highly problematic and decidedly inutile for at least two reasons. First, such an approach contravene's Sartori's own injunction that concepts should distinguish *A* from *not-A*. By including properties *A*, *B*, and *C* within the intensional domain of a concept, we address the problem of competing boundaries by incorporating all three semantic fields into a larger imperial domain and thereby defining the problem out of existence. Second, and somewhat less abstractly, to include *A*, *B*, and *C* within a concept is to confuse characteristics (which are the stuff of analytic statements) with causes or, perhaps, effects (which are central to synthetic statements), thus producing a hybrid that, as both synthetic and analytic, is really only unfocused. In most cases, an intension *A* treats *B* and *C* as causes and/or effects. Conversely, if *B* or *C* is taken as the key intension, *A* may appear as the cause or the effect. Revolutions, for example, can be viewed as forms of, say, turmoil, change, or upheaval. If it is turmoil, then upheaval may be its cause and change its effect. If it is change, then turmoil may be its cause, and upheaval its effect. And so on. To suggest, as Theda Skocpol does, that "social revolutions are rapid, basic transformations of a society's state and class structures; and they are accompanied and in part *carried through* by class-based revolts from below" (my italics—A.J.M.) is to resolve synthetic questions by analytical fiat.[9]

Another example, one closer to home, may also be useful. As Konstantin Symmons-Symonolewicz rightly points out, most definitions of nationalism fall into one of three semantic fields: nationalism as ideology, as social movement, or as group consciousness[10]—or, to use the terms employed in chapter 2, as ideas, as collective action, or as culture. Nationalism cannot be all three at the same time, nor can nationalism be defined in such a manner that the definition, like

Skocpol's of social revolutions, conveys causality. John Breuilly, for instance, falls into both traps by arguing that "the term 'nationalism' is used to refer to political movements seeking or exercising state power and justifying such actions with nationalist arguments."[11] For Breuilly, nationalism evidently is both a collective action and an ideology and, worse still, the ideology implicitly causes the action. Symmons-Symonolewicz's definition is no better: "Nationalism is the active solidarity of a larger human collectivity which shares a common culture, or a common fund of significant experiences and interests, conceives of itself as a nation, and strives for political unity and self-government."[12] Having purposely decided to include "all three basic meanings of nationalism" in his own, Symmons-Symonolewicz manages only to produce an unwieldy synthesis of causes and effects that compels social scientists to abandon explanation (or even interpretation) and retreat to mere description—of those awkwardly bounded megaphenomena that fulfill all of Symmons-Symonolewicz's conditions.

If we reject the approaches discussed above, all that is left is for us to choose some one intension and fit it into our theoretical framework as best as we can. We can base our choice on any or, preferably, all of the following three criteria:

1. some semantic fields may be less persuasive than others;
2. some semantic fields may be less useful than others;
3. some semantic fields may fit better into a theoretical framework than others.

As we shall see presently, my choice is to place nationalism within the semantic field of belief systems, partly because it is unpersuasive to view nationalism as a collective action, partly because it is of dubious utility to treat it as a form of culture or identity, and partly because collective choice theory precludes certain interpretations of associated concepts and requires others. This tyranny of conceptual frameworks is the consequence of the fact that, as I argued in chapter 1, core axioms and concepts must be logically and consistently related to produce a tight fit.

The problem with treating nationalism as collective action (or as social movement or, at the basic level, as behavior) is that there is nothing intrinsically nationalist about the behavior in which people who call themselves nationalists engage. Collective actions, like social movements, are the coordinated activities of groups. A fascist collective action differs in no way, *as a collective action*, from a Communist, Catholic, or nationalist collective action. Crowds of demonstrators, underground cells, strikes, mobs, clubs, petition drives, and so on are just that and nothing more, and, as such, they can be appropriated by any group and infused with any meaning. Even agitation and propaganda are not the property of any one ideology or movement, because it is not the act of agitation or propaganda but its content or context that imparts a certain ideological overtone to the collective action. Nationalism cannot be a social movement, a large-scale form of behavior, therefore, because all social movements merely consist of people in motion, and it is neither the people nor the motion that makes a movement nationalist, but the ideas that they have or the context in which the motion occurs. I shall return to this point below.

Nationalism as culture, cultural identity, ethnicity, or ethnic solidarity is an even worse choice, because it is so completely inutile. All these forms of communal sentiment are universally held today, and to reduce nationalism to any one of them is to convert all human beings into nationalists. Here the problem is the exact opposite of that we encountered in the preceding paragraph: nationalism as collective action seems to have no referents, whereas nationalism as culture seems to have everything and everybody as a referent. Several illustrations may be instructive. For example, to hear Sovietologists use the term nationalism, everybody in the Soviet Union must be a nationalist—surely an argument that is both counterintuitive and intellectually specious. If the likes of Mikhail Gorbachev, Chingiz Aitmatov, Aleksandr Solzhenitsyn, and muscle-bound youths in Moscow suburbs are all supposed to be nationalists, then one can but conclude that the term is merely a synonym for human being. But, surely, to be aware of one's subjective and objective ethnic markers (language, color, religion, customs, etc.) cannot be nationalism, to consider that all individuals who possess such characteristics constitute something called a nation cannot be nationalism, to love one's nation, to be proud of it, to swear loyalty to it—none of this can be nationalism, as otherwise everything involving culture or nationality must be nationalism.

Oleksandr Dovzhenko's diary entry unwittingly raises another important distinction:

My dear Comrade Stalin, even if you were God, I would not take your word that I am a nationalist who must be slandered and imprisoned. If there is no hatred in principle, and no scorn, and

50

no ill feelings toward a single nation on earth, how can love for one's own nation be nationalism? Is it nationalism to refuse to connive with stupid functionaries and cold-blooded speculators? Is it nationalism when an artist cannot hold back his tears because his nation is suffering?[13]

Correct as he was on one count, that nationalism and love of nation are not the same, Dovzhenko, like many scholars, erred on another, that of confusing ethnic chauvinism (or related manifestations, such as anti-Semitism, racism, or supremacism) with nationalism. That chauvinism is frequently utilized by nationalists is completely beside the point, as it also figures in the mobilization strategies of Communists, monarchists, and democrats, automobile manufacturers, newspaper editors, and computer makers, Christians, Jews, and Muslims. Anthony Smith is therefore quite right to insist that German National Socialism was not a species of nationalism.[14] Although Nazism drew on nationalism, Nazism's defining characteristics—the *Führerprinzip*, the corporatist organization of society, extreme chauvinism, irredentism, and imperialism—overlapped only minimally with those of nationalism. Breuilly's criticism of Smith misses the point that *pars pro toto* arguments are invalid: "Much of [Nazism's] appeal was couched in straightforward nationalist terms and it was supported more for its orthodox nationalist appeal than the obsession with racism and anti-Semitism that characterized some of its leaders. It had strong ideological and other links with earlier forms of nationalism. It seems perverse, therefore, not to regard it as itself a form of nationalism."[15] Quite the contrary, it is far more perverse to subsume something as jumbled as Nazism under a relatively straightforward category such as nationalism. Just because National Socialism drew on a variety of ideologies for inspiration does not make it reducible to them. After all, if Breuilly were right, then Nazism would also have to be considered a form of socialism.

If nationalism is neither collective action nor cultural identity, then all we are left with is belief system. That is, nationalism must be a specific type of belief, idea, doctrine, ideology, or ideal; nationalism is, in a word, a thing of the mind. I come to this conclusion partly because it is all that is left, but mostly because the collective choice perspective well-nigh demands it. If, as I have argued, rational actors pursue joint ends only on condition that selective sanctions, culture, or ideas overcome their inclinations to ride freely, then it is obviously of overriding importance to be able to identify at least the outlines of the ends that people claim to be pursuing. More specifically, we cannot study nationalism from the collective choice perspective without defining nationalism in ideational terms, as that vision leaders pursue by forcing or persuading people to join collective actions. Had I opted for nationalism as collective action or as culture, we would have found ourselves in a conceptual *cul de sac* and been forced to admit that we cannot identify the end, the notion of the public good, that motivates cultural groups or mere individuals to join collectivities.

To suggest that ideas impart meaning to actions is to argue that actions mean what actors intend them to mean: thus, to take an example, ostensibly a mass march is nationalist if its organizers and participants say that their goal is statehood. The point seems obvious, but, as a variety of scholars have stressed, intentions may be indeterminate and, consequently, meaning must be contextual.[16] That is, an action's position within the environment of meanings determines what that action actually means. Thus, to continue with the above example, a mass march is nationalist only if it occurs within a political or ideological context that brands such marches as nationalist. How, then, do we choose between these alternatives? For better or for worse, I shall not attempt to resolve what is probably an intractable philosophical problem. Rather, my approach (which, I trust, readers will consider to be Solomonic and not indecisive) will be to highlight what both approaches have in common. Thus, I shall suggest that nationalist ideas do impart meaning to actions, but only if the ideational context is appropriate and the nation these ideas address has no state, and I shall acknowledge that actions may approach the fulfillment of nationalist ideas without actually being borne by individuals or groups with such ideas. I am not ascribing priority to contextual meaning, because nationalist ideas can convert *any* action into a nationalist action in a nonnationalist context, whereas context ascribes nationalist overtones only to certain kinds of behavior. But I do believe that the environment of meanings is no less important than the ideas of actors, as I want to insist that the vast range of ideationally inspired nationalist actions can be nationalist only in a nonnationalist or antinationalist setting. In the final analysis, of course, ideas—be they inspirational or contextual—are the key.

What, then, is nationalism? What sort of thing of the mind is it? It is, as Mark Hagopian rightly suggests, an ideal—"a broad symbol that entails values and goals that make it worthy of notice and acceptance"—and not an ideology, which attempts to follow its "own logic" and reach a "level of coherence that constitutes a system." Because the "very vagueness of the ideal prevents its developing an accompanying doctrine that follows a certain logic and displays a high level of coherence," nationalism "is sometimes on the right; it is sometimes in the center; it is sometimes on the left."[17] Ideals are minimalist, ideologies are maximalist. Ideals imply only ends; ideologies also recommend means. Ideals are porous; ideologies are solid.

Nationalism is not just any ideal, but a distinctly political ideal: that is, it posits certain political ends and highlights certain optimal political relationships. Nationalism, obviously, is about nations, but it is much more than that as well. Nationalism connects nations with the "essence" of the political—states; it claims that all nations should have their own states. Nationalism, therefore, is a political ideal that views statehood as the optimal form of political organization for each nation. Nationalists are men and women who share this belief, and a nationalist collective action is a collective action that is premised on or approaches such a goal.[18]

This definition of nationalism suggests why nationalism can be so pervasive and coexist with a variety of other political doctrines and behaviors, including Communism. Except in some teleological sense concerning ultimate greatest goods, the nationalist commitment to a nation's statehood is quite compatible with ideologies that give priority to social classes.[19] This is so conceptually (we can always define, say, the Third Estate as *the* nation) and, far more important, practically: unless we define class relations as a zero-sum game, it is perfectly possible for all classes to benefit, even if unequally, from a nation's statehood. All that nationalism innately opposes are doctrines that explicitly deny the existence of nations and the possibility of states. In the twentieth century, however, such doctrines have been virtually nonexistent. Several hundred years ago, of course, conditions were different and one can easily understand why nationalism could but have had a revolutionary impact on then prevalent notions of political legitimacy and social order.

Nationalist behavior involves those forms of collective and individual activity that challenge existing states on ideationally or contextually nationalist grounds. At the basic level, individual nationalists may engage in such behavior. More complex forms of such behavior are incipient states, guerrilla struggles, political organizations, and mass movements. All four nationalist collectivities aspire to or, indeed, do challenge a state, but the kind of challenge they pose differs in terms of the positive and negative sanctions they can muster. Incipient, or fledgling, states come closest to matching a monop-olist-state's material and coercive sanctions; political organizations are furthest removed; guerrilla struggles and popular movements oc-cupy the middle ground. Individual nationalists, obviously, are not even in the running. Nationalist collectivities may thus be classified according to their capacity, as determined by the balance of resources with the state, to mount collective actions against the state.

Nationalist behavior, therefore, aspires either to the creation of an indigenous political organization with a monopoly of violence in a territory populated by a human community considered to be a nation or to the extension of state rule to an irredenta. As I argued above, nationalist activity is logically premised on the absence of a state for the entire nation or part thereof. Once the context changes and a state exists, the collective or other actions that transpire within its juris-diction, even if labeled nationalist by their initiators, acquire a dif-ferent meaning and are reduced to the everyday politics of modern states. Nationalism as ideal, however, and nationalists as individuals who accept that ideal can exist before, during, and after a state has been attained. Menachem Begin, for example, remained a nationalist after 1947. His activity, however, changed radically, both substan-tively and conceptually, from nationalist behavior that sought to ac-quire statehood to nonnationalist behavior that sought to preserve it.

The analytical distinction between nationalism as ideal and na-tionalist behavior is especially important for my purposes. The for-mer is a question of intellectual origins and persistence, the latter a question of collective action. With respect to ideals, we might want to know why people initially came to adopt nationalist beliefs and values. Elie Kedourie traces the origins of nationalism to a variety of intellectual currents in the eighteenth century, in particular to Im-manuel Kant's notions of will and self-determination. Carlton Hayes and Eric Hobsbawm view nationalism as the historical product of the French Revolution and industrialization. Smith sees its origins in the crisis of an intelligentsia confronted by the demise of religion and the challenge of the "scientific state." Ernest Gellner traces its roots and ascribes its persistence to a complex interaction among industrial-ization, modernization, education, culture, and competition.[20] For my purposes, any and all of these ontological explanations are perfectly acceptable in accounting for the emergence of nationalist ideals. There is no need for us to choose as the eighteenth and nineteenth centuries are not our concern.

The persistence of nationalism, on the other hand, is my concern, but not a primary one. Although the genetic fallacy warns us not to assume that historical origins can account for modern-day intellectual vitality, it is not unreasonable to suggest that the nationalist ideal's lasting power has something to do with the fact that the conditions of its emergence are still with us today. But far more persuasive as an explanation of nationalism's persistence is its hegemony—a proposition that sounds tautalogical but is not. If we think of hegemony in David Laitin's sense of the term as "the political forging . . . and institutionalization of group activity . . . and the concurrent idealization of that schema into a dominant symbolic framework that reigns as common sense,"[21] we can see that human beings persist in believing in the nationalist ideal precisely because nationalism has become "natural," indeed as natural as nature itself. As the current *Zeitgeist*, nationalism so thoroughly penetrates contemporary thinking, discourse, and indeed culture as to be almost an inevitable component of all that we do and say.[22] Gellner is quite right to say that, in light of contemporary conditions, nationalism is "natural and probably irresistible."[23] Thus, to account for nationalism's continued presence as an ideal is actually secondary to explaining its absence. Given such hegemonic conditions, the burden of proof is on those who insist that nationalist beliefs are an anomaly.

Why and how nationalism attained hegemony are questions beyond the scope of this study. Why nationalism's hegemony should *persist*, however, does get at my central concern: the emergence of nationalist collective actions. My answer, and it is also the one suggested by a variety of theorists working in or near the rational actor mode, is that nationalism makes sense in a world of nations and states. It is rational—which is to say that it suggests an excellent solution, statehood, to a variety of contemporary problems.

Before addressing the means-ends issue—that is, is a state a good or best means for attaining some end?—it will be useful to follow David Hume's example and ask whether the nationalist ideal in fact posits things that exist, specifically, nations and states. From the vantage point of the late twentieth and not the late eighteenth century, there can surely be no question that these core elements of nationalism are existential realities. Nations and states are no less real to millions of people than such ostensibly more material things as class, status, power, authority, and wealth, especially if we adopt the view of reality proposed in chapter 1.[24] Benedict Anderson to the contrary, if we accept the latter concepts as real, then we can but view nations and states as equally real.[25] And if the latter are imagined, then so, too, are the former. Furthermore, there is more ontological substance to nations than Gellner's disparaging comparison of nationality to noses and eyes would suggest. If Clifford Geertz is correct in arguing that culture, as a "system of significant symbols," is immanent in humanity, then it is hardly farfetched to argue that nations are particular historical carriers of culture and are thus the equivalent, to continue with the analogy, of the size or shape of facial characteristics.[26] Gellner's mistake is to overdraw the difference between physical human beings and their symbolic makeup along the lines of Descartes's attempt to think away his body.

The question of instrumentality still remains to be considered. Is a state the best way of attaining independence in a world of independent states? The question is, of course, rhetorical. And of advancing a nation's interests? The answer to this question obviously depends on how we define those interests. Insofar as the world currently consists of perpetually competing states, nationalism does have—to borrow Jon Elster's criteria—a "maximal degree of inductive plausibility" and appears to be "caused by the available evidence" "in the right way."[27] More important, nationalism may even be a necessary condition of survival in a world of competing states, atomic weapons notwithstanding. If we ask whether or not political independence advances economic interests, then the answer is, maybe yes, maybe no. If we focus on language, culture, a sense of autonomy and psychological well-being, and other such typically ethnic interests, then the answer, as Frantz Fanon would no doubt have concurred, is probably yes, at least in the contemporary world.[28] In either case, the most we can say is that sometimes a state will and sometimes it will not be in a nation's best interests, however defined. That conclusion, in turn, suggests that the rationality or irrationality of nationalist activity is contingent on environmental and historical conditions and not on the essence of nationalism *per se*.

Nationalism's behavioral *Zweckrationalität* extends to three types of goals: material, political, and national. The instrumental rationality of nationalism, as a form of behavior that believers of convenience engage in because it is well suited to the attainment of their material ends, figures most prominently in the work of Karl W. Deutsch:

> To the extent that the division of labor in a particular society is competitive and stratified, nationality can thus be used to hamper "horizontal" substitution from individuals outside the

group, and to facilitate "vertical" substitution within it. . . . Once the pressures of uprooting and insecurity are then added to these horizontal and vertical barriers, the stage is set for the rise of the political movement of modern nationalism. . . .[29]

In addition, as Breuilly argues, nationalism can be a rational means for believers of convenience to pursue the political power embodied in a state:

> Nationalism should be understood as a form of politics and . . . that form of politics makes sense only in terms of the particular political context and objectives of nationalism. Central to an understanding of that context and those objectives is the modern state. The modern state both shapes nationalist politics and provides that politics with its major objective, namely possession of the state. . . . The modern state centralises and specialises significant political action. Political opposition in turn engages in centralised and specialised political action which builds upon the institutions provided by the state. In certain situations, such as political opposition originating from outside the core territory of a multinational empire, nationalist ideology seems best to describe and promote that political opposition.[30]

Nationalism, then, may be, and clearly often is, a potent weapon of regionally or ethnically based politicians who aspire to material largesse or political power. But nationalist behavior is not just a means to, and the nationalist ideal is not just a rationalization of, nonnationalist goals: the ideal can be an end in itself and the behavior can be the most rational means for pursuing that end. That is to say, nationalist behavior may also be the rational response of *bona fide* nationalists—individuals with a sincere and strong belief in the nationalist ideal—to opportunities to pursue their goals.

Martyrs, fanatics, and true believers are always a small minority, but we should not underestimate them or commit the genetic fallacy by arguing that their faith was, after all, sparked by material or power motives. Possessing as they do what Barrington Moore calls "iron in their souls," they play a significant role in initiating political and social movements, sustaining them in critical periods, and achieving ultimate victory.[31] No explanation of the Iranian revolution, for example, can hope to be complete without giving a prominent place to the fanaticism of the Ayatollah Khomeini and the martyrdom of those of his followers who willingly sacrificed their lives for Allah.[32] The same variables are critical for a proper understanding of the political movements inspired by Mohandas Ghandi, Kemal Atatürk, Józef Piłsudski, Vladimir Jabotinsky, and many other nationalists.

Believers of convenience, true believers, fanatics, and martyrs can all serve as nationalist "entrepreneurs." Just as leaders are always and everywhere irrepressible—an empirically sound assumption that seems to be shared by such diverse authors as Joseph Rothschild, Charles Tilly, and Mostafa Rejai[33]—nationalist entrepreneurs will inevitably be available in an age of nations, states, and nationalism. Mobilizing their target audience, the putative nation, in a collective action that aspires to the public good of an independent state is their goal. As I have already argued in chapter 2, ideas and culture can be decisive at this point only. Winning *sustained* audience acquiescence and support, however, ultimately depends on the possession of relatively stable positive and negative selective sanctions. Winning the political struggle, meanwhile, depends on the balance of sanctions—or, in Soviet parlance, the correlation of resources—between the contenders for power and the state.

Although the correlation of resources depends on a variety of internal and external factors, discussed in chapter 2, nationalist contenders will be especially privileged if the state they oppose is of a particular type. In contrast to minimally constraining states, maximally constraining states with quasi-federal territorial structures offer nationalist contenders special opportunities for joining the tug-of-war with the state as well as multiple resources for transforming it into a serious contest. As chapter 4 will argue, paradoxically, nationalist success may be most possible in conditions that aim at making it least possible.

— 4 —

The Withering Away of the Totalitarian State

Everything is in the state.
— Benito Mussolini

Although imperfect, as are all theories, collective choice theory is obviously of relevance to my central concern, nationalist collective action. But, as presented in most of the literature, collective choice theory has one glaring lacuna that almost disqualifies it from use in the case of our immediate interest, the Soviet Union. Quite simply, the paradigm is premised on conditions of minimal constraint. It assumes that actors can choose freely (or more or less freely), and it is precisely because of this assumption, of course, that Mancur Olson's hypothesis regarding free actors freely choosing *not* to pursue their common interest has its attraction and force. When this premise is dropped and replaced with its opposite, maximal constraint, the terms of the intellectual experiment as well as the initial conditions of the theory change dramatically.

Where choice is maximally constrained, people still choose, and they still choose as rational actors, but the choices they make are likely to be very different from those made under conditions of minimal constraint. They will still maximize utility, but they will do so on the basis of different preference structures: that is, they will supplement their usual preference structures with two values—life and life chances—that normally are taken for granted and subordinate all other goals to maximization of life and of the material preconditions of functional existence in a maximally constraining society. Utility maximizers do not suddenly become risk minimizers under conditions of maximal constraint; they do not abandon their usual goals in order to avoid risk. Rather, they simply pursue different priorities because conditions of maximal constraint bring life and life chances to the fore of their preference structures.

We may therefore hypothesize that averagely rational actors who value life and life chances above all else will not adopt the means to pursue some lower-order end if they know that such behavior will result in, say, incarceration. Conversely, averagely rational actors told to pursue some goal via certain means or else face persecution will tend to submit even if they find both repugnant. The moral of the argument is simple: under conditions of maximal constraint, only a tiny minority of any given population will engage in consciously self-destructive behavior.[1] By and large, the rational actors in the theoretical world constructed by Hume and Olson do not confront these dilemmas.

Life and life chances are, I submit, the supreme value of most rational actors. But not of all: as I argued in chapter 2, some individuals may value religious, political, or other goals above their own earthly lives. The heroism of soldiers, the self-sacrifice of saints, and the asceticism of revolutionaries suggest that this assumption is plausible; the lives of St. Augustine and Thomas Merton, whose memoirs are as lucid and as rationally articulated as one can imagine, make this assumption necessary.[2] For rational actors such as these, who possess perfectly rational albeit nonmaterial, even seemingly irreal, values, it makes excellent sense to sacrifice their lives or life chances to the attainment of their all-consuming ends. Naturally, rational actors who value their material existence will disagree with what they are sure to condemn as irrational behavior—but that, as we know, is their privilege in light of their own radically different hierarchies of values.

Under conditions of maximal constraint we will always be able to isolate those irrational-seeming rational actors—the martyrs and fanatics—who disregard all constraints in the pursuit of their goals. But insofar as such individuals are always a tiny minority, maximal constraint precludes the emergence of collective action, which requires that more sizable numbers of rational actors, say, the true believers, also join forces. To study collective action in maximally constraining conditions, therefore, is to determine how maximal constraint can be reduced and how the autonomy, or political space, necessary for more or less free choice can emerge.

This question necessitates a shift in our analysis from collective choice *per se* to the type of state that maximally constrains rational actors. Specifically, it will be incumbent on us to determine how such maximally constraining states lose their capacity to constrain, thus permitting more or less unconstrained choice to take place in those pockets of autonomy beyond their reach. Answering this question requires that we consider how states in general exercise constraint and determine what kind of state exercises maximal constraint.

Constraint is the effective prescription and proscription of certain kinds of behavior. When people who are enjoined to do some things or forbidden to do others actually act in the manner intended by the constraining actor, their behavior may be said to have been constrained. Of course, prescription and proscription alone do not suffice for constraint to exist. People must actually feel compelled to heed such injunctions and behave accordingly. In other words, not only must we control for authoritarian political cultures or personalities, but prescription and proscription must also be effective. But they can be effective only if noncompliance carries with it the certainty of sanctions and rational actors know that sanctions will be certain. Threats have to be made *and* enforced *and* perceived as being enforced for genuine constraint to exist. For the sake of simplicity, I shall make a plausible assumption: that rational actors, who are definitionally adept at weighing costs and benefits on the basis of their bounded information of the world, *sooner or later* recognize whether or not sanctions are certain to be applied in those spheres where the authorities insist that they are in fact being applied. Averagely rational actors will come to see whether or not sanctions and constraints "fit" by observing the world, the behavior of their fellows, and the actions of the state, because they possess a convenient, if somewhat rough, measure of effectiveness: the permanent presence of martyr and fanatic populations willing to defy sanctions continually confronts the state with a test it must always and everywhere pass, lest signals of inefficiency be conveyed to rational bystanders.

In turn, enforcement requires resources—manpower, money, material and technical equipment, armaments, information, and buildings. Without these, the lives or life chances of noncompliant subjects cannot be affected: after all, at the least, paid policemen armed with guns must ferry away rebels in armored cars and transport them to distant prisons or camps. Where resources are lacking—and states are weak—enforcement will be difficult and the effective prescription and proscription of behavior will prove to be impossible, if not immediately, before perceptions have changed, then certainly in the middle term. Where resources are abundant—and states are strong— enforcement will be straightforward and choices will remain constrained. How many resources are enough? It is probably impossible to answer this question without lapsing into circularity; fortunately, it is not even necessary for us to try to do so. As our concern is conditions of maximal constraint, we may assume that such extreme forms of prescription and proscription require—other things, such as masochistic political culture, being equal—*vast* amounts of resources. How vast I neither can nor need specify, but, surely, much more than in relatively nonconstraining circumstances.[3]

What sort of political entity does maximal constraint imply? Clearly, the state makes great sense as the unit of analysis, as maximal constraint seems to necessitate an entity that actually monopolizes violence and not merely allocates values.[4] More than that, however, the maximally constraining state must be highly centralized and bureaucratically extensive. Centralization, whose polar type is decentralization, refers to the location of decision-making authority regarding all the spheres of life supervised by a maximally constraining state. Hypercentralized states concentrate all authority in some one individual, agency, or institution; in contrast, highly decentralized states disperse authority among a variety of individuals, agencies, or institutions. It appears reasonable to suggest that a high degree of centralization must characterize maximally constraining states for the simple reason that it would otherwise be impossible for them to articulate clearly what forms of behavior they prescribe and proscribe. No less important, only extreme centralization can guarantee the state the directive capacity it requires to mobilize the vast amount of resources needed to constrain society maximally. Maximally constraining states must speak with one voice—regarding rules of behavior and direction of resource accumulation.

An equally straightforward concept, *bureaucratic extent* refers to the reach of state officials into the affairs of society (by which I mean nothing more complicated than everything and everybody outside the formal institutions of the state). Obviously, such reach may be long or it may be short: in the first case, state officials supervise an enormous range of behavior; in the second case, they restrict their oversight to a few select areas such as, say, crime. It is the first type of state, that with long reach, which I term bureaucratically extensive. Like high centralization, bureaucratic extensiveness is a necessary component of a maximally constraining state: without an army of officials, both the supervision of the vast array of rules prescribing and proscribing behavior and the acquisition of immense resources would be impossible.

Such highly centralized, bureaucratically extensive states are, I suggest, best termed *totalitarian*—that is, their control of society's choices, their supervision of society's behavior, and their monopoly of economic resources all approach totality.[5] Note that my use of the term *totalitarianism*, which I maintain is no better or no worse a concept than any other in the social sciences,[6] refers only to a particular kind of authority and institutional structure. The polar type of a totalitarian state, therefore, is the laissez-faire state, one that is highly decentralized, bureaucratically condensed, and minimally involved in resource extraction. Terror, violence, rule by a single party, and all the other elements of the "totalitarian syndrome" discussed by such authors as Carl Friedrich and Zbigniew Brzezinski are at best incidental to my redefinition of the concept, although they may—but need not—function as policy means for imposing conditions of maximal constraint.[7]

As I argued above, free choice is impossible under conditions of maximal constraint, because resources are sufficiently abundant for the totalitarian state to apply sanctions effectively to all the spheres of societal life that it prescribes and proscribes. Collective action in the terms discussed in chapter 2 becomes possible if and only if constraint is reduced and political space is created, which entails that the totalitarian state's vast resources either be diminished or inefficiently applied: that is, the totalitarian state must weaken, where weakness is understood as a function of a declining resource endowment. As we shall presently see, there are two ways, the second of which is intrinsically more interesting than the first, for a reduction in state resources to come about.

The first is external and concerns the impact on the totalitarian state of disruptive outside forces. Wars and international economic crises immediately come to mind: the former represents a direct attack on the state's *raison d'être*, while the latter constrains the state in its international and domestic dealings, forcing it to divert resources from the effective pursuit of maximal internal constraint to international goals. Although wars and economic crises can debilitate totalitarian states temporarily, thereby creating the requisite autonomy for resource accumulation and collective action to occur, they are unlikely to constrain totalitarian states for long. As highly centralized, bureaucratically extensive entities with maximal control over a society's resources, totalitarian states must be assumed to be far less vulnerable to external shocks than nonconstraining ones. After all, by definition totalitarian states make quick and authoritative decisions, possess the bureaucratic machinery to mobilize society, and have enormous resources at their disposal to withstand wars and to counteract external economic crises. Thus, although political space and collective action are likely to emerge under distressing international conditions, we must conclude that totalitarian states will quickly get back on their feet, quash the collective actions, and close the space.[8]

What totalitarian states cannot do very well, however, is persist under conditions of normality. Indeed, left to their own devices, totalitarian states come to be afflicted with a number of degenerative pathologies of their own making. As I sketch below, the root of the problem is the state itself—hypercentralization, bureaucratic extensiveness, and monopoly of resources. The decay of the ideally typical totalitarian state is, I stress, a logically necessary process from which real-life approximations will of course diverge. Decay begins with the fact that extreme centralization produces horizontal bureaucratic fragmentation. Because regional officials are exclusively dependent on the center both for their material existence and for policy directives regarding prescription and proscription of behavior, the horizontal ties binding them with one another progressively erode and come to be replaced with vertical ties binding them only to the center. After all, as rational actors themselves, regional bureaucrats are best able to pursue their centrally mandated tasks as regional bureaucrats by keeping their gaze focused on the center, the giver of bread and data.

The problem of horizontal fragmentation is compounded by the fact that highly centralized decision making necessitates that all information flow to the locus of authority, thereby resulting in an information glut at the center. Insofar as it is physically impossible to process so much data, the center's ability to monitor the activity of its regional bureaucracies declines and their autonomy vis-à-vis the center increases. Endowed with autonomy, regional bureaucrats pursue their own interests. Although their interests need not be opposed to the interests of the center, the important point is that relative autonomy compels the periphery to assert its own identity.[9] Karl W. Deutsch's statement of this argument remains as persuasive now as it was in the early 1950s: "In the long run there is thus perhaps inherent in every totalitarian system of government a tendency either toward overloading of its central facilities for the making of decisions, or toward an automatic corrosion of its original centralized structure and its disintegration into increasingly separate parts."[10]

Ironically, therefore, hypercentralization and bureaucratic extensiveness create ideal conditions—horizontal fragmentation *and* vertical segmentation—for regional officials to engage in a form of localized empire building. Such political feudalization not only subverts the centralized logic of the system but, far worse, disrupts resource extraction and, thus, the ability of the state to maintain maximal constraint. As both center and periphery claim to be responsible for economic extraction, continually interfere in each other's sphere of authority, and produce a condition approaching "dual sovereignty," decision making becomes incoherent, resources are squandered, and the constraint to which the state aspires, and on the maintenance of which it is premised, cannot be effectively pursued. The state, in a word, "decays."[11]

This degenerative development, which is inherent in the logic of totalitarian states, is inevitable—*ceteris paribus*, of course. Bureaucratic empire building has such deleterious consequences for the totalitarian state because it contravenes the twofold purpose of centralization: to make authoritative decisions and to supervise resource extraction. As regional satraps hoard information for their own decision-making purposes or convey distorted information to the center so as to insulate their bailiwicks from central interference, the center is progressively deprived of the lifeblood of centralization, accurate and comprehensive information.[12] Even so, it continues, as it must, to make authoritative decisions, but woefully misinformed ones that only increase the regional incentive to build empires and undermine efficient resource extraction. Worse still, not only do satraps actually begin to hoard resources in order to promote empire building, but the feudalization of the state also makes for inefficient extraction of resources from society.[13] The upshot is that the totalitarian state becomes incapable of maintaining the conditions of maximal constraint that are its *raison d'être*. Its decay advances irresistibly as the internal logic of hypercentralization continually pushes regional satraps to oppose centralization and, thus, the internal logic of the system itself.

The inevitable consequence of such decay is that the state's capacity to supervise proscription and prescription effectively declines. As resources are squandered on empire building, remain unextracted, or are inefficiently used, the totalitarian state's capacity to enforce its own rules diminishes. And as enforcement declines and society perceives it as declining, maximal constraint gives way to greater autonomy, which enables a large number of rational actors, the true believers, to maximize their goals without regard for the effects their choices may have on life and life chances. No less important, however, conditions of reduced constraint also permit fanatics and martyrs to initiate low-level collective actions that draw on the widening circle of rational actors willing to exploit the state's weakness to pursue their ends.

What enables challengers to launch such collective actions is the factor we encountered at the end of chapter 2—culture. In their zeal to control, supervise, and exploit society, totalitarian states unintentionally reinforce the single resource that remains, however imperfectly, outside their grasp: the language, symbols, values, myths, and signs of society. Totalitarian states attempt to control these as well, of course, but they can never attain complete success, as these cultural artifacts always retain at least some independent status as things of the mind. No matter how captive, the mind cannot be fully expropriated by the state. These residues of a battered, but perhaps emboldened, culture serve antistate challengers well. It is their primary resource and, as we know, cultural solidarity can suffice to overcome the free-rider effect and launch collective actions, especially under conditions of progressive state degeneration and decay.[14]

Sooner or later, state decay—and such associated manifestations as growing individual noncompliance and the emergence of small-scale collective actions—reaches the point where it begins to undermine the continued viability of the state as a maximally constraining, hypercentralized, and bureaucratically extensive entity. Reform, logically, is called for, and inefficient totalitarian states adopt the only logical solution to their pathologies—decentralization, but only a limited kind involving the devolution of some economic authority within the framework of continued political centralization.[15] Totalitarian states opt for this course, as only it promises to reduce the bureaucratic fragmentation and information overload that brought about decay without tipping the balance of political authority from center to periphery. But the promise is hollow; indeed, it worsens things considerably. An imbalance of just this kind begins to emerge as regional elites rationally utilize the augmentation of their economic authority and resources to consolidate their empires. In response, the center can reduce the size of regional bureaucracies, but only minimally, as cutting back by too much could undermine the capacity of the state to constrain society maximally.[16] Inevitably, then, bureaucratic reductions do little to prevent intensified regional empire building, which eventually forces the hand of the center to recentralize and, thus, to begin the vicious cycle once again. Alas, recentralization does not return the state to the starting point of decay, as every turn of the cycle squanders more and more resources, aggravates center-periphery relations, and creates political space and oppositions. And at each turn of the screw societal forces independent of the center and periphery utilize the enhanced space and reduced state efficiency to accumulate resources and contemplate collective actions of their own.

There is, therefore, no systemically consistent long-term solution to the totalitarian state's contradictions, as decentralization, which is the only cure for hypercentralization, only aggravates the fragmentation, waste, and inefficiency that spurred reform. As totalitarian states inexorably "wither away,"[17] not only can collective actions emerge in the pockets of autonomy created by their decay, but they come to persist, as challengers draw on culture and the state's squandered resources to attract constituencies who act with impunity because of the state's fragmentation and inefficiency.

At some point in the process of withering away, the center may consider adopting the one remaining reform measure: a reduction in the conditions of maximal constraint. As decay undermines the state's capacity to acquire resources, process information, and apply sanctions effectively, totalitarian states countenance the possibility of reducing the constraints they impose on society, so as to bring their claimed enforcement of proscription and prescription into equilibrium with their actual capacity to do so. Simply stated, totalitarian states stop tinkering with bureaucratic reforms and abandon their commitment to maximal constraint. Once again, however, totalitarian states enter a *cul de sac*, as reductions in constraint immediately translate into vastly greater political space and resources for potential challengers, who utilize both to launch large-scale collective actions against the state.[18] As antistate challenges mount, totalitarian states finally confront a savage dilemma: either to do nothing and risk collapse, or to crack down and return to decay. We must assume that they will adopt the latter course, unless some factor, such as a supreme leader or immense international pressure, intervenes. Decay is, after all, more tolerable than destruction, and totalitarian states will choose it unless the reforming zeal or misguided policies of leaders or the interference of other states prevent them from doing so.

Reckless leaders and world actors are the *dei ex machinis* that can push the totalitarian state onto the path of collapse. Only they can prevent such states from a natural return to the degenerative condition that, although increasingly unviable, can persist for long periods of time. Supreme leaders, for one thing, can make such an enormous difference precisely because the totalitarian state is so highly centralized that the vast amounts of authority concentrated in their hands permit them to exert a far greater influence on policy than their counterparts in nonconstraining laissez-faire settings. Not surprisingly, times of crisis—when fundamental policy choices regarding, say, collapse or decay have to be made—are most likely both to invite leaders to intervene and to induce them to make hasty and ill-considered decisions, especially if they fail to distinguish between the survival of the state they lead and the survival of themselves as leaders of the state. World actors, meanwhile, who are powerless to affect totalitarian states under normal conditions, can also make a critical difference if they act to support challengers or to prevent the state from cracking down in times of stress. Like supreme leaders, other states will be most inclined to act in such a manner in times of internally generated crisis, when totalitarian states are most vulnerable to outside pressure.

One thing appears certain, however. If, for whatever reasons, totalitarian states do not crack down when collective actions are still relatively isolated small-scale phenomena, oppositions will rush forward to exploit this sudden increase in political space by initiating ever larger collective actions. At some indeterminate point, if societal collective actions continue, repression will cease to be possible and a civil society will begin to emerge.[19] Once that happens, totalitarian states cannot survive for long. When reform is ineffective and repression is impossible, the only alternative is to abdicate, to wither away and die. The events of 1989 in Poland, Czechoslovakia, and East Germany appear to substantiate this view.

But withering away may be a luxury of only certain types of totalitarian states, those with ethnically homogeneous populations. Things become far more problematic if totalitarian states rule over heterogeneous populations in general or over distinct regions populated by more or less homogeneous ethnic groups in particular. In light of the bureaucratic empire building that centralization engenders, satrapies are likely to emerge in ethnically bounded regions and turn to culture as a resource for further enhancing their independence from the center. We may expect bureaucratic empire building to be especially extensive under such conditions, and reform, of the sort described above, will only impel local bureaucrats to speak the language of ethnic solidarity and cultural authenticity. But regional bureaucrats are not alone in benefitting from multinational state structures. Nonofficial challengers also draw on culture and regional identity to attract supporters for their collective actions, and, more likely than not, coalitions will emerge between bureaucratic empire builders and challengers, both of whom share a common interest, opposition to the center. If such centrifugal forces prove to be overwhelmingly strong—and they will as the state decays and reforms fail—the center will be incapable of cracking down and retrenching, as extreme fragmentation and regional antistate alliances will be so advanced that only the equivalent of a wartime mobilization—which we may assume to be beyond the decayed state's resource endowment—could crush them. Under conditions such as these, the totalitarian state will not wither away, but collapse, unless it embarks on self-dismemberment and confines its reforms to an ethnically homogeneous population. But this remedy is temporary at best, as the reconstructed totalitarian state begins to wither away once again.

In sum, political space emerges and expands in totalitarian states in three circumstances. First and most obviously, outside shocks, such as wars, can divert and weaken a totalitarian state, thereby permitting collective action. Second and more important, the totalitarian state degenerates by squandering its resources, wallowing in its inefficiencies, and undermining its own capacity to monitor the proscription and prescription of social behavior effectively. Third, and most important, totalitarian states embark on self-reform. They purposefully attempt to address the primary source of their pathologies—hypercentralization—by devolving some authority to peripheral bureaucracies, hoping thereby to reduce the bureaucratic fragmentation and information glut that brought about the symptoms in the first place.

It is only when a modicum of political space exists under maximally constraining conditions that we can consider the possibility of the emergence, persistence, and consummation of collective actions. I have already discussed these three phenomena as they relate to states in general in chapter 2. Insofar as the state was then assumed not to be maximally constraining, the political autonomy requisite for collective action was taken as a given. Emergence could then be explained in terms of sanctions, intense ideas, and cultural solidarity. Persistence appeared to necessitate an indeterminately appropriate level of resources that would make the costs of continuing in a collective action no larger than the costs of dropping out and accepting the status quo: such resources, I argued, were acquired by virtue of the everyday problems that befell states and the opportunities that awaited oppositions. Finally, consummation required a massive shift in the balance of resources due to external interventions that tip the scale against the state.

Not unexpectedly, these conclusions apply to the totalitarian state only in highly modified form. The first difference concerns political space. As totalitarian states are maximally constraining states, collective actions, which are the order of the day in nonconstraining settings, obviously are impossible until totalitarian pathologies produce pockets of autonomy. The second difference involves persistence: it takes little more than the normal vicissitudes of modern socioeconomic and political life to assure persistence in nonconstraining states, while under maximally constraining conditions, prolonged state decay is necessary. Finally, whereas massive external assaults can tip the balance against nonconstraining states, totalitarian states are quite adept at surviving military and economic shocks. Instead, internal shocks by system-transforming elites can so weaken the totalitarian state as to enable oppositions to pursue antistate collective actions to complete victory.

Ironically, then, totalitarian states are least susceptible to pressure from the outside and most likely to undertake change on their own—conclusions that flatly contradict the conventional wisdom on the subject. Quite the contrary, totalitarian states are forced, over time of course and other things being equal, by virtue of their own contradictions, to permit a civil society to emerge. But—and this, to quote Stephen Crane, is the "strange thing"—totalitarian states not only create their own grave diggers, they also dig their own grave.

Naturally, totalitarian states are an ideal type, and the dynamics discussed in this chapter have been deduced only from their institutional characteristics. True totalitarian states, if such there be, will only approximate the dynamics of the ideal totalitarian state, but, as the case of the Soviet Union suggests, falling short of ideal totalitarianism can actually enhance an imperfectly totalitarian state's tendency toward self-destruction.

70

I take it to be self-evident that the Soviet state more or less fits my definition of totalitarianism. It has been a highly centralized, bureaucratically extensive, maximally constraining monopolizer of resources since at least the late 1920s, and, as Soviet reformers currently acknowledge, these are the very institutional distortions that *perestroika* seeks to address. G. Arbatov, E. Batalov, A. Migranian, and A. Burganov have even gone so far as to call this type of system totalitarian,[20] in recognition of, I presume, the fact that the term makes eminent sense in the Soviet context and that they, surely, cannot be accused of harboring Cold War sentiments or of being "inveterate anti-Communists."[21]

Paradoxically, the imperfectly totalitarian nature of the Soviet state is its Achilles' heel. Were its bureaucracy less extensive, its centralization of authority less extreme, and its exploitation of resources less complete, the Soviet state would stand to benefit and might, as a result, be less susceptible to the pathologies discussed above. Alas, the imperfection in the Soviet state's brand of totalitarianism is just the sort that aggravates, rather than ameliorates, its pathologies. The bureaucratic apparatus reaches deep into society—so much so that any semblance of civil society was absent before the onset of *glasnost* and *perestroika*—while authoritative decision making was highly centralized within state agencies based in Moscow. Yet, there was one sphere that was purposefully consigned to regional bureaucracies—culture. To a greater or lesser extent, regional Soviet bureaucracies have always been permitted to decide some cultural issues, a far cry from full autonomy, of course, but no less a striking contrast to the virtual monopoly on political, economic, and social decision making held by the center. Not only have regional bureaucrats thus been armed with a critical resource, but their incentive to collaborate with nonofficial challengers against the center has been high, as the grounds for collaboration—the availability and utility of culture—have been built into their relationship with the center. Endowing the USSR's regional bureaucracies with relative control of culture is, therefore, the fatal flaw of the Soviet system. As we shall see, it was an inevitable flaw, and it had its origins in Marxism's original confrontation with, and inability to deal with, the nationality question.

71

— 5 —

The Contradictions of the Soviet State

Arbeiter aller Länder, vereinigt Euch!
— Marx and Engels

From today's perspective, the convoluted discussions held by Marxists in the late nineteenth and early twentieth centuries on the relationship between socialism and the nationality question seem obscure, if not quite obscurantist. This century has forcefully demonstrated that some of the most successful national liberation struggles have been led and inspired by Communists—note China, Yugoslavia, Albania, Cuba, Nicaragua, and Vietnam. Moreover, once in power, all Communists appear to have adjusted quite well to the realities of the nation-state, with some, such as Nicolae Ceausescu, adopting the kind of irredentist posturing that would have made even nineteenth-century nationalists blush. Border conflicts, as between the USSR and China, the USSR and Rumania, Hungary and Rumania, and Armenia and Azerbaidzhan, are also not intrinsically alien to people with allegedly Communist convictions. Indeed, Peter Zwick goes so far as to speak of the "contemporary marriage of communism and nationalism."[1]

72

Contradictions

Walker Connor suggests that this development is paradoxical—after all, it was the founders of Communism, Karl Marx and Friedrich Engels, who declared that proletarians have no countries, who placed class above nation, and who saw national struggles as either irrelevant, or obstructive, or at best tactically useful for the furtherance of the cause of socialism.[2] As I argued in chapter 3, however, the paradox vanishes on closer inspection. It is not quite the case, as Richard Pipes states, that "Marx and Engels left their followers little guidance in matters of nationality and nationalism."[3] Rather, Marx and Engels left their heirs a mixed intellectual legacy that could be used in support of a plethora of positions on the nationality question. The three dominant elements of this legacy may be referred to as the strategic primacy of class struggle, the tactical utility of nationalism, and ethnocentrism.[4]

The first element is obvious and requires little elaboration. We know from the *Communist Manifesto* that the "history of all hitherto existing society is the history of class struggles."[5] We also know from *The German Ideology* that "all struggles within the State, the struggle between democracy, aristocracy, and monarchy, the struggle for the franchise, etc., etc., arc merely the illusory forms in which the real struggles of the different classes are fought out among one another."[6] The viewpoint encapsulated by these two brief quotations runs through and informs all of Marx and Engels' writings to a greater or lesser degree. To be sure, politics is, as *The 18th Brumaire of Louis Bonaparte*, *The Civil War in France*, and, of course, the *Communist Manifesto*—as well as Marx's own activity as a revolutionary politician—assure us, important. Occasional zigs and zags in the actions of the bourgeoisie can be explained with reference to the autonomy of the state, imperial intrigues, power grabbing, and so on (indeed, Marx's writings on Russia for all practical purposes abandon the class framework), but—to use a hoary phrase Marxists love—"in the last analysis" class and class struggle is primary. The following quotation from the *Manifesto* says it all:

> National differences and antagonisms between peoples are daily more and more vanishing, owing to the development of the bourgeoisie, to freedom of commerce, to the world-market, to uniformity in the mode of production and in the conditions of life corresponding thereto.
>
> The supremacy of the proletariat will cause them to vanish still faster. United action, of the leading civilised countries at

least, is one of the first conditions for the emancipation of the proletariat.

In proportion as the exploitation of one individual by another is put an end to, the exploitation of one nation by another will also be put an end to. In proportion as the antagonism between classes within the nation vanishes, the hostility of one nation to another will come to an end.[7]

Rightly or wrongly, a perspective such as this relegates nationalism to a decidedly epiphenomenal position. Those of Marx and Engels' followers who dogmatically insisted that Marxists should not concern themselves with such trivial issues as nations and nationalism were not being faithless to their legacy.

Yet, their opponents, who argued that socialists should confront and solve the nationality question, could also draw on Marx and Engels for inspiration, and this set of Marxian exegetes brings me to the second element of the founders' legacy, the tactical utility of nationalism. The inevitability of capitalism and socialism notwithstanding, Marx and Engels were obviously astute enough to realize that they lived in a complex world characterized by different degrees of economic and political development, one in which superstructural phenomena had a nasty habit of getting in the way of theoretical predictions. Insofar as they expected the revolutionary process to be consummated in the most advanced capitalist countries, viz., England and Germany, it made good tactical sense to do everything possible to hasten the "birthpangs" of history. On the one hand, this meant taking part in propagandistic and organizational activity—accelerating the development of a proletarian consciousness and expediting the proletariat's capacity to fight for its political, economic, and social rights. Every blow against capitalism, even a shorter working day (perhaps especially a shorter day in view of Marx's theory of surplus value), was a blow for socialism. On the other hand, hastening the revolution meant removing obstacles to it, and it is here that the nationality question could and did in fact play a major role.

Starting with the late 1850s–early 1860s, both Marx and Engels became consistent supporters of Irish and Polish independence, not because they saw any particular value in Irish and Polish states as such, but because the separation of these nations from Great Britain and Russia, respectively, would be to the benefit of the English and European, and especially the German, working classes. As Marx wrote of the conflictual state of English-Irish relations: "This antagonism is artificially kept alive and intensified by the press, the pulpit, the comic papers, in short, by all the means at the disposal of the ruling classes. This antagonism is the secret of the impotence of the English working class, despite its organisation. It is the secret by which the capitalist class maintains its power."[8] The message is clear: remove the Irish competitor and the English worker will focus his antagonism on the real enemy, the English capitalist.

Similar logic pervades Marx and Engels' evaluation of the Polish struggle for independence. Here, too, a Polish nation-state held no innate attraction for them. Rather, Polish independence would strike a twofold blow against geopolitical obstacles to socialism. The first would be against Russia, which Marx and Engels considered a bastion of reaction and an expansionist power. Rolling Russia back from Poland would decrease its influence in Europe and give revolutionary forces more leeway. By the same token, an independent Poland would also strike a blow against Prussia, drive it into Germany's arms, and thereby hasten German unification—which, in turn, could but facilitate the class struggle in Germany as well as simplify capitalist relations in Europe.[9]

In the spirit of tactical utility—and somewhat in the manner of Karl W. Deutsch and Michael Hechter—Marx and Engels explicitly treat nationalism as only a geopolitical means toward the attainment of class ends. Implicitly, however, their position grants nationalism existential legitimacy and manifests a definite preference for the English and German working classes—not just as any old classes, but as specifically English and German ones. It is no surprise that Marx and Engels' followers could find support for at least two less-than-pure positions in their writings: that indigenous nationalism was also a logical means of hastening indigenous class struggle and that national working classes were the logical units of socialist strategy. Indeed, although the *Manifesto* solemnly intoned that "the working men have no country," it immediately hastened to add: "We cannot take from them what they have not got. Since the proletariat must first of all acquire political supremacy, must rise to be the leading class of the nation, must constitute itself *the* nation, it is, so far, itself national, though not in the bourgeois sense of the word."[10]

Marx and Engels' preference for the working classes of the leading civilized nations, England and Germany, brings me to the third element of their legacy, their ethnic chauvinism. Primarily evident in their earlier public writings, it is also apparent in much of their lifelong private correspondence. Clearly, they were products of the nineteenth century. As Europeans, they shared the conviction that European values and culture were the wave of the future. As socialists, they also had a marked preference for consolidation, for large states and large nations. And, as former Hegelians, they may have been inclined to view with impatience the historical meddling of stateless nations. Marx's essays on the Jewish question could be considered anti-Semitic today. His pieces on imperialism in India show a flagrant disregard for the peculiarities of outlying regions.[11] Finally, Engels's notion of nations with and without history, his casual references to *Völkerabfälle* consigned—to use pre-*perestroika* Soviet terminology—to the "garbage heap of history" reveal much more than a conviction that minority nationalism is pernicious to the cause of socialism.[12]

Marx and Engels' legacy on the nationality question is, then, mixed. No one line, no one interpretation stands out. Class is paramount, but nations can be important. Big is generally better, but small can have its uses. Should Communists ignore nations and nationalism? Clearly, no. Should they embrace them? Well, no. Should they utilize them for the good of the cause? Of course. But how? Marx and Engels give no specific answers, or, to state it more exactly, they give a variety of answers: some working classes, such as the English and German, apparently do have a country; some manifestations of nationalism, like that of the Irish, can accelerate working-class consciousness; other forms of nationalism, like that of the Poles, can have geopolitical importance. The overall message seems to be that nations and nationalism can be utilized in a variety of ways for the cause of socialism. The vagueness of this injunction permits a broad range of interpretations, all of which are more or less compatible with the teachings of the masters. To say that it all depends on the concrete historical conditions is no help, as perceptions of concrete historical conditions will vary from group to group and from party to party. Late-nineteenth- and early-twentieth-century Marxists were therefore to a large extent free to pursue the interpretation they deemed most useful for their particular ends.

But the freedom to choose was not the issue, as it became increasingly obvious to most socialists, and particularly those in Eastern Europe, that an interpretation of some kind had become imperative. Nations and nationalism could not simply be confined to the upper recesses of the superstructure, especially in Austria-Hungary and Russia. The Habsburg monarchy had experienced the shock of national rebellions in 1848, was forced to conclude a compromise with the Hungarians in 1867, and came increasingly in conflict with Czech, Polish, Ukrainian (Ruthenian), and South Slav national aspirations. For Russia, Poland remained the major problem for most of the nineteenth century, to be joined by the Balts, Ukrainians, Caucasians, and Tatars in the twentieth, especially after the near-revolution of 1905 and the limited reforms it generated. Not surprisingly, the approaches socialists adopted to the nationality problem were informed by the two dominant intellectual strands in the legacy of Marx and Engels—the strategic socialist and the tactical national. It will be best to begin with the latter.

The tactical national school and various variations thereof encompass what is generally referred to as the "right" wing of Marxist thought on the nationality question. Right or not, it represented the tendency that was most fully aware of the complexities involved in reconciling nationalism with socialism. True to the explicit Marx, the "tactical nationalists"—I shall call them that although they were not necessarily nationalists—saw national aspirations as a means for achieving socialist goals. But, true to the implicit Marx, they argued that national working classes represented the proper focus for their activities. At the forefront of this school were the Austrian Social Democrats and their leading theoreticians, Karl Renner and Otto Bauer. Inspired by them were a variety of "minority" socialist parties in Russia, in particular the Jewish Bund, the Ukrainian Social Democratic Workers' Party, and Baltic and Transcaucasian socialists.[13]

The Austrian socialists led the tactical national group by virtue of the programmatic innovations they adopted at their 1899 party congress in Brünn, where they considered two possible solutions to their country's nationality problem and, somewhat in the spirit of the Hofburg's incessant search for compromises, finally opted for a third. Neither territorial national-cultural autonomy, nor extraterritorial national-cultural autonomy, but a "federation of nationalities" was the answer. The first option would have converted the empire into a set of ethnically self-ruling provinces; the second option foresaw self-rule as encompassing all the members of a nation regardless of where they happened to live; the final option combined the two approaches and is worth quoting at greater length:

1. Austria is to be transformed into a democratic federation of nationalities (*Nationalitätenbundesstaat*).
2. The historic Crown lands are to be replaced by nationally homogeneous self-ruling bodies, whose legislation and

administration shall be in the hands of national chambers, elected on the basis of universal, equal, and direct franchise.

3. All self-governing regions of one and the same nation are to form together a nationally distinct union, which shall take care of this union's affairs autonomously.
4. A special law should be adopted by the parliament to safeguard the rights of national minorities.
5. We do not recognize any national privilege; therefore we reject the demand for a state language. Whether a common language is needed, a federal parliament can decide.[14]

All three options were premised on the continued existence of the Habsburg state, and all represented a conscious effort to separate culture from politics. By letting nationalities decide their own national-cultural affairs, such as language, press, and education, the Austrians hoped to defuse nationality conflicts politically and thereby preserve the unity of the monarchy. Was the plan viable? Insofar as the Habsburgs could legitimately claim to represent all the empire's peoples— "An meine Völker" began Franz Josef's 1914 proclamation regarding the war—it was not unreasonable for the socialists to have thought that the state would be preserved if, to use neo-Marxist terminology, its relative autonomy could be reinforced. At the same time, the socialist scheme was based on a fundamental contradiction. Culture and politics cannot be so easily separated as the Austrians assumed: culture spills over into politics, and politics involves culture. Even if the two realms did not overlap, some of the Habsburgs' national subjects inevitably would have utilized the space allotted to them for cultural affairs for political ends as well. In a word, the socialist plan may have been able to save the empire, but only at the cost of institutionalizing conflict among ethnic groups and between them and the state. Naturally, acknowledging the permanence of ethnic tensions would have been a small price to pay for perpetuating the state.

Renner and Bauer eventually raised the banner of extraterritorial national-cultural autonomy, and in doing so they reaffirmed their belief that nations were not just a passing fancy, but here to stay. Indeed, Bauer went so far as to place Marx on his head and conclude that "socialism leads necessarily to the realization of the principle of nationality."[15] The process by which this would happen, said Bauer, went as follows:

Modern capitalism begins gradually to distinguish the lower classes in each nation more sharply from each other, for these

78

classes too gain access to national education, to the cultural life
of their nation, and to the national language. The tendency toward unification also affects the labouring masses. But only socialist society will bring this tendency to fruition. It will distinguish whole peoples from each other by the diversity of national
education and civilization, in the same way as at present only
the educated classes of the different nations are distinguished.[16]

What sounds remarkably like Ernest Gellner's theory of nationalism could but have enormous appeal to the non-Russian socialists
trying to justify their inclination to work among the laboring classes
of their own nationality.[17] The Bund had already adopted the slogan
of extraterritorial national-cultural autonomy at its Fourth Congress
in 1901. Its choice was logical as the Jews of Russia were spread
throughout the Pale of Settlement and could claim no one compact
territory as unquestionably their own. The slogan was also appealing
to Armenian and Georgian socialists who, like the Bundists, had to
cope with an ethnic mosaic, the Caucasus. A dissonant voice belonged
to Ukrainian Social Democrats, who, at their founding congress in
1905, adopted a form of territorial national-cultural autonomy that
bordered on political autonomy. Compactly situated and possessing
the advantage of size, Ukrainians logically opted for an "autonomous
Ukraine . . . with a legislative right in those areas that concern only
the people living on the territory of the Ukraine."[18] None of these
groups could yet be considered nationalist, insofar as their aspirations stopped far short of a state, but the solutions to the nationality
question that they adopted were all premised on the view that nationality and class were hopelessly intertwined and therefore inseparable. Their "strategically national" argument was not that a national road to socialism was a good way of attaining socialism, but
that it was the only way. It is noteworthy that the national Communists of the 1920s (as well as most Third World socialists of the
present) eventually adopted and amplified this theme.
    The quintessentially strategic socialist answer to the nationality
question was formulated by Rosa Luxemburg. Not only does class
take priority over nation and socialism over nationalism in her writings, but they stand almost in contradiction to each other. In her po-
lemic against the Bolsheviks' adoption in 1903 of the slogan of "the
right of nations to self-determination," Luxemburg argued that, as
"there are no 'eternal' truths and . . . no 'rights'," to insist on the
"right of nations to self-determination" was to violate the basic Marxist

tenet, namely, that phenomena have to be understood within their specific material and historical context.[19] In other words, it is not necessarily true that all nations either should or should not enjoy self-determination. Rather, each case has to be settled on the basis of its own merits. Where self-determination, as with Ireland or Poland in the nineteenth century, furthers socialism, then it merits support. Where it does not, as with early-twentieth-century Poland, the "right" should be disavowed.

Second, said Luxemburg, it is a mistake to treat nations as units. After all, as nations consist of the working class *and* the bourgeoisie, it would be ludicrous for socialists to support the bourgeoisie, even in so indirect a manner. And if the working class is what socialists are concerned about anyway, then why obfuscate matters by speaking of something as nebulous as a nation? Indeed, why encourage workers to pursue something that is so obviously not in their interests? As she wrote in 1918: "Instead of warning the proletariat in the border countries against all forms of separatism as mere bourgeois traps, they [the Bolsheviks] did nothing but confuse the masses in all the border countries by their slogan and delivered them up to the demagogy of the bourgeois classes."[20]

It seems fair to say that, although Luxemburg may have been true to the spirit of Marx—or truer, say, than the Austrians or Lenin— her approach to the nationality question was doomed to failure in an age of nationalism and national consciousness. Irrespective of her total misassessment of the future of ever larger states (bright) and of national struggles (dim), Luxemburg's scheme could not work because it was sure to infuriate all those who cherished their nations and, thus, to incite them to oppose the national nihilism of her brand of socialism. Luxemburg's was, quite simply, a recipe for political suicide.[21]

Straddling the strategic socialist and tactical national positions was the early Lenin, who proffered an uneasy—some might say sophistic—synthesis of the two. His protestations in "The Right of Nations to Self-Determination" to the contrary, Lenin clearly sympathized with Luxemburg's strategic goals. Class struggle and socialism were primary, nations and nationalism were secondary. Yet Lenin realized that closing one's eyes to nationalism was no solution; the problem had to be addressed. But how was nationalism to be dealt with and Luxemburg's goals still retained? Both extraterritorial and territorial national-cultural autonomy appeared to lead to the break-up of large states, to divide the vanguard party into equivalent units, and to en-

courage the working class to pursue nationalist goals. Political autonomy was no less pernicious an option for the very same reasons.

Lenin's solution, that all nations have the right to self-determination via separation, was calculated to square this political circle.
Arguing in the Austro-Marxist mode, Lenin stated that Bolshevik support of the *right* to self-determination was unconditional. Arguing in
the Luxemburgian mode, however, he noted that their support of *self-
determination* as such was not unconditional: rather, support was
contingent on whether or not separation advanced the proletariat's
interests — foremost of which was, of course, unity.[22] How, then, could
national separation ever foster proletarian unity? Only under conditions of bourgeois entrenchment or colonial rule. In countries where
"progressive bourgeois national movements came to an end long ago,"
the "tasks of the proletariat of these ruling nations are the same as
those in England in the nineteenth century in relation to Ireland." In
the "semi-colonial countries" and colonies, meanwhile,

> Socialists must not only demand the unconditional and imme-
> diate liberation of the colonies without compensation — and this
> demand in its political expression signifies nothing else than the
> recognition of the right to self-determination; they must also
> render determined support to the more revolutionary elements
> in the bourgeois democratic movements for national liberation
> in these countries and assist their uprising — or revolutionary
> war, in the event of one — *against* the imperialist powers that
> oppress them.[23]

Separation, then, was to be supported by the most advanced countries and pursued in the least advanced ones. In those countries in
the middle, however, such as "Austria, the Balkans and particularly
Russia," where "bourgeois-democratic national movements" were
relatively recent, self-determination was to remain only a right. Thus,
it was obviously too late to pursue proletarian unity in advanced nation-states; too early in undeveloped colonies with weak bourgeoisies
and tiny proletariats; and timely only in transitional multinational
societies where both bourgeoisie and proletariat were still in the process of consolidation. Under the latter conditions, "the most difficult
and most important task . . . is to unite the class struggle of the
workers of the oppressor nations with that of the workers of the op-
pressed nations."[24]

While Lenin's proposals for developed and undeveloped countries
offered socialists an unambiguous conceptual framework for com-

prehending the colonizer-colonized relationship, his suggestions for the middle-range countries were both ambiguous and unworkable. Lenin's exhortation that dominant-nationality socialists support the right to self-determination, while subordinate-nationality socialists reject it, was a nonsolution to a complicated problem, because it seemed to suggest that socialists alone were involved in deciding the nationality question. Once nonsocialist nationalists enter the picture, as they inevitably do, it is not at all clear what the socialist policy toward a genuine national liberation struggle should be. Supporting it undermines proletarian unity; resisting it strengthens the hand of the hegemonic nation and ruling class; ignoring it, while speaking of rights, is to consign oneself to political irrelevance. Like Luxemburg's principled stand, Lenin's position was practically useless.

No less problematic was Lenin's entire tripartite classification. While the developed and undeveloped categories are relatively straightforward, the middle one is not. Although transitional, these countries were not uniformly so. Serbia, Greece, Bulgaria, and Rumania were neither colonizers nor colonized. Austria and Russia, however, were both. Galicia was little more than a colony,[25] as was Turkestan. Were their socialists to demand separation — as M. S. Sultan Galiev was to do — on the grounds that they were colonies, or were they to work for proletarian unity, as their purportedly transitional status required of them? Things became even more complex with quasi-colonies such as the Ukraine, which was clearly positioned somewhere above Turkestan but far below the central Russian provinces. Those Ukrainian social democrats who emphasized the colonial half of the equation, such as Lev Iurkevych, not unreasonably demanded independence, only to be denounced by a furious Lenin for bourgeois nationalism.[26] In cases such as these the Bolshevik position dovetailed so neatly with that of the Tsarist government that many non-Russian socialists concluded that Lenin's approach to the nationality question was merely a ruse to perpetuate Great Russian hegemony. Justified or not, such misunderstandings were the inevitable product of Lenin's ambiguity about the central issue in all his writings — political power. Uncharacteristically, although perhaps not accidentally, Lenin had nothing to say to those non-Russian socialists who desired a practical program with realistic political options regarding the nationality question.

The ambiguities in Lenin's nationality policy became most apparent, even to him, during and after the Civil War. Despite their training in the "school of Bolshevism," numerous non- Russian socialists, including those with no previous autonomist inclinations, began insisting on some political power, be it in the form of independent Party organizations or maximally autonomous states. A Volga Tatar, Sultan Galiev, and two Ukrainians, Serhii Mazlakh and Vasyl' Shakhrai, demanded both on the grounds that their nations could embark on genuine proletarian unity only after they had shed the baggage of their colonial relationship with Russia. Mazlakh and Shakhrai's arguments recall Frantz Fanon's:

> Many socio-economic and cultural-spiritual links have been forged during the two and a half centuries of the Ukraine's confinement within the boundaries of tsarist and autocratic Russia, but, at the same time, so much filth has collected on these links that they have lost their elasticity and become stiff, incapable of bending with the turns of history. . . . Instead of clearing away individual rails and beams and wasting energy attaching supports to walls which may fall in today or tomorrow, it is better to clear out the whole place, removing the old and installing new rafters. . . . Relations with the Ukraine must find a new set of foundations; they must be based on a real and alive— not a verbal— international unity. . . . For respect to develop it is not enough for all peoples to be equal. It is still necessary that one have respect for oneself and that one compel others to respect one's will, one's language, one's person. . . . And when this is done you will have such an ally as cannot be acquired from any kind of one and indivisible [Russia].[27]

Sultan Galiev went even further, arguing that the Russian proletariat was no better than the Russian bourgeoisie in its relationship with colonially exploited non-Russian borderlands. Indeed, according to Sultan Galiev, a genuinely revolutionary socialist impetus could come only from the "proletarian nations," and it was up to them to impose a dictatorship on the colonizers— the Russians: "Old Russia, still alive under the new mask of the Union of Soviet Socialist Republics, cannot last forever. Soviet Russia is a transitory phenomenon. The hegemony of the Russian people over other nations necessarily must be replaced by the dictatorship of these same nations over the Russians."[28]

These autonomist strivings were crushed, of course, while the formal independence of non-Russian republics and parties was progressively undermined. Their military, foreign policy, and economic prerogatives were circumscribed in a series of bilateral treaties with Soviet

Russia in 1920–1921. More important, such national parties as the Russian Party of Muslim-Communists (Bolsheviks), the Turkic Communist Party, the Ukrainian Communist Party (UKP), the Borot'bist version of the UKP, and the Socialist Party of Turkestan ERK (Party of Freedom) were abolished and/or merged with territorial branches of the Russian Communist Party.[29] Merger, to be sure, was a step forward, in that it recognized the existence of actual national regions, but a very small step nonetheless. Insofar as actual power was in the hands of the central Party, and not the state, Moscow's preference for a unitary party with regional branches in all the republics except Soviet Russia was tantamount to continued Russian institutional hegemony and a rejection of local self-rule. Once this battle was lost, the fight over the extent of states' rights was inevitably hopeless for the non-Russians.

It may be worth stressing that it is the location and distribution of authoritative institutions that determine the national character of a state, and not the putative nationality of politicians—a designation of more than dubious value in the Soviet context, anyway—or the state's treatment of ethnic groups. The Communist Party was and still is Russian by virtue of the fact that it consists of territorial subunits corresponding to all the republics except the RSFSR: that is, the Party explicitly rejects the federalist principle and indirectly asserts the primacy of Russia.[30] Similarly, the Soviet government apparatus in general and the secret police in particular are Russian because most of their decision-making authority is lodged in the bureaucracies of Moscow. In contrast, Stalin's being Georgian is as much beside the point as Disraeli's being Jewish or Catherine the Great's being German. By the same token, states need not be beneficient to the nationality they claim to represent. (Indeed, as the jealous monopolizers of the means of violence in some territory, how could they?) The fact that, as Aleksandr Solzhenitsyn argues, the Russians bore their share of Stalinism is as immaterial as the fact that the English working classes suffered from industrialization, that the Italians were involved in costly tropical adventures by Mussolini, or that Mao Zedong—as much a nationalist as Mazzini—was responsible for the death of millions of Chinese during the Great Leap Forward and the Cultural Revolution.[31] In the Soviet case as elsewhere, ethnic or policy inclinations hold a back seat to the institutional centrality of Moscow and the strategic importance of the Party and the secret police.

The tug-of-war between the Russian state and the non-Russians continued unabated until 1922–1924, when the Union of Soviet Socialist Republics was founded. Significantly, its establishment represented a repudiation of the obfuscatory ballyhoo surrounding the right to self-determination, which had clearly proved to be useless in regulating Russian-non-Russian relations, even under such ostensibly ideal conditions as existed after the consolidation of Bolshevik rule in 1921–1923. Confronted with the persistent autonomist demands of non-Russian Communists, the Bolshevik solution to the nationality question simply disintegrated. Both Stalin and Lenin abandoned this mostly empty formula for alternatives with more practical substance. At the risk of only some exaggeration, I venture to say that, in effect, Stalin adopted Luxemburg's approach, whereas Lenin turned to the Austro-Marxists for inspiration. *Tertium non datur.*

The story is familiar. Arguing that the interests of the proletariat were paramount, Stalin demanded that the non-Russians be harnessed as closely as possible to the Russian center. He proposed incorporating the heretofore quasi-independent Soviet republics into a unitary Russian state, granting them autonomous status, and subjecting them to the central government. Lenin, on the other hand, argued for creating a federation, including Soviet Russia and the non-Russian republics, to be headed by governmental organs separate from those of Russia.[32] As both men agreed that the Party should remain centralized and institutionally Russian, their disagreement was not over the distribution of political power, but over the allocation of administrative authority, with Stalin opting for a very narrow interpretation and Lenin for a wider one. It is for this reason that Lenin's approach was quintessentially Austro-Marxist in inspiration. It represented nothing less than a weaker Soviet version of the Brünn Congress's call for some form of "territorial national-cultural autonomy." As Austria was supposed to have been, the Soviet Union claimed to have become a "democratic federation of nationalities" administered by organs of self-rule whose prerogatives were largely of a national-cultural kind. To be sure, the analogy is not quite exact for two reasons: the USSR was never democratic, certainly not in the sense intended by Renner and Bauer, and Soviet republics had and still have some decision-making authority in a few noncultural realms as well. Nevertheless, the analogy is neither inaccurate, as Moscow does decide all major political and economic issues, nor misleading, as the Austro-Marxist and Soviet solutions are both premised on a separation of national-cultural concerns from military, political, and most economic ones.

Only Lenin's solution was consistent with the Bolshevik claim to be the true defenders of the right of nations to self-determination. As Lenin had to reconcile this right with the reality of a *de facto* Russian-dominated state formation, he had in effect to hoist himself and his followers with their own petard. To deprive the non-Russians of even the pretense of self-rule, as Stalin suggested, was to pretend that the ethnic energies unleashed by the Revolution and Civil War did not exist. The only viable course was to proclaim a federation and channel nationality aspirations into nonpolitical directions, thereby separating politics from culture, an impossible task, as we already know. Ironically, by granting non-Russians cultural autonomy, Lenin guaranteed that they would utilize this nonconstraint to voice preferences that exceeded their mandate. And by permitting the non-Russians to pursue national-cultural goals within the framework of a quasi-federal, highly centralized, and bureaucratically extensive state, Lenin made certain that they would, sooner or later, rationally utilize that framework in a manner that could threaten the political foundations of the state. The Soviet version of Austro-Marxism created national Communism. Lenin succeeded in squaring the circle, but keeping it squared meant continually having to resist built-in pressures by national Communists to return it to its original shape.

— 6 —

The Inevitability of National Communism

Ukraino nasha radians'ka.
— Petro Shelest

National Communism is a political ideal that claims that Communism, however defined, can be pursued best by acknowledging "national specificities" and by following "national paths." In the Soviet context, national Communists are individuals who share this ideal or act as if they shared it by pursuing their own republics' interests, even to the detriment of all-Union interests. Soviet national Communism is distinguished from mere localism (*mestnichestvo*) by being focused, not on oblasts or regions, but on symbolically sovereign republics. Soviet national Communism also differs from nationalism in explicitly rejecting political independence. And yet, in the appropriate circumstances, Soviet national Communism may be contextually nationalist and, thus, can pose no less of a threat to the integrity of the Soviet state than genuine nationalism. Ironically, it is none other than the imperfectly totalitarian Soviet state itself that permits national Communist behavior to emerge and creates the conditions that compel it to acquire contextually nationalist dimensions.

Coming to Grips

As an inevitable consequence of the contradiction between a centralized Communist Party and an Austro-Marxist state, national Communism has been a recurrent and irrepressible feature of Soviet history. Only during the period of entrenched Stalinism—the late 1930s, the late 1940s, and the early 1950s—did extreme centralization largely succeed in repressing the national Communist symptoms of the USSR's Janus-like nature. Otherwise, the pattern of national Communism has always been the same, irrespective of who its spokesmen happen to be—Oleksandr Shums'kyi, Mykola Skrypnyk, Veli Ibragimov, Galimdzhan Ibragimov, Faizullah Khodzhaev, Turar Ryskulov, Jānis Kalnbērziņš, Petro Shelest, Vasilii Mzhavanadze, Sharaf Rashidov, or Dinmukhamed Kunaev.[1] Other things being equal, republican Communists assert themselves in one form or another whenever circumstances permit, and the greater their autonomy, the greater, usually, their self-assertiveness.

Although irrepressible, national Communists have always met the same fate. When the political center has perceived them as going too far in their pursuit of republican interests—as it inevitably has—the national Communists have been either dismissed or repressed or both, and their policies have been halted or reversed. Iosef Stalin's was the bloodiest response, involving the wholesale physical liquidation of scores of non-Russian cadres. Leonid Brezhnev's, second in severity, was focused on the Ukraine and Shelest. His successors, and Mikhail Gorbachev in particular, have responded most mildly, turning their attention to the intractable republican Party organizations while encouraging cultural and economic initiative. As chapter 12 argues, Moscow's current struggle with national Communism has only just begun, but if history is any guide to the future (which it may not be, thanks to the intervention of Mikhail Gorbachev), its outcome is not in doubt.

Why this cyclical pattern? Why does national Communism emerge in periods of systemic decentralization and why does its repression herald systemic recentralization? Indeed, why does its repression occur with a monotonous, if not indeed inevitable, regularity? The underlying answer lies, as chapters 4 and 5 suggested, in the contradiction between the imperfectly Austro-Marxist Soviet state and the Russian-dominated and politically centralized Communist Party. Austro-Marxism grants republican Communist elites limited national-cultural authority and resources within the boundaries of their symbolically sovereign republics. Political and economic power, on the other hand, remains concentrated in a centralized and institu-

88

tionally Russian Party, which claims to be and is the core of an imperfectly totalitarian state that exerts maximal constraint on virtually all spheres of life. As long as the center's political and economic monopoly is maintained—as long as authority is centralized—bureaucratic fragmentation will be inevitable, but republican elites will have little opportunity to pursue their own interests if these interests are contrary to all-Union interests. But just this will happen once that monopoly is broken and greater amounts of political and/or economic authority are devolved to already fragmented peripheral bureaucracies.

Determining exactly how and why the devolution of Soviet central authority results in national Communism requires going deeper into the theoretical framework discussed in previous chapters. As will shortly be evident, the actual working out of the contradiction between the Austro-Marxist state and the centralized Party can best be understood in terms of how regional satraps pursue their interests by mobilizing resources under conditions of enlarged political space. There are three questions that I shall address in light of these concerns:

1. Is systemic decentralization a rational way to reform the centralized Soviet system and, if so, why?
2. Does systemic decentralization inevitably result in the emergence of national Communism, perhaps even of nationalism?
3. Are national Communism and decentralization incompatible with stability and, if so, why?

The first question is answered most easily. As Alec Nove has argued for many years, highly centralized political-economic systems, especially those that, like the USSR, approximate totalitarianism, suffer from a number of built-in weaknesses that impede the rational choice and implementation of policies.[2] Most debilitating is the fact that central authorities (or planners) can never fully assimilate all the information that they receive from lower levels of the system. Even if we assume that they receive all available information and that all of it is accurate, planners would still be physically incapable of absorbing it, ordering it, and using it in accordance with their preferences, even with the help of powerful computers. The problem becomes especially evident when one appreciates that there are millions of workers and housing units, thousands of enterprises and stores, and millions of products and prices in the USSR and all other large economies. Even doers of research would have to admit that the combinations and permutations are staggering. Under conditions such as these, efficient planning becomes problematic as the information required for such planning is inevitably deficient.

Complicating the problem are two additional factors. First, even if central planners could process all available information, they could never determine the optimal economic arrangements for all the regions of a country, especially one so vast as the Soviet Union. Raw data, no matter how accurate and how extensive, can never replace the firsthand knowledge of local conditions, the "feel" for a region and its inhabitants, that only local officials and entrepreneurs can have. And second, because central preferences will inevitably diverge from local ones, at some times and over some issues at least, local officials will always be subject to two powerful temptations: to subvert, undermine, or resist central preferences and, thus, to prevent the implementation of central policies in their bailiwicks; and to provide the central authorities with inaccurate data, in order either to obstruct central planning or to enhance their own standing in the hierarchical chain of command. The inherent difficulties of central planning become even more substantial when the preferences and activities of plant managers, workers, and farmers are thrown into the equation. There are obviously many more deficiencies of (as well as, of course, advantages to) centralized political-economic systems but, as I have suggested above, the fundamental ones appear to involve their inability to find optimal—or rational—solutions to any but exceedingly macroeconomic problems.[3] Once we descend to lower levels of the economy, the inability of planners to process data, understand local preferences, and overcome the interference of local officials results in inefficiency, waste, and general economic malaise, especially under conditions of the so-called scientific-technical revolution. As these problems accumulate, the initial response of the center generally is to assert even greater control, which simply makes things worse. Instead, as a variety of economists in the West and in formerly state socialist societies argue, the logical solution to such overcentralization is decentralization, permitting local officials and entrepreneurs greater leeway in making the decisions that their preferences, their better knowledge of local circumstances, and their more accurate data suggest are rational.[4]

Decentralization in Soviet-type economic systems can be one of two kinds: the introduction of elements of the market or the transfer of decision-making authority from central institutions to republican ones—or what Franz Schurmann calls Decentralization I and II, respectively.[5] The first approach represents complete decentralization to the level of individual consumers and producers and is clearly the antipode of a centralized planning system. The second approach lowers the locus of decision making and, arguably, retains some of the worst features of overcentralization. The second approach directly enhances the authority of republican institutions, but so does the first one, if somewhat less so. A Union-wide pure market system might function best without the cumbersome interference of republics, but, as it is well-nigh impossible to imagine that they might be abolished in the foreseeable future,[6] an expanded market system would inevitably align itself along republican lines, thus leading to the emergence of some fifteen internal Soviet markets and to the enhancement of the economic and political institutions whose job it is to regulate and oversee them.

We are not amiss, then, in suggesting that decentralization is the best way to reform the overcentralized Soviet economic system. We are now in a position to inquire whether decentralization, in one or both of the forms discussed above, inevitably produces national Communism or, worse still, nationalism. The case of Yugoslavia suggests that the answer is an emphatic yes, but such an analogy is obviously insufficient for our purposes. The place to start our inquiry is with a more general discussion of the relationship between polyarchies and markets, in order to determine, at the highest level of abstraction, whether or not economic forces alone logically lead to the disintegration of dictatorial and, hence, of ethnically coercive systems.

Charles Lindblom defines polyarchies as consisting of the following elements:

Freedom to form and join organizations
Freedom of expression
Right to vote
Eligibility for public office
Right of political leaders to compete for support
Right of political leaders to compete for votes
Alternative sources of information
Free and fair elections (open, honestly conducted, one man one
    vote), which decide who is to hold top authority
Institutions for making government policies depend on votes and
    other expressions of preference.[7]

What is the relationship between such a system and markets in general and marketization in particular? Lindblom convincingly argues that, because all polyarchies have markets, while not all market systems are polyarchies, there is no logical connection between the two. Indeed, as he writes, the fact that existing polyarchies all have markets appears to be due to the peculiarities of their historical development: both polyarchies and markets arose in conjunction with struggles for constitutional liberalism in particular historical circumstances.[8] Lindblom concludes:

> If we understand that polyarchy is a component of a highly developed form of constitutional liberalism and that constitutional liberalism in turn is a set of institutions assuring individuals of their liberty to enter into trade in order to develop their own life opportunities, we would not expect a polyarchy without a market. But we would expect markets without polyarchies. For short of polyarchy, some nations would be expected to develop a form of constitutional liberalism sufficient to guarantee the rights of an elite or middle class to try to enrich itself. Such a set of guarantees might be protected by agreement within an elite or by constitutional tradition short of polyarchy.[9]

In a similar vein, Wlodzimierz Brus suggests that marketization, or what he more broadly terms decentralization, does not lead directly to polyarchy in economically centralized socialist systems and therefore has no logical connection with the diminution of "monoarchy." Because, as he argues, the decision to decentralize is a politically motivated calculation to increase the political system's chances of survival, economic decentralization cannot in and of itself initiate a shift away from monoarchy. A political struggle has to take place; without that, monoarchy will remain—a point seemingly confirmed by the 1989 massacre in Tienanmen Square.[10]

Brus does concede two points that are of enormous importance to our subject. The first is:

> Perhaps the political value of marketization lies therefore not so much in its active role as an engine of destruction of mono-archy but in the creation of an economic environment more propitious for the maintenance of polyarchal elements won in direct political struggles. This interpretation looks plausible in light of our analysis. It affords new significance to the role of the market as a factor reducing the *area* of political authority and hence providing greater independence for the individual, as well as a basis for the grouping of interests.[11]

Decentralization, in other words, reduces the scope of state control and increases autonomy. Both elements, as we know, are critical to the emergence of political opposition, nonnationalist and nationalist. Brus's second point injects the ethnic angle I am looking for:

> One aspect that perhaps deserves separate mention is the new dimension opened by market socialism for pursuit of local (especially regional) interests as a result of the decentralization of investment decisions. Local interests are now able to manifest themselves not only in pressing the centre for favourable allocations, but also in the promotion of development plans backed by their own resources. An element of independence is hereby created with political significance for political pluralisation, particularly when regional aspects interact with national (ethnic) ones.[12]

The key words here are, of course, resources and independence. Decentralization not only increases autonomy, but it also permits locals to utilize their *own resources* for their *own ends*. Decentralization, therefore, may not be the engine of monoarchal destruction, but—and this is critical—it does create the conditions for individuals and groups to pursue what they perceive as their own interests. More important, as I shall argue, decentralization permits, enables, and actually compels the periphery to act independently. In a word, systemic decentralization does indeed appear inevitably to result in the emergence of national Communism and contextual nationalism.

A logical reconstruction of this descent into the national Communist and contextually nationalist maelstrom would start with the fact that, at its basic level, decentralization represents a devolution to local levels of information and of decision making.[13] Both are significant expansions of peripheral authority on their own terms, but they are especially important for three additional reasons. First, they cannot be confined to the economic sector alone, to the system of ministries and to the factories attached to them. Politics and economics are intertwined in socialist systems, and it is inevitable that economic decentralization will be accompanied by the devolution of information and decision making to peripheral Party organizations. Second and no less important, a genuine devolution to the periphery of information and decision making necessarily goes hand in hand with increased popular participation and initiative. If the periphery is now to solve centrally defined problems, it is impossible for it not to involve greater numbers of people in its information-gathering and decision-making processes. Just as the center depends on peripheral inputs in order to make decisions, so, too, the periphery now depends on its own "periphery" for inputs. Third and perhaps most important, none of these developments is feasible if central and/or coercive organs continue to exert exceedingly close supervision of peripheral goings-on. Some kind of "thaw" is logically necessary for peripheral information processing, decision making, and participation to function half-effectively. For decentralization to work, the center has to reproduce at the peripheral level the conditions of decision making that it itself enjoys, that is, it must expand the periphery's autonomy.

Expanded autonomy permits individuals to pursue their own preferences and rational actors will do just that. With the changed structure of incentives—reduced negative sanctions and increased positive ones—they will more freely pursue their interests as they define them. But, except for fanatics and martyrs, who are indifferent to sanctions, as well as a smattering of true believers, most peripheral actors will still eschew nationalist behavior even if they believe in nationalism. After all, to be consistent we must assume that, even under conditions of economic decentralization, the state will continue to be richly endowed with resources and be willing to impose severe penalties on nationalist dissent. If the impact of decentralization stopped here, our inquiry would be at an end.

It is our good fortune that economic decentralization increases the autonomy not only of individuals, but also of elite collectivities. As Brus insists, marketization does not create new autonomous groups, because such a polyarchal development is contingent on a political decision of the center, and if the center is determined to prevent such groups from arising, we must assume that it can do so without undermining decentralization. But economic decentralization does expand the autonomy of already existing peripheral elites and institutions. To what effect, however? After all, such Communist elites will not be ideologically inclined to engage in national Communist and nationalist behavior, because their official status definitionally excludes the possibility of their having such sentiments. And even if they were clandestine national Communists and nationalists, the state's negative sanctions would dissuade most of them from translating their beliefs into behavior.

How, then, is it possible for peripheral elites to engage in national Communist and, perhaps, even contextually nationalist behavior when our assumption—continued state power and hostility to national Communism and nationalism—precludes such activity on their part?

Evidently, a *deus ex machina* is now in order, and mine bears the barbarian name of Austro-Marxism.

Economic decentralization affects Austro-Marxist elites in three ways. As we know, decentralization permits them to engage in greater interest formulation, articulation, and implementation in the republic. But, second and more important, decentralization forces peripheral elites to pursue *only* their own interests. The purpose and logic of decentralization compel peripheral elites to focus their initiative and energies on the territorial unit they administer, the republic; otherwise, they would be incapable of implementing decentralization's original mandate—improved efficiency, better decisions, and a better system. Finally, and most important, decentralization arms the periphery. It gives local elites the means to pursue their goals effectively. That is, it provides them with resources or with greater control of resources. Resources, in turn, convert into positive and negative sanctions and permit peripheral elites to mobilize rational actors by overcoming the free-rider problem.

More specifically, the three areas in which national Communists have invariably asserted themselves are—as Austro-Marxism would lead us to expect—language and culture, cadres, and investments. National Communists have been almost unanimous in supporting measures that enhance local cultures and languages, promote local cadres to positions of prominence within the republican elite, and divert monies to their own economies. In turn, the center's crackdown on national Communism has always involved centripetal policies that encourage Russian language and culture, Russian-Slavic cadre primacy, and the subordination of republic economic interests to all-Union ones. All three resources figured prominently in the period of the New Economic Policy (NEP) and the First Five-Year Plan, as well as during Khrushchev's "Thaw" and the Sovnarkhoz experiment. Even under the Brezhnev retrenchment, which primarily affected the cultural and economic spheres, the promotion of local cadres continued unabated, with the result that, by the 1980s, formidable local machines had developed, especially in the Ukraine, Kazakhstan, and Central Asia. Not surprisingly, the same three issues have acquired a high profile in the era of *perestroika* under Gorbachev.

What do republican elites do when they are allotted the space, authority, and resources to implement decentralization? Naturally, in such optimal circumstances, they pursue their own interests, even to the detriment of all-Union ones. Pursuing their own interests, however, inevitably involves enhancing not only their own political and economic authority, but also their political and economic sovereignty. In this sense, when taken to its logical end, national Communist behavior becomes a zero-sum game with the center. The periphery converts the authority granted to it under conditions of systemic decentralization into greater sovereignty. The periphery *must* act in this manner if it wants to fulfill the center's mandate; it *must* pursue its own interests, accumulate resources, and mobilize constituencies if it hopes to succeed. Ironically, however, in acting in this manner, the periphery begins to undermine the center's position of political and economic dominance vis-à-vis itself.[14]

National Communist behavior of such magnitude is, I submit, contextually nationalist behavior, little different from that pursued by, say, Armenian, Georgian, and Azerbaidzhani elites in 1917–1921. Decentralization and Austro-Marxism turn the tables on the normal structure of sanctions—they reward efficient self-centered behavior and punish inefficient self-centered behavior—and rational, nonnationalist republican elites react accordingly. Indeed, they act *as if* they believed that their unit of governance should be sovereign and its interests paramount, and by acting as if they were nationalists they become nationalists *malgré soi;* that is, they become contextual nationalists. Significantly, Russian elites are exempt from such deviations—a fact that underlines their exceptional status vis-à-vis the state, a point I discuss in chapter 11. Because of the overlapping of Soviet and Russian elites and institutions, the interests and actions of the two are definitionally identical. Russia in general and Moscow in particular are the center, and the center, obviously, cannot be decentralized. Consequently, decentralization is meaningful only in relation to them, that is, in the periphery, while contextually nationalist behavior is impossible in Moscow.

We see now why the mixture of decentralization and national Communism is so unsettling for the imperfectly totalitarian Soviet state as it is currently constituted in its highly centralized, bureaucratically extensive, and quasi-federal form. Needless to say, contextually nationalist elite behavior affects the Soviet system in the same manner as the subjectively nationalist behavior of true believers, martyrs, fanatics, and believers of convenience. It accelerates centrifugal tendencies and aggravates the system's fundamental contradiction between the Party's institutionally Russian political monopoly and the cultural bases of Austro-Marxism. Economic centralization thus bears the seeds of its own destruction. Because decentralization, if pursued far enough and long enough, is likely to lead to the break-up of the Soviet system, the center has never permitted decentralization to run its course. At some empirically indeterminable point, when it perceives that centrifugal tendencies are increasing more than it can bear, the center recentralizes, revokes peripheral autonomy, and reduces peripheral resources. In other words, it "cracks down." The exact timing of a crackdown depends on a host of circumstances—international relations, intraelite conflicts, successions, economic trends, and so on—but at some point a turnaround logically must occur if the system is to survive.

The logic described above holds with equal force if the conditions of the intellectual exercise are changed: if economic centralization is held constant and political decentralization is assumed to take place. The diminution of Party control and supervision of local political organs translates directly into increased peripheral prerogatives, political resources, and contextually nationalist behavior for the reasons already discussed with regard to economic decentralization. That political decentralization has political consequences is true by definition, however, and therefore represents rather less of an intellectual challenge than the economy-nationalism connection. Nevertheless, it is no less important both logically and empirically, as political de-Stalinization means that some political decentralization has been built into the Soviet system since the early 1960s. Attempts at economic decentralization under conditions of some political decentralization are all the more likely to encourage national Communism and produce contextually nationalist behavior.

Both forms of decentralization coincided in the 1920s, with nativization (*korenizatsiia*) and the New Economic Policy, and in the late 1950s and early 1960s, with de-Stalinization and the Sovnarkhoz reform—periods that, not incidentally, witnessed a flowering of national Communism. Since Khrushchev's demise, political and economic decentralization have not overlapped to so great an extent. Wholly in fact and partly in intention, the Kosygin reforms and their offspring were tantamount to economic recentralization, whereas Brezhnevism represented a selective reassertion of some central political control in recalcitrant republics such as the Ukraine and Georgia and the institutionalization of peripheral political prerogatives regarding cadre selection and promotion. This latter fact, together with the political turmoil that accompanied the Brezhnev succession, enabled Uzbekistan's Rashidov, Kazakhstan's Kunaev, Kirgizia's

Usubaliev, and other local satraps to engage in national Communism and convert their republics into modern-day principalities on the order of prerevolutionary Khiva and Bukhara.

The current Soviet leadership is treading on especially thin ice because Gorbachev's program of *perestroika* combined all the necessary ingredients for an acceleration of national Communism and contextually nationalist behavior. *Glasnost* and *demokratizatsiia* are equivalent to political liberalization and decentralization, while the introduction of republican cost accounting (*khozraschet*), economic sovereignty, and the "socialist market" entails economic decentralization. The combination is potent, and the visible growth in 1987–1990 of aggressively national and nationalist sentiments in all the republics was the first sign of the immense dangers that lie ahead. Despite the fact that Gorbachev placed his own supporters into key positions within the center and periphery, the logic of decentralization plus Austro-Marxism will drive these individuals and elites increasingly to pursue contextually nationalist behavior. If so, Gorbachev or his successor will come face to face with the contradictory essence of the Soviet multinational state. And unless they are willing to preside over the empire's disintegration, recentralization of some kind will be inevitable.

To the extent that, as most economists argue, centralization inevitably leads to crisis-like situations demanding economic decentralization as a cure, the Soviet state would appear to be caught in a vicious circle of its own making. Just as decentralization effectively addresses the problems inherent in economic centralization, so, too, it inevitably sets loose forces that threaten the stability of the system. Can the USSR continue indefinitely in such a vicious circle? The answer is a conditional yes. As long as systemic survival is not an issue (a point the conclusion considers in greater detail), temporary decentralization can alleviate certain problems and recurrent recentralization is always quite plausible. After all, some states muddle through for centuries, while others can decay for decades. In order to answer this question negatively, we would have to assume that the crisis necessitating decentralization is so severe that anything but complete decentralization would lead to immediate collapse.[15] Of course, as I argued in chapter 4, the reforming zeal or misguided policies of leaders can create such a crisis—and if they do, then radical decentralization and breakdown may be the only alternatives.

The possibility of system breakdown aside, can the vicious circle ever be broken? In principle, yes, but one of three conditions would have to be met. Either Austro-Marxism would have to be replaced with a more unitary state structure that dissociates administrative units from ethnic groups. Or, Austro-Marxism would have to be transcended and a genuine federation or, even, a confederation involving the abolition of the political and economic hegemony of an institutionally Russian Party would have to be established. Or, finally, Soviet socialism would have to work sufficiently well—perhaps with some element of low-level marketization—so as to forestall the emergence of hypercentralization.

We may dismiss the third alternative, as socialism's near-term revitalization appears unlikely. The second alternative, a genuine federation or a confederation, will be impermissible as long as the Party continues to make an effective claim on a "leading role" in the political system. The third alternative—a unitary state structure—may be most conducive to economic reform, but least acceptable to the country's increasingly powerful Austro-Marxist elites. *Quo vadis?* Nowhere apparently, as the Soviet Union appears to be faced with a no-win situation on all sides. Lenin's solution, which may have been the best, or the best available one at the time, has condemned both center and periphery to a neverending series of hot and cold wars punctuated by moments of détente: a stagnant condition that may be incompatible with the USSR's rapid modernization and entry into the twenty-first century. Indeed, the moral of the story seems to be that, as long as the Party remains dominant and Moscow refuses to countenance the USSR's dismemberment, graceful economic decline to the level of an advanced Third World country and military retrenchment to the level of a third-rate great power may be the only solution to Lenin's awkward grafting of Austro-Marxism onto the Communist Party's version of the Russian empire. Even the dour Franz Josef might have been amused to learn that his empire's predicament was not unique.

— II —
WITH NATIONALISM IN THE USSR

— 7 —

State Building, States, and Incipient States

Building nation-states, even in the best of circumstances, is not, to use Mao Zedong's phrase, a tea party. Attaining and maintaining political independence require time, material resources, people, and some nonconstraint—relative freedom of action or, the term I prefer, political space. Most important, nationalist entrepreneurs who aspire to break away from states must first create a condition of "parallel sovereignty" by converting these factors into incipient states—political organizations that effectively challenge an existing state's monopoly on administration, extraction, and coercion in a part of the territory it claims for itself. Once they exist, the main task of incipient states is to extend their claim on some territory (parallel sovereignty) to all the territory (dual sovereignty) administered by the state, to acquire exclusive sovereignty, and, finally, to consolidate their statehood.[1]

Incipient states are challenger states. They meet, and hope to beat, the existing state on its own terms. In light of their lofty ambitions, incipient states—unlike guerrilla struggles, which I consider in chapter 8—are rational political options for nationalist entrepreneurs only if the existing state is already so weakened or so distracted as to permit them to lay the foundations for a state in relative peace. As Hannah Arendt and Theda Skocpol suggest, wars create the most propitious conditions for the emergence of incipient states.[2] If external adversaries debilitate a state without destroying it and occupying all of its territory, its internal opponents will be ideally positioned to advance their own claims to sovereignty in some "liberated" pockets of autonomy. To paraphrase Charles Tilly, states are war makers, and wars are incipient-state makers.[3]

But wars alone cannot assure the victory of incipient states. In order ultimately to prevail, the balance of resources between them and existing states must be in and remain in the incipient states' favor. And that can transpire only if outside pressure enables them to enjoy political space indefinitely and engage in the uninterrupted accumulation of resources, or if outside assistance is forthcoming to such a degree that it helps them to survive the inevitable counterattacks of rejuvenated states. In other words, external interference is critical: it may not be necessary for nationalist challengers to mount collective actions, but it is necessary and can be sufficient for incipient states to succeed in their secessionist schemes. To continue with the above paraphrasing of Tilly: Wars may be incipient-state makers, but only other states are new-state makers. Great-power gatherings at Vienna, Berlin, Versailles, Teheran, and Yalta testify to the accuracy of this observation.

It should not surprise us, therefore, that state building became a distinct possibility for non-Russians only during World War I and especially during the Civil War that followed. The war with the Central Powers severely weakened the tsarist state; the Bolshevik coup d'état in Petrograd effectively split it into Red and White factions and the Civil War witnessed the bloody struggle for sovereignty between the two heirs of tsarism. The Bolshevik inheritance may indeed be termed a state, as they controlled the former empire's industrial heartland, the larger part of its transportation network, the major population centers, the lion's share of tsarism's governmental structure—the buildings, offices, and other necessities of bureaucracy, and the organizational structure of the soviets and of the Party itself. No less important, the Bolshevik state could draw on the active support of large Russian working-class constituencies, who were ideologically motivated, culturally and ethnically homogeneous, and attracted by substantial positive sanctions: peace, bread, and land.

The White inheritance was at best a militarily strong incipient state. The Whites lacked industry and were confined to the borderlands, where transport and infrastructure were much more tenuous. Popular support was no less problematic, as monarchist fervor, ethnic solidarity, and programmatic appeal were hard to find among the frequently non-Russian peasantries that served as the Whites' potential popular base. Most debilitating for the White incipient state, however, was its lack of unity and coordination. The Whites were divided among the forces of Admiral A. V. Kolchak, General A. I. Denikin, Baron P. N. Wrangel, and General N. N. Iudenich, and, lacking an effective supreme command or sovereign, they proved incapable of coordinating their assaults against the Bolsheviks. Their strength lay in their armed forces, which consisted of well-trained and for the most part highly motivated troops led by skilled officers. Nonetheless, even with popular support, the Whites probably would not have won.[4] Only massive external intervention could have tipped the balance in their favor and against that of the far more richly endowed Bolshevik state.

World War I and and its aftermath are the environment that both spawned and quashed the non-Russian incipient states. The tsarist state's collapse and the subsequent Civil War created the space that all manner of non-Russian elites rushed to fill. Conflict between the center and the periphery was a foregone conclusion in such propitious circumstances, as close to a Hobbesian state of nature as Russia had been in since the Time of Troubles. The course of the conflict, however, and, most important, its outcome were contingent on the capacity of local entrepreneurs to transform incipient states into actual states. Their ability to do so was, in turn, a function of factors largely beyond their control.

By 1917–1918, incipient states of one sort or another had emerged in all the borderland regions of Russia: Finland, Poland, Estonia, Latvia, Lithuania, Belorussia, the Ukraine, Bessarabia, the Crimea, Armenia, Georgia, Azerbaidzhan, the Volga Tatar region, Bashkiria, Turkestan, and the Kazakh-Kirgiz steppe (contemporary Kazakhstan). These regions varied greatly in terms of geography, culture, ethnicity, and economy, but they did share certain characteristics of relevance to our concerns. All of them were what we would today call underdeveloped, irrespective of pockets of development such as the

Donbass, Baku, the Baltic ports, Helsingfors, and sections of Poland. They were overwhelmingly rural, and their economies were largely agricultural, be the base wheat, flax, cotton, livestock, or something else. Their working classes were minuscule in the west and in the Caucasus and nonexistent in Central Asia. All could boast of a small, but growing, and increasingly vigorous bourgeoisie and intelligentsia. In all these regions, a variety of local parties, organizations, and press organs had emerged after 1905. Finally, all throughout the empire, national if not quite nationalist demands had already been voiced before 1917, so that the calls for autonomy, which were heard with growing volume after the Tsar's downfall, were not unexpected. Clearly, there were also enormous differences. Then as now, political and economic development was greatest in the northwest of the empire and least in the southeast. Nonetheless, the overall differences do not appear to be greater than the similarities and therefore do not disqualify these regions from comparison.[5]

By 1921, when the dust had settled, the non-Russian incipient states that emerged in 1917–1918 had attained quite different and rather surprising outcomes. With the benefit of hindsight, we can group participant states in the following three categories. The first consists of those incipient states that attained complete statehood (i.e., for the duration of the interwar period): Finland, Poland, Estonia, Latvia, Lithuania, and Bessarabia (a special case insofar as it successfully seceded from Russia and joined Rumania). The second group contains countries that attained or enjoyed incipient statehood for a period of several years, at least one year and generally no more than three or four: Bukhara, Khiva, Georgia, Armenia, Azerbaidzhan, and the Ukraine. (I exclude the Far East People's Republic because it obviously was only a creation of the center.) The last group consists of those regions that enjoyed independence either not at all or very briefly or in very truncated form: Belorussia, the Crimea, Bashkiria, the Volga Tatar region, and the Kazakh-Kirgiz steppe. As we shall see, none of the variables traditionally considered to be decisive in accounting for national independence consistently correlates with the following three sets of outcomes:

Nationalist Outcomes, 1917–1939, by Country.

GROUP 1. Political independence, 1917–1939: Finland, Poland, Estonia, Latvia, Lithuania, Bessarabia

GROUP 2. Prolonged incipient statehood, 1 to 3–4 years: Bu-

khara, Khiva, Georgia, Armenia, Azerbaidzhan, the
Ukraine

GROUP 3. Minimal incipient statehood, less than 1 year: Belorussia, the Crimea, Bashkiria, Volga Tatar region, Kazakh-Kirgiz steppe

Consider the degree of self-rule that these regions enjoyed under
tsarism. Regional autonomy could be important not only because of
its potential impact on political culture and its direct impact on political space, but also because it represents concrete resources, which
potential nationalists can utilize. Buildings, bureaucrats, armies, ar-
istocracies, elites, institutions, and symbols translate into positive and
negative sanctions and are all instruments of state building. Although
such conditions clearly facilitated the emergence of parallel sovereignty after the breakdown of authority in 1917, a glance at Finland,
Poland, the Baltic, and the principalities of Khiva and Bukhara, all
of which shared the distinction of enjoying a greater or lesser degree
of autonomy under tsarism, suggests that they were neither necessary
nor sufficient for the attainment of statehood.

Finland was a grand duchy with a legislature, constitution, and,
for a long time, its own army. Although it came under increasing central pressure in the late nineteenth and early twentieth centuries, it
never lost its special status, to which Lenin and other revolutionaries
bore witness by invariably seeking refuge in Finland. Poland, although increasingly subject to repression and Russification after the
revolt of 1863, still possessed an aristocracy, an intelligentsia, international prestige, and a long tradition of independence. Poles also
had the good fortune of being partly under Habsburg rule in western
Galicia, where relatively liberal conditions permitted national activists to emerge.[6] The Baltic region, consisting of Kurland, Livland, and
Estland, was the preserve of the so-called Baltic barons, a regional
German elite that enjoyed both self-rule and substantial access to top
political, military, and diplomatic posts within the empire.[7] Estonians and Latvians, however, were largely excluded from the privileges enjoyed by the barons. Finally, Khiva and Bukhara, both feudal
states ruled by a khan and an emir respectively, had been transformed into Russian protectorates in the second half of the nineteenth
century.[8] While neighboring states in Turkestan had been annexed
outright, these two remained relatively autonomous in their internal
affairs.

107

Although all these regions possessed some autonomy and were endowed with resources, their incipient states enjoyed differing degrees of success. Finland and Poland should have attained, and did attain, permanent statehood; Khiva and Bukhara should have, but did not; while the Estonians and Latvians, who were excluded from the barons' privileges, should not have, but did. The connection between accoutrements of self-rule and nationalist success evidently is quite tenuous.

National consciousness and nationalist beliefs fare no better. Poland and Finland appear to have enjoyed substantial amounts of both among elites and masses. In Estonia, Latvia, Lithuania, and Bessarabia, however, such feelings were far weaker and largely confined to the intelligentsia. In the Ukraine, national consciousness and nationalism were fairly widespread among local elites, while the former sentiment may even have made substantial inroads into the peasantry as well.[9] On the other hand, the Armenian, Georgian, and Azerbaidzhani elites appear to have been far more indifferent to nationalism, even as late as mid–1918, than Volga Tatar, Bashkir, Crimean Tatar, and Alash Orda elites. The evidence, clearly, does not fit the pattern.

The presence or absence of urban populations—bourgeoisie and proletariat—is often invoked for its explanatory powers. Peasantries, according to this interpretation, are a drawback, while urban populations have the consciousness, resources, and skills to embark successfully on revolutionary struggles—a view that, wittingly or not, reflects a Marxist bias against peasantries as "sacks of potatoes."[10] Although twentieth-century revolutions have shown not only that peasantries are quite capable of participating in national-liberation struggles, but that usually they are the only social class that can be mobilized successfully,[11] it is hard to argue that there is a clear-cut correlation between social structure and nationalist outcome in the Russian case. Poland, Finland, and the Baltic region possessed relatively large cities with nascent bourgeoisies and proletariats, but, then, so did the Ukraine, the Volga Tatar region, and Azerbaidzhan. In contrast, Lithuania, Bessarabia, Khiva, and Bukhara were all overwhelmingly rural.

The strength of local pro-Bolshevik or Bolshevik forces is an obvious candidate for an explanatory variable. Alas, it, too, collapses under closer scrutiny. We would expect fewest local sympathizers in the first category, most in the third. But Finland, Estonia, Latvia, and Poland had large and well-established social democratic parties. In

1918, the Finnish socialists even managed to win control of the southern portion of the country until they were beaten by the nationalists under General C. G. E. Mannerheim. So, too, in Latvia, the local social democrats were sufficiently strong to win, in 1917, 41 percent of the vote in municipal elections in Riga and 72 percent of the vote in elections to the Constituent Assembly in Livonia.[12] No less important, pro-Bolshevik forces were relatively weak in much of the Ukraine, except for the Donbass; they were relatively strong in Baku, virtually nonexistent in Khiva and Bukhara, and, most telling of all, nonexistent in Georgia, which was a Menshevik stronghold.[13]

The size of native armed forces also fails as an explanatory variable. Finland had virtually no army to speak of in early 1918; Poland fared much better, insofar as Józef Piłsudski had received German approval to organize an armed force in 1916. The Ukrainians were able, several times in 1917–1921, to muster close to a hundred thousand men, but to no avail. Indeed, after 1918 the eastern Ukrainians were joined by the well-trained Ukrainian Galician Army.[14] The Belorussians, Crimean Tatars, and Turkestanis had no army, but neither did the Bessarabians. Most important perhaps, the armed forces of the Estonians, Latvians, Lithuanians, Armenians, Georgians, Bashkirs, and Kazakhs were all quite small, generally no more than several thousand men. Admittedly, even small forces can play large roles in civil wars, but it is not at all evident why those of the Balts should have been consistently more effective than those of the unsuccessful non-Russians.[15]

Was the presence or absence of a national elite the critical factor? No obvious differences stand out. All non-Russians had capable political, cultural, and religious elites: there were progressive and traditional counterparts to jaddids and mullahs in all the borderlands. National, socialist, and various other kinds of parties and organizations existed in all the Empire's peripheral regions before the revolution. Most nationalities had representatives to the Duma; most also succeeded in establishing autonomous organs aspiring to self-rule in 1917–1918: the Maapäev in Estonia, the National Council in Latvia, the Taryba in Lithuania, Central Radas in both Belorussia and the Ukraine, the Sfatul Tarii in Bessarabia, the Milli Shura among the Muslims, the Milli Firka in the Crimea, the Alash Orda in the Kazakh-Kirgiz steppe, the Armenian National Council, the Transcaucasian Commissariat, and so on.

Elite effectiveness—the ability to win battles, attract popular support, and lead well—is always critical in any but the most deterministic of explanatory schemes. But here, too, differences are smaller than one would think and do not fit the expected pattern. Piłsudski and Mannerheim were exceptional generals, but even Piłsudski managed to commit an enormous strategic blunder by invading Russia and the Ukraine in 1920.[16] Moreover, although the Balts, Khivans, Bukharans, Bessarabians, Ukrainians, and Transcaucasians all lacked distinguished military leaders and indecision, mistakes, and lack of will were common to all their military elites, these nations still attained qualitatively different nationalist outcomes.

The ability to win popular support is frequently highlighted as the key difference between the Bolsheviks, whose promises of bread, land, and peace were positive sanctions *par excellence*, and their adversaries, who temporized about social reform. The contrast is overdrawn and, even if it were not, it is of little help in explaining the different nationalist outcomes. As their initially unsuccessful campaigns in the Ukraine and Central Asia illustrate, the Bolsheviks were hardly the objects of peasant veneration in the borderlands.[17] Their agricultural policies were so catastrophic, especially during the Civil War, as to prompt them to adopt the New Economic Policy in 1921. Moreover, their successful non-Russian adversaries were no more inclined to implement reforms during the Civil War than the unsuccessful ones. Poland, Latvia, Estonia, and Lithuania embarked on land reform only after the fighting had stopped, while Khiva and Bukhara never even considered it.[18]

Finally, all the non-Russians possessed able political leaders. Piłsudski was outstanding, of course, but he may also be the exception that proves the rule. P. E. Svinhufvud and Mannerheim of Finland, Konstantin Päts of Estonia, Kārlis Ulmanis of Latvia, Antanas Smetona and Augustinas Voldemaras of Lithuania, Mykhailo Hrushevs'kyi and Symon Petliura of the Ukraine, Mehmed Emin Resul-zade of Azerbaidzhan, Noi Zhordaniia of Georgia, Noman Celebi Cihan of the Crimea, Alikhan Bukeikhanov and Akhmed Baitursunov of the Kazakh-Kirgiz, Mustafa Chokaev of Turkestan, and Zeki Validov of Bashkiria appear to have been more or less equally competent national leaders.

Although my analysis of the above factors has admittedly been static, it serves to underline their lack of explanatory power. Most important, these factors are unpersuasive because they focus only on the *internal* characteristics of the incipient states. In addition to adopting a more dynamic mode of analysis, we would do well to consider how external factors related to the ebb and flow of the various forms of conflict and intervention taking place in 1917–1921 might explain the outcomes. As we shall see, the location of the world war, the location of the civil war, and the extent of external prodding or support were critical. They materially affected the balance of resources and thus permitted incipient states to withstand or bypass the inevitable Soviet assault.

The war between Russia and the Central Powers and the Civil War between the Red and White heirs of tsarism influenced the non-Russians in general and their political elites in particular in several ways. Armed conflict weakened the center and thereby automatically expanded the periphery's autonomy. But the war also had a direct impact on the borderlands: it devastated them, as in Belorussia, due to the continual to and fro movement of the front; it weakened them by forcing the non-Russians to choose sides in and commit scarce resources to an intra-Russian conflict; or it strengthened them by virtue of the external assistance they received from actual or potential occupiers. There were thus four main players in the drama: the Red state, the White incipient state, the non-Russian incipient states, and foreign states. As we shall see, the manner and timing of the conflict between the two Russian entities and between them and outside forces set the parameters for peripheral maneuverability and largely determined how the non-Russian incipient states would fare.

The pattern of German expansion and the fact of Germany's enormous power are of critical importance. By the end of 1915, Germany was in control of most of Poland and Lithuania; Latvia went to the Germans by the end of 1917, and Estonia by the beginning of 1918. Finally, as a consequence of the Brest-Litovsk Treaty, most of Belorussia and the Ukraine fell into German hands in March 1918. The consequences of the German-Austrian advance and of the peace with Russia were far-reaching.

In particular, Berlin and Vienna explicitly courted Polish nationalism in the hope of acquiring recruits for the war against Russia and, on November 5, 1916, they proclaimed their intention to establish a fully independent Kingdom of Poland. "The declaration of the two emperors," writes M. K. Dziewanowski, "—a hesitant, reluctant, and modest tactical gesture—proved to be a turning point in the story of Poland's reappearance on the map of Europe as a sovereign state."[19] As a consequence of this important geopolitical step, the Central Powers, Russia, and the Entente, and especially President Woodrow Wilson, all came to vie for Polish support, thereby legitimating and boosting Polish nationalist aspirations. Most important, all three sides promoted the establishment of distinctly Polish armed forces. Concludes Dziewanowski:

Thus, by the spring of 1917, because of the steps undertaken by the former partitioning powers, the Poles had a nucleus of a state administration in Warsaw and Lublin as well as the beginnings of two armed forces, one in Russia and another in Poland. To this one should add the existence of the Polish National Committee headed by Dmowski, active in the West and trying to connect Poland's national cause with that of the Allies. The committee was soon to embark on organizing a third Polish armed force, composed partly of Polish volunteers from America. The pro-Russians [sic] and the pro-Austrian orientations, although outwardly working at cross purposes, were basically complementing each other and preparing, step by step, the eventual reconstruction of an independent Polish state.[20]

Although Finland remained outside the war zone, it benefited from Germany's advance both indirectly and directly. Civil war with Finland's socialists broke out soon after independence was declared in December 1917; in these critical months, the local Red Guards enjoyed the support of Russian troops garrisoned in Finland, while the nationalists under Svinhufvud and Mannerheim were only just beginning to mobilize. But thanks to the drawn-out negotiations at Brest-Litovsk, their eventual breakdown, and the rapid German offensive that followed, Soviet troops were tied down in Russia and could not be dispatched to help their comrades to the north. The Finnish nationalists used this breathing space to raise an army, beat back the socialists, and acquire German military assistance in the form of some 12,000 well-trained troops who "played a conspicuous although not a decisive part . . . in the closing stages of the war."[21] Decisive or not, the Germans did capture Helsingfors. Finally, Berlin insisted at Brest-Litovsk that Soviet Russia accept Finnish independence.

Germany's occupation of the Baltic also redounded to the advantage of local nationalists. Partly as a counterweight to Polish territorial appetites, Germany authorized some Lithuanian self-rule in mid-1917, acquiesced in nationalist demands for independence in December, and approved the establishment of an independent Lithuanian state in March 1918. Germany's impact on Latvia and Estonia was less a function of length of occupation than of timing. By coming when it did—late 1917, early 1918—the occupation turned the tide against the hitherto ascendant local Bolsheviks and permitted the nationalists to recoup their forces. Unlike Lithuania, Latvia and Estonia remained occupied territories, but, from the nationalist perspective, the important thing was that they had not turned Soviet.[22]

The direct beneficiaries of Brest-Litovsk were, of course, Belorussia, the Ukraine, the Crimea, and Bessarabia. Prodded by Germany, Belorussian nationalists declared the independence of the Belorussian People's Republic on March 25, 1918 and then utilized the months of occupation to establish a rudimentary administration, school system, and press. The German advance was, thus, an enormous boon for Belorussian nationalism, no less than it was for Polish, Finnish, or Baltic nationalism. The fact that independent Belorussia was, as a result, a German creation is beside the point in evaluating the legitimacy of Belorussian nationalism, as the vast majority of modern states are, after all, the product of external forces beyond their control.[23] Brest-Litovsk had equally salutary nationalist consequences for Bessarabia, the Crimea, and the Ukraine. Germany acquiesced in Bessarabia's annexation to Rumania, established Suleiman Sulkiewicz as head of a makeshift Crimean national government,[24] and saved the Central Rada from imminent collapse by signing a separate treaty with it and subsequently occupying the Ukraine. To be sure, the Rada's days were numbered, as Berlin soon installed General Pavlo Skoropads'kyi as putative Hetman of the Ukrainian state. Ironically, although a puppet and a dictator who did much to discredit the idea of Ukrainian independence among the peasantry he exploited, Skoropads'kyi, as John Reshetar argues, may have done more to lay the foundations of a state than his patriotic critics on the left.[25]

While Kazakhstan and Central Asia were largely outside the war zone, developments in the Caucasus proceeded along the lines of Russia's western territories. The Turkish massacre of Armenians in 1915, their pell-mell flight to Russian Armenia, and the subsequent Turkish advance on Transcaucasia in 1917–1918 impelled the Armenians, Georgians, and Azerbaidzhanis to band together and reluctantly declare an independent Democratic Federative Republic of Transcaucasia in April 1918. The federation's *raison d'être* was not nationalism—as none of the local elites desired to leave Russia's fold—but fear.[26] Unwilling to accept Bolshevik rule, while clinging to a vision of a Russia one and undivided, the Transcaucasians had no legal basis for negotiating with the Ottomans and therefore were literally forced to opt for independence as a last resort. Their unity was short-lived, however. The Georgians soon broke ranks and sought German protection for an independent Georgia. The Armenians and Azerbaidzhanis had no choice but to follow suit, so that, by the end of May 1918, the native elites of all three countries had become nationalists *malgré soi*. David Marshall Lang's comments apply also to Armenia and Azerbaidzhan: "It is in fact ironic to observe how the Georgian Social-Democrats, whose leaders were working as late as 1918 for the triumph of democratic socialism in a Russia united and undivided, were at length transformed by the force of circumstances into nationalists of chauvinistic fervour and of an intransigence common in countries where independence has recently been regained after a long spell of alien rule."[27] The Azerbaidzhani Muslims proceeded to ally themselves with Turkey, and together they smashed the Baku Commune, while the desperate Armenians signed a Treaty of Peace and Friendship with the Ottoman Empire and thereby managed to salvage some territory.

Although Hohenzollern Germany, Habsburg Austria-Hungary, and the Ottoman Empire had collapsed at war's end, their intrusions into Russia considerably altered the political map. As hostilities with Soviet Russia resumed in late 1918, *bona fide* incipient states already existed in Finland, Poland, Lithuania, the Ukraine, Georgia, Armenia, and Azerbaidzhan, while Latvia and Estonia had at least been denied the Bolsheviks. *Ceteris paribus,* only Poland would probably have been strong enough to maintain statehood on its own. But other things were not equal, and the pattern of the Civil War and continued outside intervention decisively influenced the course of future events by drawing Bolshevik attention away from the extreme periphery and closer to the country's center, which the Whites were attempting to storm.

While the eastern nationalities largely escaped the ravages of World War I, their chances of attaining independence were directly affected by the Civil War, in some cases negatively, in others positively. The Bolshevik campaign against Kolchak and the Czech Legion effectively undermined the fledgling efforts of the Volga Tatars, Bashkirs, and Alash Orda to attain and retain autonomy. (Indeed, the Volga Tatar Communist, Mulla Nur Vakhitov, was executed by the Czechs in 1918.) The conflict deprived these nationalities of the conditions of nonconstraint necessary to organize an incipient state and embroiled them in a foreign conflict that depleted their energies and resources. The fate of the Alash Orda typifies the dilemma. First, the Kazakh nationalists sided with Kolchak; then, after his animosity toward them became too obvious to be ignored, they went over to the Bolsheviks. By that time, however, they had lost the opportunity to build and consolidate an autonomous state entity of their own and had become mere appendages of one of the two Russian sides engaged in the Civil War.[28]

The Civil War in Siberia did, however, have a relatively salutary impact on the Turkestanis. In effect, it insulated Turkestan from the rest of Russia, thereby preventing the Red Army from intervening directly until 1920. Insulation meant that the local Turks and Russians had to rely on their own resources, which were far from tilted in the latter's favor. Not surprisingly, the Bukharans were able to inflict a resounding defeat on General Kolesov in 1918, while Bukhara and Khiva managed to survive as independent states until 1920, when the Young Bukharans and Young Khivans conspired with the Bolsheviks to overthrow them. Conversely, the collapse of the Kokand Muslim government in February 1918 was in large measure due to the Bolsheviks' success in piercing the Orenburg front of the Whites and laying seige to the city.[29]

Denikin represented the most serious threat to the Bolsheviks, reaching as far as Orel in the summer of 1919. Like Kolchak, Denikin had a salutary effect on those non-Russians situated behind his offensive and a detrimental one on those who stood in his path. Thus, Denikin objectively protected the weak Transcaucasian states from Bolshevik takeover while undermining nationalist efforts in the Ukraine and even more so in the Crimea. To be sure, he drove out the Bolsheviks and in so doing permitted Petliura, the Supreme Otaman of the Ukrainian People's Republic, to advance as far as Kiev. But this was a mixed blessing, as it added fuel to the fire of the country's chaos and turned the eastern Ukrainians against their Galician allies, who, by joining Denikin, had seemingly betrayed socialist ideals.[30] By the same token, the Red counteroffensive against Denikin embroiled the Ukraine and the Crimea in a devastating war that further depleted nationalist resources and constrained their autonomy.[31]

No less important than his catastrophic impact on south Russia, however, was the fact that Denikin diverted Soviet forces from the east and the west, thereby enhancing the survivability of the Khivans, Bukharans, Poles, Finns, and particularly the Estonians, Latvians, and Lithuanians. Baltic prospects appeared hopeless in early 1919, but German intervention stopped the Soviet advance and permitted the Baltic nationalists to mobilize, so that by mid–1919, at the height of Denikin's offensive, the small Estonian, Latvian, and Lithuanian armies actually succeeded in driving out the Bolsheviks and the Germans. Naturally, patriotic fervor played its part, but enthusiasm alone cannot explain how such "mininations" could have warded off a great power such as Soviet Russia.[32] Subsequent Bolshevik willingness to recognize Baltic and especially Estonian independence was largely motivated—not by fear of the Balts—but by the desire to deprive the counterrevolutionary forces of Iudenich and Bermondt-Avalov of havens in the area.

After Denikin's defeat, the road lay open to Bolshevik occupation of the Transcaucasus, the only restraining consideration being international socialist support for the Georgian Mensheviks. But after the USSR and Kemal Atatürk agreed on an alliance in the winter of 1919–1920, the Transcaucasian states' utility as a buffer between the Soviets and their enemies diminished. Azerbaidzhan fell first, in mid–1920; Armenia, which had needlessly embroiled itself in a war with Turkey, fell next in late 1920. Georgia offered the stiffest resistance but succumbed to the Red Army in March 1921.[33]

The final element to be considered is the Polish-Soviet War, which began with Piłsudski's foolhardy advance in May 1920. Polish occupation of Belorussia and the Ukraine permitted local nationalists to enjoy a last hurrah and diverted Bolshevik attention from the Caucasus. Once again, as with the German occupation, had the Poles remained long enough and had they been genuinely committed to Belorussian and Ukrainian independence, even as puppet states—two very big ifs, to be sure—the Belorussians and Ukrainians might have acquired enough time, space, and resources to mobilize and build genuine states. But the occupation was short-lived and the Bolshevik counteroffensive completely crushed Belorussian and Ukrainian nationalist aspirations.[34]

My tripartite division of countries now appears more explicable and we can group our findings in the form of three conclusions:

1. Irrespective of their own resources, those countries that remained longest outside the Russian-Soviet orbit, largely escaped the Civil War, and enjoyed substantial external assistance attained and maintained independence. These are the Group 1 countries: Finland, Poland, Estonia, Latvia, Lithuania, and Bessarabia.
2. Those countries that briefly escaped Russian and/or Soviet control and received little or no external support were forced to rely on their own undeveloped resources and succeeded in attaining independence only temporarily. Inevitably, they were too weak to resist the Bolshevik invasion. These are the Group

2 countries: Bukhara, Khiva, the Ukraine, Georgia, Armenia, and Azerbaidzhan.
3. Those regions that bore the brunt of the Civil War, received no foreign aid, and had few or no resources of their own to start with succumbed most easily. These include the Group 3 countries: Belorussia, the Crimea, Bashkiria, the Volga Tatar region, and the Kazakh-Kirgiz steppe.

Nationalist goals were achieved where the balance of resources and therefore the structure of incentives permitted it. Insofar as local forces were inherently disadvantaged against either the Reds or the Whites, survival meant receiving requisite outside assistance and/or succumbing to externally generated proindependence pressures. Where such assistance or pressure was not forthcoming, nonconstraint helped locals, but only temporarily, as its lifting meant that they had to face superior Bolshevik forces on their own. Where assistance or pressure coincided with nonconstraint, permanent independence was the outcome.

Neither self-rule, nationalist sentiment, national consciousness, social structure, leadership, organization, nor popular support was crucial in determining outcomes. Rather, the honor belongs to external forces and the manner in which they affected the balance of resources. World War, Civil War, and outside intervention created a complex set of constraints, incentives, and resources that propelled certain regions in one direction and others in another. Some nationalist entrepreneurs could pursue desired nationalist ends, others could not; still others who rejected nationalism completely had no choice but to act against their own wishes. The choices that elites made were to a large degree a function of the kind of choices that could and/or had to be made.

These conclusions should not surprise us. The vast majority of post-World War II anticolonialist struggles succeeded, not, as their leaders and ideologues would have us believe, because of discipline, determination, and popular support, but because of the external intervention of distant political and economic forces. Since the independence wave that swept the 1950s and 1960s, virtually no separatist movement has managed to upset existing boundaries and create a state on its own. Bangladesh succeeded only because of India's military support; Algeria was granted independence by General de Gaulle only after its independence movement was crushed; Biafra failed as a result of international isolation and British hostility. The Basques, South

117

Tyroleans, Catalans, Scots, Quebecois, and many others can affect a state's stability, but—on their own—they are generally powerless to be more than a major nuisance.[35]

If nations contribute relatively little to nationalist outcomes, then, clearly, it should be possible for such outcomes to occur regardless of whether or not full-fledged nations or nationalist ideals even exist. Almost every country in Africa is testimony to the validity of this proposition. But this conclusion, too, should not surprise us. It is, after all, only a restatement of Ernest Gellner's proposition that "it is not the aspirations of nations which create nationalism: it is nationalism which creates nations."[36]

— 8 —

Guerrilla Struggles Against the Soviet State

Incipient states bring institutions, armies, and officials to mind, whereas guerrillas connote inchoate bands of armed irregulars. Although these images accurately reflect the reality, they confuse the issue conceptually. The key difference between incipient states and guerrilla forces is that the former exert continuous control over some territory and can therefore create a condition of parallel sovereignty, while the latter do not. Guerrilla forces, like incipient states, are political and coercive organizations. But unlike incipient states, guerrillas possess no coercive monopoly in some area claimed by the state. Just as guerrillas aspire to such a monopoly, so, too, they aspire to become incipient states.

Like incipient states, guerrilla struggles are the rational response of oppositionists to the structure of the political environment, its incentives and constraints. Incipient states arise only if existing states are severely weakened or destroyed. Being definitionally more circumscribed, guerrillas emerge under a larger variety of nonconstraining circumstances. Wars are obviously most conducive to both incipient states and guerrilla struggles, but unlike incipient states, guerrillas also thrive under occupations and reoccupations. Occupiers never seem to have sufficient resources to control both the strategically vital cities and roads and the countryside. Germany and Japan encountered this problem during World War II—especially in Yugoslavia and China—as did the United States in Vietnam. The same set of difficulties faces reoccupiers. Equally preoccupied with the ongoing war effort, formerly sovereign states are physically unable to extend their rule throughout all the territory they are in the process of reoccupying. No less important, even after wars are officially over, reoccupiers are likely to face a period of instability and transition, during which oppositionists will be able to maneuver with some impunity. Such conditions faced the Soviets after both wars, as well as the French, Greeks, and Italians after World War II, when they had to contend with large and well-armed Communist resistance forces.[1]

Naturally, weak states—those endowed with insufficient resources to safeguard their sovereignty in some territory—cannot extend effective control to the entire area they claim as theirs, thereby facilitating guerrilla activity even in the absence of war. State resources can be insufficient for a variety of reasons that need not concern us, such as elite incompetence, bureaucratic parasitism, military adventurism, economic degeneration, international constraints, or the sheer difficulty of controlling a huge or impassable territory. Whatever the reasons for their being so, extremely weak states are incapable of preventing and containing challenges to their sovereignty.[2] In such propitious circumstances the fine line between guerrillas and incipient states begins to blur.

Finally, guerrillas can emerge or find refuge in neighboring states. Polisario, the Nicaraguan contras, and the Vietcong are typical examples. In contrast, incipient states generally opt for flight abroad only as a very last resort. As we shall see in chapter 9, exile governments abound, of course, but to the degree that states without territory command little respect in the international arena, few governments willingly embark on this road. Naturally, refuge is only a temporary solution for guerrillas as well. Cut off from their homeland, guerrillas cannot afford to sit back for too long: the longer they remain out of the political game, the more they assume the defining characteristics of émigrés and the greater the likelihood that their opponent will consolidate power and prevent their return.

While nonconstraint is necessary for emergence, resources are necessary for survival and, of course, for victory. As Joel Migdal argues, "For revolutionaries to succeed in building a powerful movement, they must routinize peasant action so that powerful, complex organizations are built. This comes about in a process of social exchange, in which peasant support and participation are traded off initially for individual rewards. . . . Even more than other political organizers, revolutionaries must provide rewards and sanctions that can *overcome* the costs and risks to the peasant of participating" (my italics— A.J.M.).[3] The last line is critical. Because they possess far fewer resources than states by definition, however, guerrillas cannot coexist for long with strong, resource-endowed states. Indeed, other things being equal, long-term survival is impossible under such conditions. Guerrillas can outfight a superior army and outbid the state with respect to the populace only if the balance of coercive, instrumental, and normative resources is radically altered, usually as a result of some intrusion from the outside.

Both sides can coerce populations, as indeed they do, state soldiers during the day, and guerrillas at night. But strong states can coerce more people at any one time and, unlike guerrillas, they can deport people, resettle them, and thereby deprive guerrillas of their popular base. The establishment of protected villages in South Vietnam, Sandinista resettlement of the Miskitos, and Soviet deportation of Balts and Ukrainians after World War II are examples of this approach. In instrumental terms, strong states also hold the upper hand. They have more money to dispense, they can provide education, services, and employment, they can build beneficial projects. Guerrillas correctly perceive their ideological and/or cultural appeal as one of their strongest points, and they often succeed in drumming up some support on this basis alone. As we know, however, ideals, ideology, and culture do not suffice for collective actions to persist, as positive and negative sanctions become increasingly imperative to counter the state's determination to maintain effective sovereignty. No less important, states also utilize normative appeals, especially nationalist ones. These may be not be enough to attract the fanatics and martyrs, but often they suffice to sway the minds of the disinterested observers standing on the sidelines. All in all, the balance sheet looks gloomy for guerrillas. They thrive when states are weak and autonomy is substantial; they degenerate when states are strong and space is minimal. Given the odds against them, can guerrillas succeed in attaining their goals? The answer, obviously, is yes, as the Vietnamese, Algerians, Sandinistas, and many others can testify. In all these instances, however, the opposing state was hobbled by a variety of internal and external constraints that made it incapable of opposing the guerrillas effectively. At the same time, most of these guerrillas received significant amounts of foreign aid.

Nationalist and national guerrilla movements in the USSR fit the patterns discussed above exactly. As expected, all of the guerrilla struggles under consideration emerged under conditions of relative nonconstraint and attained their peak strength at times when state power—Soviet or other—was weakest, especially during wars and/or immediately after them. The Basmachi were most formidable between 1918 and 1924, they persisted until 1928 and then flared up once again in the early 1930s. The Daghestani jihad was confined to 1920–1921. The Ukrainian, Lithuanian, Latvian, and Estonian nationalists were most active in 1944–1947/8, surviving in much weakened condition into the early 1950s, when all four struggles were terminated.[4]

Of all the guerrillas the Balts were most advantaged in terms of resources and political space, as they had enjoyed independence in the interwar period (an independence the demise of which, not insignificantly, was as much the product of international forces as was its emergence). Statehood endowed Estonia, Latvia, and Lithuania with, among other things, the military and political elites who were to initiate much of the military activity in subsequent years: revolts against the Soviets in June 1941, the creation of underground umbrella opposition organizations in 1943–1944 (the Supreme Committee for the Liberation of Lithuania, the Latvian Central Council, and the Estonian Republic National Committee), and the postwar guerrilla struggles.[5] Two decades of independence also gave the Balts political experience, military training, and cultural solidarity. In turn, Stalin's flagrant aggression inculcated them with an uncompromising anti-Sovietism. Finally, Germany pursued relatively lenient occupation policies in all three countries: human and material resources were less brutally exploited than in Belorussia and the Ukraine, Baltic civil society was not fully dismantled, and elites were not destroyed.[6] Once the front passed and the Soviets returned, massive Baltic resistance to the Stalinist reoccupier was a foregone conclusion.

The Ukrainian nationalists traced their origins to the imperfectly democratic conditions of interwar Poland, which tolerated, if not quite encouraged, legal Ukrainian parties, a well-developed press, a strong Uniate Catholic church, and an extensive system of cooperatives and schools, and to the unconstrained environment of the émigré colonies in Central and Western Europe. The first radical nationalist grouping was the Ukrainian Military Organization, an underground association of former soldiers who terrorized Polish officialdom and landlords for much of the 1920s. Fated to play a far more important role was the Organization of Ukrainian Nationalists (OUN), founded in Vienna in 1929 by émigrés and eventually dominated by Galician students whose visions of "permanent revolution" succeeded in attracting large numbers of young people in the 1930s.[7] Although the Polish police decimated the nationalists in the mid–1930s, as did the Bolsheviks in 1939–1940 and the Germans in 1941–1942, the OUN survived in the underground and, in contrast to the legal parties, which had been disbanded and never revived, the radical nationalists emerged during the war as the only organized west Ukrainian political group. Unchallenged by any Ukrainian competitors, except for occasional intrusions by Soviet partisans, the OUN managed to develop an extensive network, penetrated areas of the Soviet Ukraine, effectively set the Ukrainian national political agenda, and came to lead the anti-German, and eventually anti-Soviet, resistance known as the Ukrainian Insurgent Army (UPA). The UPA developed into a formidable army in the heavily forested pockets of autonomy beyond German control—indeed, it even approached the status of an incipient state by establishing "insurgent republics" in some areas—and survived the passing of the front in 1944–1945. The nationalist claim to parallel sovereignty did not survive several crushing encounters with the Red Army, however, and, after 1945, the OUN and UPA were transformed into *bona fide* guerrilla forces. Nevertheless, although the Soviet state disabused the nationalists of their pretensions to incipient statehood, the protracted process of Sovietization in those west Ukrainian areas that had their first encounter with Soviet power only in 1939–1941 permitted the nationalists to survive for almost a decade after the war.[8]

As devotees of the Naqshbandiya Sufi sect, which had a long tradition of waging holy war against infidels, the North Caucasian rebels had even longer organizational roots than the Balts and Ukrainians. In addition, the Sufi base provided the rebellion with legitimacy, fanatical discipline, an established system of recruitment, highly respected clerical leaders with prestige extending far beyond the region, ideological and cultural solidarity, and a political program which consisted of the "expulsion of the Infidels and the establishment of a theocratic state."[9] Not surprisingly, the Sufi jihad erupted during the Soviet reoccupation of Daghestan in the spring of 1920. Fortunately for the rebels, their uprising coincided with the attack on Russia of Józef Piłsudski and Symon Petliura and therefore remained a secondary Soviet concern until after the western front had stabilized.

Finally, the Basmachi had their origins in the pre-Soviet "phenomenon of *basmachilik*, highway robbery with a vague political colouring, which consisted of robbing the Russians (preferably) and those Muslims who supported them."[10] Tsarist Russia had left the Turkestanis alone, thereby permitting an unpoliticized *basmachilik* to thrive; in contrast, the Bolsheviks had a program and a plan for transforming Turkestani society, thus politicizing the Basmachi. Like "primitive rebels" elsewhere, the Basmachi were ideally positioned to lead popular resistance to a state determined to impose political and ideological control on their homelands.[11] Although initially an uncoordinated set of disparate fighting groups based on tribal, regional, or personal loyalties, the Basmachi acquired a mass political character after the Russian takeover of Kokand in 1918 and the resultant flight into the mountains of numerous nationally conscious Turkestanis committed to driving out the Russians. The very same reasons that permitted the Khanate of Khiva and the Emirate of Bukhara to survive relatively long—the comparative weakness of local Soviet Russian forces and the cutting off of the region from Moscow by the Civil War front with the Whites—also enabled the Basmachi to operate with substantial impunity until 1921. Thereafter, although Moscow's rule was formally reestablished, the protracted nature of reoccupation let the Basmachi survive for several more years.

The similarities among the Baltic, Ukrainian, Daghestani, and Turkestani guerrillas are striking. In all four regions, the guerrillas traced their roots to previously existing organizational structures, emerged in pockets of autonomy during or after wars, and drew on the support of ideologically hostile and culturally distinct populations. The returning Soviets encountered nationalist and national entrepreneurs who possessed the organization, skills, resources, and popular base to wage an effective resistance. Not surprisingly, Soviet strategy was identical in all four regions: first, to defeat the guerrillas militarily, and, second, to erode their popular base. As we would expect from a strong, though imperfectly totalitarian state, the Soviets succeeded in both respects. Sadly for the guerrillas, the denouements of their unhappy encounters with Soviet power were also the same—complete destruction.

The gross coercive imbalance between a major power and guerrilla bands ensured that the guerrillas could not survive for long as a significant force. The various guerrilla forces possessed the following manpower at their peak: Lithuanians (1945–46): 30–40,000; Latvians (1945–1946): 10–15,000; Estonians (1945–1946): 10,000; Ukrainians (1944–1945): 90,000; Daghestanis (1920): 10,000; and Basmachi (1922): 18,000.[12] These numbers are impressive, but deceptive, as they fluctuated continually. In the Ukrainian and Baltic cases, especially, the figures include large numbers of deserters and refugees, many of whom were to return to their normal lives as soon as the war ended and the Soviets offered amnesties. Furthermore, many of the Basmachi were "winter Reds," collaborators with the regime during the winter and opponents during the rest of the year.

The Soviets, meanwhile, were vastly superior not only in terms of military equipment and supplies, but also in terms of troop size. According to a variety of estimates, the Soviets appear to have fielded some 120–160,000 troops in Turkestan, 35–40,000 in Daghestan, 110,000 in Lithuania, and, if we are to believe a possibly questionable source, 585,000 in the western Ukraine.[13] The Daghestanis were crushed after the Soviets methodically reconquered the rebellious region valley by valley. Similar tactics, along with sealing off of the border with Afghanistan, were employed in Central Asia. The Balts and Ukrainians were smothered, as Soviet army and police units occupied every suspicious village and town, thereby forcing the opposition literally to go underground.[14] There were, quite simply, too many Soviets with too many guns.

Despite the overwhelming numerical advantage enjoyed by the Soviets, the guerrillas appear to have inflicted substantial damage on them—testimony to their commitment or, perhaps, to their desperation. In Lithuania, the nationalists lost some 20–50,000 fighters, while the Soviets suffered 20–80,000 casualties.[15] Ukrainian nationalist sources claim that 1,350 Soviets were killed and wounded in 1947, 1,240 in 1948, and 283 in the first half of 1949. The corresponding figures for the OUN and UPA were supposed to have been 350, 369, and 110.[16] In turn, a recent Soviet source plausibly claims that 72,000 Ukrainian nationalists were either killed, captured, or surrendered in 1944–1945, the period of the most intense fighting between the nationalist incipient state and the advancing Red Army.[17] Whatever the exact numbers, it is obvious that, in relation to the overall size of the contenders, the insurgents lost a far higher percentage of soldiers than did the Soviets.

The balance sheet is clear. Although the guerrillas put up a brave effort and probably succeeded in imposing a high toll on the Soviet armed forces, they could not overcome such imposing odds. Their end was preordained, especially as virtually no outside military assistance was forthcoming. The Basmachi leader, Ibrahim Beg, received some aid from Afghanistan and the former Emir of Bukhara; the Ukrainians and Lithuanians acquired some money, armaments, and supplies from the withdrawing German Wehrmacht during the war and, after 1945, from émigrés and the American, British, and German secret services. Cold War rhetoric notwithstanding, however, decisive amounts of aid were not forthcoming from the West, and the Ukrainians and Balts, like the Basmachi and Daghestanis before them, were left to fend for themselves.[18] Not surprisingly, by 1924 in Central Asia, and by 1947 in the Baltic republics and the Ukraine, the local guerrilla movements had been pulverized militarily and reduced to political nuisances on the order of embryonic guerrilla struggles. At this point, with the military outcome having been decided, Soviet tactics shifted and the ongoing competition for peasant neutrality or support assumed paramount importance. This, too, the guerrillas were fated to lose.

Initially, the peasant populations of all four regions supported the guerrillas. Nationalist beliefs and values, cultural homogeneity, anti-Russian sentiments, and religious opposition to a self-styled atheist state inclined Balts, Ukrainians, Daghestanis, and Turkestanis to oppose the Soviets. Equally important, however, the guerrillas offered the peasants important material gains. The guerrillas could rightly claim to be defending their constituents' physical survival and material well-being in the face of foreign onslaughts. The Ukrainians actually protected the local population from the encroachment of German troops, Soviet partisans, and Polish nationalists. The Baltic and Ukrainian guerrillas offered refuge to Red Army deserters, reluctant draftees, frightened peasants, and all manner of individuals with ties to the occupation regime. All six guerrilla groups resisted Soviet reoccupation and hoped to save their constituents from the encroachments of an infidel or, what is the same thing, a Stalinist state—for true Muslims, as the Daghestanis and Turkestanis certainly were, and for people who had experienced Soviet terror in 1940–1941, a goal that very much concerned their physical survival.[19] Finally, all six struggles offered the peasantry a continuation of their traditional mode of life, a promise of great importance to the Balts and Ukrainians who rightly feared collectivization. Naturally, the guerrillas also made use of negative sanctions—not the least of which were killings of alleged collaborators—but these paled in comparison with the good things they had to offer and came into their own only after the Soviet reoccupation.

The postwar Soviet presence confronted all the guerrillas with a dilemma. Unlike the Whites, Germans, or other power contenders operating under wartime conditions, once the war ended the Soviets could concentrate their full resources on the guerrilla-infested territories. Moreover, unlike mere occupiers, the Soviets were also intent on integrating, and not just exploiting or benignly neglecting, the non-Russian populations. The Soviets came with a program, and not only with destruction. Their substantial resource endowment translated into negative sanctions against active guerrilla supporters and positive sanctions for passive guerrilla supporters and neutrals. Most distressing for the guerrillas, Soviet positive and negative sanctions increased immensely at the same time that their own were entering into decline. The guerrillas' fighting capacity was being progressively undermined, while their instrumental appeal—survival during war, the prevention of a Soviet takeover—was now either irrelevant or unconvincing. After all, war had ended and the Soviets were manifestly here. Unless the guerrillas could stop the Soviets, and they could not, there was little for the guerrillas to do except play an exclusively obstructive role. They could impede Sovietization, but they could not bring it to a halt. As a consequence, despite the continued popularity of anti-Sovietism, anti-Communism, and nationalism, the guerrilla struggles appeared increasingly hopeless, pointless, and destructive for much of the population.

The more thoroughly the Soviets established themselves, the larger the number of people they involved in the emerging new order. Those peasants, workers, or intellectuals who resisted were ruthlessly repressed. Arrests, executions, job dismissals, and other reprisals were an all too common feature of the Sovietization of the Baltic republics, western Ukraine, and Turkestan. Perhaps even more effective was the Soviet willingness to deport actually and potentially troublesome elements. The number included some 80,000 Estonians, 100,000 Latvians, 260,000 Lithuanians, and up to 500,000 western Ukrainians in 1945–1955.[20] In the 1920s, meanwhile, close to 900,000 Turkestanis either fled or were driven out to Afghanistan as a result of the fighting with the Basmachi.[21]

Those non-Russians who did not resist soon discovered that the Soviets had positive incentives to offer as well. The first and most obvious was peace, the appeal of which became ever greater as it became increasingly obvious to all civilians, even those who hated collectivization, that the guerrillas were pursuing a hopeless military cause. The second was social advancement, educational opportunities, and employment within the structures of the Soviet state, all measures with not inconsiderable appeal for illiterate peasant youths desperate to escape the confinement and hardships of a war-ravaged countryside.

Last but not least, the Soviets also proved adept at stealing some of the guerrillas' ideological and cultural thunder. In Central Asia and Kazakhstan, the *Turkkommissiia* wisely reversed some of the harsher anti-Islamic measures imposed in the early 1920s, while Soviet power appealed to jaddid sympathies by providing the Turkic peoples with national identities, republics, and written languages. In the Ukraine, the Soviets could rightfully state that it was they, and not the nationalists, who had "ingathered" the ethnically Ukrainian lands and created a single Ukrainian national organism. Naturally, no such claims could be made in the Baltic republics, as the memory of Soviet imperialism was much too recent. But here, as in the Ukraine, some political capital could be and was made by accusing the nationalists of collaborating with the Germans or of objectively delaying liberation by opposing the Soviet advance, as well as by labelling *bona fide* Nazi hirelings as nationalists. All three ploys also proved to be effective in undermining the credibility of East European nationalists, in particular the unfortunate Chetnik leader, Draža Mihajlović.

The guerrillas had little that was positive to offer in return. Because they could not win, they could not promise better times ahead. All the guerrillas could do was to impede the normalization that the Soviets were promoting, but doing so put them in the unenviable position of appearing to be a purely negative force. Killing individual collaborators, for example, may have made great sense during the initial stages of the reoccupation, but it proved senseless after the battle against the Soviets had been lost and the nationalists went underground. Whereas loss of a friend or relative could have been rationalized as being for the good of a viable cause, it seemed pointless once the cause was obviously lost. The same logic held for guerrilla attacks on collective farms, local soviets, and other symbols of power. What seemed to be a reasonable form of resistance at the beginning appeared increasingly unreasonable as Sovietization proceeded inexorably and became part of the fabric of daily life. Ironically, creeping Sovietization and guerrilla military defeat turned the tables on the guerrillas: from defenders of the traditional way of life they were progressively transformed into the destroyers of the present way of life, and, traditional or not, the present way of life was the only one there was.

The tragic dilemmas confronting nationalists and peasants alike became most transparent during collectivization. Nationalists opposed it, because collectivization represented the consolidation of Soviet rule, the immiseration of the nation, and the elimination of the guerrilla food supply. Most peasants also opposed collectivization, because it deprived them of land and promised only poverty in return. In response, the Soviets radically altered the structure of incentives. First, they imposed ruinous taxes on noncollectivized farms. Second, they deported recalcitrant peasants en masse. And third, they collectivized homesteads forcibly.[22] Under such conditions, a peasant could either embark on suicide by resisting, join the valiant but hopeless underground, or enter the collective farm. Rational peasants, even if true believers in nationalism, would have chosen the latter. Only martyrs and fanatics would have opted for the second option, but they probably would have joined the guerrillas much earlier anyway.

Given these alternatives, programmatic statements such as the following by the Ukrainian nationalists appear completely irrelevant to the daily concerns of a desperate peasantry:

> The UHVR [Ukrainian Supreme Liberation Council] is for the complete destruction of the Bolshevik collective farm system in the Ukraine, for the complete liberation of the Ukrainian peasantry from the collective farm yoke. . . . The UHVR calls on the Ukrainian peasantry to struggle against the collective farms both in the long since collectivized east Ukrainian oblasts as well as in the still not completely collectivized western oblasts. . . . The Ukrainian liberation-revolutionary movement conducts its struggle against the collective system in the Ukraine under the slogan: "Down with the collective farms! The land to the peasants!"[23]

Ukrainian peasants may have agreed with these noble sentiments, but it would have been irrational for them, especially in the eastern oblasts, to tell collective farm chairmen that the land was actually theirs and that the farms were null and void.

The following example from a Lithuanian underground document also illustrates how continued nationalist resistance was objectively driving the peasantry into an impossible position:

The attack was carried out by an LFA [Lithuanian Freedom Army] platoon of 47 men. During that day, the freedom fighters thoroughly reconnoitered the sovkhoz and its environment, in order to be certain that no concealed NKVD units were in the vicinity. Next, some thirty farmers with wagons were mobilized. When darkness fell, guards were posted on the roads leading to the sovkhoz, while the majority of the freedom fighters surrounded the sovkhoz itself. Three men drove in one of the wagons to the sovkhoz office building. Their task was to prevent the two Russian officials, the only armed men in the sovkhoz, from sounding the alarm. Although the trio spoke good Russian and stated that they were NKVD officers from a neighboring town, the Russians would not unlock the door. Only when the sovkhoz night watchman came to the door, pistol at his back, to verify their identities, did the door open. The two officials were then disarmed and bound. In the warehouse sovkhoz workers were mobilized to fill sacks of grain and load them onto the wagons. Thus some thirteen tons of grain were acquired, together with several cows and hogs, added for a balanced diet. The sovkhoz laborers were paid for their work in sovkhoz grain. By dawn the wagons and the freedom fighters had vanished without a trace. NKVD units in several neighboring regions were dispatched to search, but without result. Soon, however, as the night guards were reinforced, night raids on the sovkhozes became very difficult. The LFA then switched to daytime raids, some of which were disguised as criminal holdups, in order to avoid NKVD searches and reprisals.[24]

Consider what happened. The LFA unit mobilized thirty Lithuanian farmers with wagons, forced the presumably Lithuanian night watchman to lie to his superiors, mobilized additional Lithuanians to load the wagons, and finally paid them all with state-farm grain. In view of NKVD brutality, it is hard to believe that these individuals were not subjected to severe reprisals as bourgeois nationalists, and the LFA's adoption of criminal disguises indicates that the nationalists were fully aware of this danger. But while holdups may have alleviated one problem, they only aggravated another. By staging daytime raids, the guerrillas were disrupting the work of the state farm, reducing its output, impoverishing an already overtaxed peasantry, and provoking the wrath of police and Party officials concerned with productivity. As Soviet, Yugoslav, and Chinese Communist partisans learned in World War II, reprisals can radicalize a peasantry and force it to choose sides, but only if there are viable sides to choose from. The mistake of the Lithuanians, Ukrainians, and other guerrillas was to provoke reprisals when they no longer represented a viable force. Under such conditions, reprisals were unlikely to induce peasants to join the underground; rather, they merely complicated an already sufficiently complex peasant life. The guerrilla tragedy, however, consisted in the fact that they, too, had no choice. Not to raid collective farms was to surrender and to starve. Collectivization, in a word, was a no-win situation for the guerrillas.

Although their end was never in doubt, it is nonetheless remarkable that the guerrillas survived for as long as they did. Martha Brill Olcott attributes the longevity of the Basmachi to "the diverse nature of the *Basmachi* leadership, the availability of a large fighting force, their advantage as guerrillas in their knowledge of the terrain; and finally, and most critically, they enjoyed the support of virtually all sectors of Turkestani society."[25] To be sure, these resources were as important in Turkestan as in the Baltic republics and the western Ukraine, but, on their own, they explain little. Instead, guerrilla resources must be seen in comparison to those possessed by the Soviets. When Soviet resources were small, as in the initial years of reoccupation, the guerrillas survived; when Soviet resources became larger, as they inevitably did in the course of Sovietization, the guerrillas were outmaneuvered and outfought. In other words, the longevity of all the guerrilla movements considered above, excepting the Daghestanis, was due to initial Soviet weakness and to the difficulties that reoccupation entailed.

The Muslim, Baltic, and Ukrainian guerrillas lost active popular support because they lost on the battlefield. As Che Guevara's misadventures in the jungles of Bolivia suggest, guerrillas cannot take root if they cannot stop running.[26] Once Sovietization seemed inexorable, as it did by 1923–1924 and 1947–1948, the Basmachi, Balts, and Ukrainians had no positive incentives to offer. Unable to force compliance or to win support, the guerrillas faded into irrelevance. But the key to their demise was military defeat, not lack of popular support. Had they been able to escape to a Yenan, they could have survived.[27] Had another world war erupted, as the Lithuanians and Ukrainians hoped, their star might have risen once again.[28] But in conditions of relative weakness and normalization, they were, alas, condemned to destruction or to flight abroad, whence they could— and would—continue the struggle from afar as émigrés.

— 9 —

The Triumph of the Émigrés

Ours is a bias for victors, for successful political actors. Willfully or not, we consign the losers of political struggles to the "garbage heap of history" and reduce them to the status of curiosities and relics of the past. As a consequence, émigrés are rarely studied. Occasionally, historians will delve into their intrigues and produce gossipy books; more often, students of intelligence services will refer to the role that émigrés play in the murky world of espionage.[1] Most of the time, émigrés are either ignored or denounced for failing to share the political views of scholars.[2]

Testimony to this bias is the fact that we do study those émigrés who turn out to be victors. I have in mind that émigré political grouping *par excellence*—Lenin and his exile Bolshevik comrades. A disinterested observer looking at the exiled Russian social democrats of the early twentieth century would surely have concluded that they were merely a rag-tag bunch of squabbling, chess-playing, coffee-drinking intriguers, penetrated by the secret police, lacking any future, and incapable of effective action. Indeed, one Austrian socialist, upon being asked whether a revolution in Russia was possible, is supposed to have said, "And who's supposed to lead it? Herr Trotsky of the Cafe Central?" Of course, the Bolsheviks succeeded, but we should not lose sight of the fact that their success is at least partly attributable to their being émigrés who could continue to hatch plans and mobilize forces, albeit far from home.

Just as émigré Bolsheviks are critical to an understanding of the Russian Revolution, so, too, Russian and non-Russian émigrés cannot be excluded from the study of Soviet politics. In this respect, Soviet scholars—or former Soviets, such as Aleksandr Nekrich and Michael Heller[3]—are ahead of their Western colleagues: recognizing that émigrés in general and émigré nationalists in particular remain an integral part of the political dynamics of the USSR, they almost invariably devote at least a chapter to émigrés in their studies of the Soviet state's domestic politics.[4] And they do so with good reason, as, to paraphrase von Clausewitz, emigration is not the end of the political struggle against the state, but its continuation by different—but not too different—means, an unpleasant fact of life that all revolutionary regimes have always confronted.[5] Indeed, as Albert O. Hirschman suggests, one can oppose the state legally, construct an incipient state, become a guerrilla, join a popular movement, engage in dissent, or one can "exit" and pursue one's political goals as an émigré.[6] In a word, émigrés must be seen as part of the political process that is taking place at home. Although they are removed from the scene of conflict, they have the advantage of autonomy, of being able to pursue their goals more or less unhindered by the adversary state. In this sense, they are like guerrillas who have found refuge across the border.

The part émigrés play in the political process is very much a function of the resources they can mobilize and of the international environment. All participants in a political struggle must, as we know, have resources in order to be able to wage it. Not only must they resist their opponents, but they must also mobilize their rational constituencies to support them actively. Émigrés, quite simply, have resources in relative abundance. They have money, contacts with interested foreign agencies, propaganda, firearms, and some diplomatic clout. They can utilize these resources against the state directly, by means of their own antistate activities, or indirectly, by supporting the activities of home-grown oppositionists to the state or by attempting to inculcate the state's subject population with antistate attitudes. Naturally, as holders of resources, émigrés are perceived to be and in fact are genuine opponents of the state, which, sensibly enough, adopts a variety of measures to combat their pernicious influence. Intelligence services are mobilized against émigrés and their supporters at home; propaganda, border controls, jamming, surveillance, and attempts to curb émigré activities by pressuring foreign governments also come into play. All these efforts are costly: they siphon off the state's resources and negatively affect its effective pursuit of domestic and foreign policies. All émigrés, even the most irrelevant ones, weaken the state by reducing its resource endowment.

How important are émigrés? Their impact obviously depends on the correlation of resources between themselves and the state. When the state is richly endowed with resources and the émigrés, comparatively, are not, they tend to confine their efforts to indirect influence and support. At times of systemic distress, however, such as wars or during periods of economic or social turmoil, resource-endowed émigrés can assume a significant role in domestic political developments. The case of the Bolsheviks is instructive. The war in general and the February Revolution in particular permitted them to intervene decisively in the revolutionary process. Lenin's arrival at the Finland Station is an excellent symbol of how, as Sidney Hook suggests, even a single émigré can impose himself on internal political events and come to dominate them.[7] Analogously, the Ayatollah Khomeini's appearance at Teheran airport turned the tables on the defenders of the *ancien régime* in Iran.

Perhaps the key determinant of the extent of the émigré threat to the Soviet state is the size of the émigré population, and that, of course, has traditionally been a function of Soviet success in crushing incipient states and dispersing guerrillas. Where numbers are concerned, political émigrés from Tsarist Russia and the Soviet Union represent a formidable force that came to the West in four waves: before World War I, during and immediately after the first and second world wars, and in the 1970s. Jews were the largest prerevolutionary emigration, numbering some two million.[8] Most came to the United States, and the organizations they established, although no longer considered émigré, have played, and continue to play, an enormous role in the life of Jews in the USSR. If we include prisoners of war and evacuees, Russians and Ukrainians were the two largest emigrations during the second and third waves. After the Revolution, over one million Russians settled largely in Germany and France, while several hundred thousand Ukrainians went mostly to Austria, Czecho-Slovakia, and

Poland: there is surely much overlap between these two figures, as the Ukrainians who served in White armies were generally counted as Russian by Russians and as Ukrainian by Ukrainians.[9] The number of Russians leaving during World War II was much smaller, some 60,000, while that of Ukrainians reached about 135,000. Approximately 85,000 Latvians, 50,000 Lithuanians, 36,000 Estonians, and 24,000 Belorussians joined the third wave, most of which came to rest in the United States, Canada, Australia, and Great Britain.[10] Finally, the fourth wave, consisting of 225,500 Jews, 56,600 Germans, 20,000 Armenians, several thousand Russians, and a smattering of Ukrainian and other dissidents, swept into Israel, West Germany, and the United States in the 1970s.[11] A fifth wave began in 1988–1990 with the loosening of emigration regulations under Mikhail Gorbachev. All of these political waves were, of course, accompanied by hundreds of thousands of economic refugees, who, after coming under the influence of the politicals, often provided them with the material base for their anti-Soviet activities.

The manner in which they continue the political struggle has been remarkably alike for all émigrés, as has the Soviet response. Comparison is especially appropriate, because what anti-Soviet émigrés do and how they do it is no different from the activity of nationalist émigrés. All émigrés immediately form organizations: most are cultural, religious, social, economic, and educational, ranging from choirs to churches to philatelist societies to business clubs to free universities. Many, however, are overtly political or have political overtones and span the entire ideological spectrum from far right to far left. Some are strictly émigré creations, others are carryovers from the homeland, foreign representations, foreign delegations, and the like. Still others are governments in exile, "supreme" liberation committees, or the coteries of some pretender to the throne.[12] Although most émigré organizations were and are insignificant, some, such as Leon Trotsky's followers, the Russian People's Labor Union (NTS), the Organization of Ukrainian Nationalists (OUN), and the exiled representatives of the Helsinki Groups have managed to be a permanent thorn in the side of the Soviet body politic.

Traditionally, émigré activities have ranged from attempts at armed struggle to propaganda and agitation. The first tends to be most common during periods of political instability, when the Soviet border is most porous; the latter two predominate during times of relative tranquility. Russians, Ukrainians, and Belorussians were particularly active in organizing interventionist schemes in the early 1920s. Most

135

involved the crossing of the Soviet border by armed bands that were soon caught and destroyed. Once Soviet control of the border solidified, by the late 1920s, émigrés could at most hope to send couriers into the USSR. It was only on the eve of World War II that interventionist Russians, Ukrainians, Belorussians, and Balts came into their own. Some served in the German Abwehr; others cooperated with the Wehrmacht, oftentimes as translators; most simply followed in the German army's wake and hoped to reap the political benefits of its military victories. The Lithuanian Activist Front under Colonel Kazys Škirpa enjoyed German aid, as did, for various lengths of time, the NTS, the OUN, and the Belorussian National Republic in exile. The latter three also established armed units in cooperation with the German military authorities.[13] After the war, the émigrés lodged in the Displaced Person camps in Germany—Russians, Ukrainians, Balts, Belorussians, and others—continued their assaults against the USSR, not so much directly as in the form of assistance to resistance movements at home. Various groupings cooperated with the Central Intelligence Agency, the British Secret Service, and the Bundesnachrichtendienst: they received training, were parachuted into the USSR, and attempted to make contacts. Generally, all were quickly discovered, as the NKVD, thanks to its many infiltrators and, above all, to Kim Philby, often knew of their missions beforehand.[14] Thereafter, in the 1960s and 1970s, émigrés funneled minimal amounts of money, printing technology, and other paraphernalia to dissidents.

Despite the glamor associated with infiltration and intervention, émigrés influence developments within the USSR for the most part by means of propaganda and its effect on the values and beliefs of Soviet constituencies. The most traditional form of propaganda is, of course, the printed word—journals, newspapers, and books. Until recently, such materials could only be smuggled into the USSR, presumably by tourists, journalists, and diplomats, so that their availability was limited beyond Moscow and Leningrad. Nevertheless, émigré publications did mold perceptions in some indeterminate manner, as their audience tended to consist of official and unofficial Soviet elites who avidly followed émigré developments. The former kept track of what the "enemy" was doing, while the latter, the dissidents, read émigré literature for inspiration. And inspiration there was, as émigré propaganda invariably addressed the "blank spots" in Soviet history, such as the Molotov-Ribbentrop Pact, the 1932–1933 Famine, and the Great Terror, which official Soviet media persistently ignored.

Since World War II, what the Soviets call radio infiltration has also assumed a prominent place in the émigré war of ideas. The NTS and OUN at one time ran clandestine radio stations,[15] but the most important "air-wave pirates" are, by far, Radio Liberty and Radio Free Europe, both American organizations staffed primarily by émigrés. Radio Liberty audience surveys, the testimony of dissidents and emigrants, and incessant Soviet denunciations of both media persuasively suggest that their impact on Soviet intellectual strata was substantial.[16] In their detailed reporting of international news, East European developments, and Soviet dissent, and in their in-depth examinations of controversial aspects of Soviet history and culture, Radio Liberty and Radio Free Europe not only predated the revelations of *glasnost* by several decades but also helped set the intellectual agenda for Soviet dissidents and reformers during the "era of stagnation" as well as during *perestroika*.

Least appreciated—and most difficult to quantify in any meaningful sense—is the passive influence that émigrés exert on cultural, and by extension national, processes in the USSR, simply by travelling to their homelands or by setting intellectual agendas through their belles lettres, scholarship, and journalism. Obviously, western clothes, music, and technology did not convert any non-Russians into nationalist fanatics, but they did affect Soviet values subtly and unquestionably complicated official efforts at creating "new Soviet men and women." The massive resources spent under Brezhnev on combatting bourgeois decadence were testimony to this fact. No less important, Soviet political, cultural, and academic elites have often had to modify their own work so as to keep up with émigré agenda-setting. One of the first examples of this curious relationship occurred in 1923, when the Ukrainian socialists Volodymyr Vynnychenko and Mykyta Shapoval began publishing an impressive literary-political journal, New Ukraine, in Prague; one year later, the Soviet Ukrainians explicitly responded to their challenge with their own fat journal, *New Path*,[17] thereby giving, willy-nilly, an enormous boost to the fledging Ukrainization campaign then just initiated in the republic. Significantly, after cultural and academic ties expanded dramatically after 1988, to the point where it seemed possible to speak of a normalization in Soviet-émigré relations, émigré agenda-setting was openly embraced by Soviet elites who saw it as the fastest and easiest route to Western culture, science, and business, a fact that can but enhance the émigré impact on cultural processes in their homelands.

Historically, the third component of émigré activity, agitation, has been directed at *bona fide* states, international organizations, private associations, and the media. In general, émigré success in influencing these bodies has been directly proportional to their political importance, either as intrinsically ethnic lobbies or as instruments of foreign policy. Governments tend to utilize émigrés only when it is convenient for them to do so—as did Germany in the 1930s and Great Britain, the United States, and West Germany in the 1940s and 1950s—or when it is necessary to respond to ethnic interest groups with substantial political clout. The Jackson-Vanik and Stevenson amendments are the classic examples of government response to ethnic lobbying.[18] Not surprisingly, rational émigrés seek less fickle alliances with those government agencies that have a permanent interest in anti-Soviet activities: militaries and intelligence services. One can only speculate how much both sides have benefited from such partnerships, although we can be certain that they have functioned to deplete, however minimally, Soviet resources—if only the scarce newsprint wasted on brochures that denounce émigré connections with the military-industrial complex. Such alliances, obviously, do not make émigrés agents of Western imperialism, any more than they convert Daniel Ortega or Ho Chi Minh into agents of Soviet totalitarianism.

International bodies, such as the Socialist International, the League of Nations, the United Nations, the International Labor Organization, and others, have not been much more receptive to agitation. Although émigrés have actively lobbied in them since the 1920s, their influence has been minuscule, as few such organizations are willing to countenance the dismemberment of member states. Rather more accessible are such recently prominent nongovernmental organizations concerned with human rights as Amnesty International, Freedom House, Helsinki Watch, and the International League of Jurists. If their campaigns for Soviet political prisoners are any measure of émigré input, then the latter has been substantial. Although these organizations generally have little political influence, they can affect international opinion and thus exert some pressure on the Soviet state.

Finally, the media are of special importance to émigrés. They publish their own foreign-language newsletters and books, write letters to the editor, and attempt to influence prominent journalists. One Ukrainian political activist describes the ideal contours of such activity as follows:

It is necessary to acquaint oneself with the mechanism of the given political system in some country, with the mainsprings of

138

public opinion, the methods of mass communication, the social-political mentality of various sectors of the population, the financial-economic motors and the dimensions of socio-political forces, the relationship between various state and private institutions, the condition of Sovietological and Slavic disciplines at universities, scholarly institutions, research institutes, and specific professional organizations such as the Council on Foreign Relations in the USA or the Royal Society for International Relations in England. Only on the basis of so broad a knowledge of and acquaintance with the structure and bases of the internal and external political world of a given country can one proceed to master the main elements, directions, and content of its foreign policy in general and with respect to our adversary in particular.[19]

Whether émigrés actually are as methodical as the above quotation suggests they should be is doubtful, but there can be no question that most aspire to the status of effective lobbies and disseminators of information.

Émigrés influence Soviet political processes in two analytically distinct ways involving norms and sanctions. With respect to their Soviet target audiences, émigrés can and do shape values and beliefs. The strong ties that Baltic, Ukrainian, Jewish, and Armenian émigrés traditionally have maintained with their brethren in the USSR surely have contributed to the retention of national culture and nationalist ideals by significant segments of all six ethnic groups. Because they usually lack the opportunity to affect populations with their own positive and negative sanctions, however, émigrés, as émigrés, rarely counteract the Soviet state's structure of incentives and thus do not affect behavior. Nevertheless, changes in values and beliefs are significant (especially if they occur among the intelligentsia, the social group most likely to be interested in émigré goings-on), because personal preferences will tend to be pursued in the absence of constraints. And, as we know, constraints have fluctuated throughout Soviet history and there is no reason to think that they will not continue to do so.

With respect to the Soviet authorities, émigrés presumably have had no effect on values and beliefs (although this proposition seems less obvious in view of the remarkable similarity between Gorbachev's analysis of the USSR's ills and that held traditionally by émigrés), but they can affect, even if minimally, the environment of incentives and constraints within which the Soviets must operate. By cooperating with foreign militaries and intelligence services and by creating a climate of hostile international public opinion (say, with regard to psychiatric abuse or human rights), émigrés force the Soviets to divert scarce resources from potentially productive domestic concerns to decidedly unproductive foreign ones. In addition, while denunciations of brutal Soviet practices cannot topple the Soviet state, they do constrain and embarrass it, thereby compelling it to increase the space available to oppositionists in the USSR. Émigré human rights interventions, for example, appear to have eased significantly the lot of some Soviet dissidents and political prisoners in the past and may have been indispensable to mobilizing Western public opinion against the USSR, a strategy that appears to have payed off in 1988 with Gorbachev's decision to court the very human rights public previously scorned by his predecessors.

We can get some idea of just how many Soviet resources have been drained by émigrés by examining how the Soviet authorities have combatted émigré influence in the past. Until *glasnost* changed things dramatically, an enormously expensive system of jamming, counter-propaganda and propaganda, strict border controls, and hundreds of thousands of informers served to shield the Soviet population from the émigrés.[20] Technology, manpower, and money were diverted to such wasteful pursuits as following tourists, eavesdropping on conversations, and monitoring information flows. The KGB obviously benefited from such subsidies, but the state itself lost billions of rubles on what Adam Smith would have decried as wholly unproductive labor.

Even more resources have been expended on émigré organizations themselves, which have been the targets of assassination, infiltration, cooptation, and disinformation. The heyday of Soviet "wet affairs" was the 1930s, 1940s, and 1950s, and their victims included, among many others, General Aleksandr Kutepov (1930) and General Evgenii Miller (1937) of the Russian All-Military Union, Colonel Ievhen Konovalets' (1938), Lev Rebet (1957), and Stepan Bandera (1959) of the Organization of Ukrainian Nationalists, Leon Trotsky (1940), and Aleksandr Trushnovich and Valerian Tremmel (1954) of the People's Labor Union.[21] After Rebet and Bandera's assassin, Bohdan Stashyns'kyi, defected to the West and was tried in Düsseldorf amidst much embarrassing publicity in 1962, assassination appears to have been dropped from the USSR's repertory of anti-émigré measures.[22] Changing with the times, the Soviet authorities began placing far more emphasis on infiltration, disinformation, and cooptation in the Brezhnev era, their "primary aims" being, according to Tönu Parming,

- Political discreditation of the émigré communities and their political leaders in the eyes of their host societies.
- Sowing of general discontent in the émigré communities in order to weaken their political effectiveness.
- Driving of a wedge between community leaders and the mass of their members.
- Active cultivation of contacts with those elements of the communities that are not strongly anti-Communist or anti-Soviet, including youth born and reared in the West.[23]

It is impossible to tell how much émigré infighting, backstabbing, youth alienation, and lack of unity are the product of KGB conspiracies or the natural consequence of growing political irrelevance, frustration, and assimilation.[24] Still, there does seem to be some soft evidence for the view that Soviet disinformation did mold the émigré image in host societies.[25] The legitimate concern over East European war criminals, for example, was obviously not a Soviet invention, but the jaundiced Western perception of certain groups, especially the Balts, Belorussians, and Ukrainians, appears to have been affected by Soviet propaganda.[26]

Although calculating how many resources the Soviets have wasted on anti-émigré efforts is a hopeless task, the amounts involved clearly are not inconsiderable, surely no less than émigré expenditures on anti-Soviet activities. In this sense, émigrés have functioned to weaken the Soviet state and, thus, to enhance the relative resources of potential oppositionists at home. Like other international actors, therefore, émigrés can facilitate antistate collective action. Although they are generally too weak to create political space and too distant to bestow vast amounts of resources on state opponents, paradoxically, their weakness is also their strength as it guarantees that the Soviets can never crush them. Indeed, Soviet measures have turned out to be as unlikely to undermine the émigrés as émigré measures were unlikely to subvert the USSR. The two contestants were locked in a perpetual tug-of-war, which neither side could win: the Soviets were too strong for the émigrés, while the émigrés were too far away for the Soviets. The upshot was that a balance of sorts existed between the two sides for most of the 1960s, 1970s, and 1980s.

Much to everyone's surprise, this stalemate ended in 1988–1989.

Events under Gorbachev suggested that the Soviet authorities admitted defeat: in a functional equivalent of their withdrawal from Afghanistan, they appeared to recognize that the émigrés had prevailed and that continuing hostilities, of the sort outlined by Parming, was counterproductive. This development was remarkable, not only because it represented the Soviet state's capitulation to distant grouplets with no divisions at their disposal, but also because it was accompanied by a virtually blanket rejection of the "werewolf" terminology formerly favored by Soviet propagandists.[27] But the "new thinking" went even further, and the evolving Gorbachevian strategy toward émigrés could be best described as "bridge building"—the active solicitation of all émigré cultural, political, and academic groupings that were not overtly hostile to contacts with the Soviets.[28]

The Soviet rationale appears to have been simple: because resources were scarce and the émigrés could not be beaten, they should be approached, if not quite joined. A policy such as this, which was openly premised on Soviet recognition of their weakness vis-à-vis the émigrés, had several potential benefits. First, it might appeal to the cultural and technical elites who desired contacts with the West and who formed the base of Gorbachev's pro-*perestroika* coalition. Second, it might mollify national and nationalist sentiments among discontented groups in the non-Russian republics by permitting them to travel, see relatives, and acquire consumer goods. Third, it might even defuse some of the émigré threat by blunting the appeal of uncompromisingly anti-Soviet groupings. Fourth, bridge building held open the possibility of utilizing émigré contacts for establishing more profitable ties with foreign firms. And last, it would permit the state to divert the resources spent on fighting émigrés to more productive internal uses.

Logically, the émigré response to the Soviet hasty retreat was to follow in hot pursuit. Intransigently anti-Soviet émigré groups, initially caught off guard by the Soviet efforts at rapprochement, felt vindicated by 1989, when their symbols and slogans became commonplace in the USSR.[29] Together with the émigré moderates, who welcomed *perestroika* on its own terms, the radical émigrés jumped at the opportunity to follow the Soviets into the Soviet Union. Different groups pursued different agendas, but the overall effect was the same. Business, cultural, academic, journalistic, and political contacts expanded rapidly, and émigré influence on Soviet internal developments boomed as a result. An émigré Baltic document published in 1988 reflected this shift in strategy:

We in exile have long waited for significant internal changes in the Soviet Union. These are now starting to take place, and it is likely that whatever the major changes, they will occur in the next year or two. The hour of decision seems to be near! . . .

Baltic communities in exile [should] develop a more positive and aggressive approach regarding cultural exchange with visiting artists, writers, intellectuals, educationalists and other creative professionals to diminish any cultural divide that has grown up between exiles and people in the homelands. . . .

The exile communities have large numbers of capable people with knowledge and experience of Western business and management. . . . The time may be approaching when the Baltic communities in the West could help. . . . The appropriate time would have to be judged on the progress towards independence and self-financing. . . .

It is important to foster closer links (in particular, among the younger generations) between Baltic exiles and the people in the homelands. For the time being ideological differences should not constitute a barrier to closer links. For instance, a member of the Communist Party of Estonia, Latvia, or Lithuania who is a patriot and supports the same goals for achieving independence should not be shunned by the exile community just because of CP membership.[30]

Increased contacts, such as those outlined above, could enhance *perestroika's* chances of success by contributing to the regeneration of Soviet society, but they were also extremely risky. The open courting of émigrés could unleash an uncontrolled flood of critical information on the non-Russian (and Russian) populations, thereby contributing to the further delegitimation of the state and of the Party. Most important perhaps, émigrés proceeded to develop direct political links with domestic opponents of the Soviet state and contributed significantly to the technological, monetary, and propaganda resources of openly anti-Soviet and anti-Communist nationalist groups and movements. In particular, émigrés provided critical material support both to the non-Russian popular fronts and to a host of more explicitly nationalist groupings as well as sponsored visits to the West by leading representatives.

What, then, does the future hold for émigrés? If *perestroika* continues, the days ahead look quite rosy indeed—a fact that, in turn, may bode ill for *perestroika*. The first reason for this optimistic assessment concerns the USSR's determination to join the international community of states by becoming a full-fledged member of the world economy, establishing extensive relations with the advanced industrial democracies, and adopting a variety of internationally recognized human rights norms. For émigrés, all these developments mean that their isolation from their homelands has come to an end: with open borders, liberalized internal conditions, and greater international exposure, the Soviet state will find it impossible to prevent their continued interventions.

The second reason for optimism is the virtual certainty that Soviet systemic health will remain poor for many years to come. Soviet resources will continue to be far smaller than in the recent past, while popular discontent with the system will probably remain more or less near the astronomically high levels registered in late 1989.[31] Audience receptivity to alternative political and socioeconomic programs in general and to those of the émigrés in particular are sure to grow, especially in light of the first factor noted above, the certainty that émigrés will be able to establish beachheads in the USSR.

The final reason for émigré optimism is especially important in light of the first two points. If it is true that the émigré presence in the USSR will grow, then their capacity to have a long-term political impact on the Soviet system becomes a function of their ability to form alliances with Soviet opposition elites. As chapter 10 argues, de-Stalinization, and the permanent weakening of the coercive apparatus that it entailed, guaranteed that individual opposition would become endemic to the USSR. In turn, *glasnost* and democratization signify that organized opposition will now become a permanent feature of the Soviet political landscape. Both trends augur well for the émigrés, as there will always be Soviet elites willing to join forces with them, pool resources, develop common strategies, and mount coordinated assaults on the state.

Glasnost, demokratizatsiia, and *perestroika* have not only sparked a Soviet renaissance but have also invigorated the émigrés, who, for better or for worse, will affect the course of the reforms initiated by Mikhail Gorbachev in a manner that neither the Soviet leadership nor the émigrés can yet foresee. At present, it no longer seems outlandish to suggest that Russian and non-Russian émigrés will interpret literally Gorbachev's call to follow in Lenin's footsteps and return to the USSR, where, as in the 1920s, they will expect to play a direct role in the political process. Can the Soviet state survive the impact of so unavoidable, yet so destabilizing, a force? The answer depends on the internal Soviet conditions that accompany the émigré charge. Had Lenin returned to Russia a year earlier or later, his impact on events might have been radically different—not because Lenin or the Bolsheviks would necessarily have been different, but because a revolutionary situation might have been lacking. Like Lenin, present-day émigrés can exert greatest influence under conditions of chaos—which none other than the reckless and hapless Gorbachev so graciously created in 1989–1990.

— 10 —

Rational Nationalist Dissent

Historically, the heyday of nationalism as a form of collective action passed with the destruction of the Lithuanian and Ukrainian guerrilla struggles in the early 1950s. For the three and a half decades that followed, nationalist collective action virtually disappeared, reemerging only in 1988–1989. Instead, the dominant mode of nationalist behavior in this interim period was individual: incipient states, guerrilla struggles, and organizations were supplanted by genuinely heroic men and women who by and large formed collectivities only after being repressed and incarcerated in concentration camps.[1]

Individual nationalist behavior represents a very different analytical problem from collective nationalist behavior. Whereas the latter is primarily a question of the balance of resources that the state and its competitors can mobilize, the former is quintessentially a question of personal choice. As such, individual nationalist behavior is inseparable from the larger phenomenon of dissent. But what, ex-

146

actly, is dissent? Although much has been written on dissent as a product of strain, modernization, frustration, constriction, social mobilization, and the like, the rational choice framework suggests that dissent must be, above all, behavior that is premised on a decision to transgress official norms.[2] Dissent does not just happen; it is neither inevitable nor automatic. It requires a conscious choice on the part of the potential dissident. At some point every dissident, whom we must presume to be rational, thinks one of two thoughts: "Something is forbidden, but I will do it anyway" or "Even though I now know that my previous actions violated certain norms, I will persist." Dissent, then, is the product of a dynamic relationship between behavior and norms, and, as with the tango, it takes two to dissent: the setter of norms, the state, and the potential dissident. Behavior alone can never be dissenting; norms are necessary and they must be violated for behavior to become dissident.

The case of Andrei Sakharov is illustrative. His behavior was dissident under Leonid Brezhnev, Iurii Andropov, and Konstantin Chernenko. Once Mikhail Gorbachev permitted him to return to Moscow, give press conferences to Western journalists, and even travel to the West, Sakharov's behavior ceased to be dissident. It might have become so again had Gorbachev abandoned *glasnost* and democratization or had Sakharov decided to violate some current norm. Clearly, liberalization makes it more difficult for an individual to be a dissident nowadays than it was before *perestroika*; other things being equal, there is less dissident behavior to engage in if norms are relaxed or are lax; alternatively, more behavior qualifies as dissident if norms are tightened or are strict.

What are the norms that Soviet dissidents chose to violate in the "era of stagnation," the 1960s, 1970s, and 1980s? They were not constitutional, as the Soviet Constitution arguably is one of the most democratic in the world, a point the dissidents always emphasized. They were only partly legal, as Soviet criminal codes never specified what "anti-Soviet agitation and propaganda" and "slandering the state" meant. Soviet citizens knew of official norms less from legal and other documents than from official pronouncements, the pattern of past and present secret police repression, and the semiotically conveyed signals and cues they received from Party and state officials, ideological workers, and the like.[3] And, by and large, with their exquisitely refined sense of what was and what was not permissible in Soviet society, they would fashion their behavior according to these official expectations.[4] In general, such explicit and implicit official norms concerned three major forms of behavior: nationalism, democracy, and religion. Nationalist behavior was taboo, democracy was permitted only within the confines of a dictatorial Party, and religion was scorned as unworthy of Soviet man.

Why did individuals choose to violate official norms? Because their choice to do so must, according to my assumptions, be considered rational, their behavior was presumably the best means for attaining their ends in light of given environmental constraints, in particular, the state's sanctions. The decision to dissent is, thus, a function of personal preferences, state norms, and state sanctions: norms must be violated for dissent to occur, but dissent can occur only if sanctions—the actual penalties one is likely to incur for violating norms—are disregarded. Sanctions, obviously, are different from norms: the latter are discernible from official "signs"—statements, cues, and patterns of repression; the former refer to the actual repressive measures that will or will not be employed to counter some form of behavior.

Unlike other forms of behavior, however, to dissent in the imperfectly totalitarian Soviet context traditionally has been a conscious choice to ignore all positive sanctions and to incur severely negative ones. Dissent is a very specific form of rational behavior: it directly pits beliefs and values against negative sanctions. Moreover, by ignoring the state's positive sanctions, dissent eliminates instrumental considerations from the factors that can motivate it. In other words, dissenters do not *really* seek material gain or power, as those could much more easily, and rationally, be had by accepting the state's positive inducements or indulging in officially sanctioned behavior.

For dissenters consciously to court negative sanctions and ignore positive ones, they must regard their ends as ends in themselves. That is, their preferences must be intensely held. Robert Conquest appears to share this view by arguing that "dissenters are those who claim the right to think for themselves, to seek the truth directly."[5] Valentyn Moroz, a Ukrainian nationalist now living in the West, spoke of just this kind of intensity in an earlier *samizdat* piece:

Rome was revived by the Christians. What gave the illiterate Christian with his naive sermons the power to overcome the Roman philosopher, burdened with the weight of Greek and pre-Greek wisdom? Perhaps the Christian disciple had knowledge not possessed by the Roman philosopher? No, the explanation lies elsewhere. The philosopher's knowledge exceeded that of the Christian disciple. In general, the essential difference is not in what one knows and [what] the other does not know. The essence lies in the degree of feeling with which a person relates to one truth or another. One *knows* something, while the other *lives* by it. For one person a given truth is simply information, knowledge. For another it is a revelation, without which life loses meaning. A truth incubated in the soul to a certain degree becomes a treasure. Knowledge is transformed into faith. And only then does a person begin to live. Lesya Ukrayinka christened this state—*inspiration*.[6]

For preferences to be directly determinant of behavior, their intensity will have to outweigh the severity and efficiency of sanctions—the size of penalties involved and the perceived likelihood that they actually will be incurred. That is, the relationship between preference intensity and sanction severity and efficiency will largely determine when and where dissent is likely to occur. Naturally, for this proposition to hold, popular perceptions of severity and efficiency must more or less accurately reflect actual severity and efficiency: this is, I submit, a safe assumption as Soviet citizens, who are rational actors *par excellence*, sense such things almost uncannily, as anyone familiar with the USSR can testify.

If intense preferences are absent, we expect little or no dissident behavior; where negative sanctions are severe and efficient, we expect the spectrum of dissent to be narrow, as only the preferences of martyrs and fanatics will violate norms and translate into dissent; where sanctions are less severe and efficient, we expect a wider spectrum as the preferences of true believers will also motivate dissent. Believers of convenience, individuals who value things as means toward other ends, are excluded from the dissident pool because the mere threat of negative sanctions and the absence of positive ones deters them from dissident behavior. Clearly, as only a tiny minority of any population fanatically or self-destructively believes in some nonmaterial goal, dissent should be a minority phenomenon in any circumstances, as indeed it is.

How do individuals acquire particularly intense preferences? And why do the severity and efficiency of sanctions fluctuate? We know from Clifford Geertz that cultural communities transmit systems of significant symbols from generation to generation.[7] And, as Milton Rokeach tells us, particular social institutions, such as religion or science, also transmit values:

> Social institutions . . . provide frameworks for *value specialization*, that is, frameworks for the transmission and implementation mainly of those subsets of values that are especially implicated in their own particular spheres of activity. It is as if the total spectrum of human values has, through a process of evolution or historical development, been divided up and "assigned" to the several social institutions for their specialized transmission and implementation.[8]

Other things being equal, we expect the members of a community or institution to be most exposed to and therefore most likely to adopt the symbols, beliefs, meanings, and values transmitted by those corporate bodies. Naturally, not all individuals will be equally exposed or equally likely to do so, as a variety of psychological, social, economic, generational, and other factors can intervene to determine who will and who will not adopt the preferences in question and to what degree.

It is for this reason that Robin M. Williams reminds us that, as values continually interact with human experience, they can and do change in a host of ways, which he terms creation, abrupt destruction, attenuation, extension, elaboration, specification, limitation, explication, consistency, and intensity.[9] Logically, it follows that individual preferences must be the product of some combination of collective preferences and personal experience, such that, to put it all too simply, the former dominate the latter, the latter outweigh the former, or both are more or less equally determinative. If we proceed along these lines and, as always, insist on the *ceteris paribus* clause, we can reasonably expect intense individual preferences to result from intense collective preferences, from intense individual experience, whether sudden and dramatic or drawn-out and banal, or from some combination of the two involving the reinforcement of one by the other. Although it is impossible to determine which possibility will be decisive for any particular individual, in the aggregate, and other things being equal, collectivities with intense preferences should hold the largest pool of potential martyrs, fanatics, and true believers, to be followed by collectivities with nonintense preferences, and, last and least, by sets of otherwise unconnected individuals with shared experiences. The first type of collectivity can accommodate all three

150

combinations of collective preferences and individual experiences noted above, the second type encompasses two, the third only one.

There are two exceptions to this rule, and both can occur only if other things—regarding the kind of human experiences that collectivities and their members undergo—are not equal. As we know, personal experiences vary with the context within which a collectivity exists as well as with the context within which individual members of the collectivity exist. If contexts are appropriate, it may be perfectly possible for the above hierarchy to be altered. If, say, collectivities with equally intense values undergo manifestly different socioeconomic and political developments, then we would expect their value systems to be affected accordingly. On the other hand, a reversal of the hierarchy is unlikely if the communities in question are the objects of broadly similar socioeconomic and political developments. For instance, if nationalist, nationally conscious, and nationally indifferent communities undergo similar rates of industrialization, social mobilization, secularization, and other processes generally assumed to enhance or diminish national or nationalist sentiments, then it is reasonable to hold the latter factors constant and focus only on differences in intrinsic collective preferences, as in the case of the non-Russians. Although huge developmental disparities continue to exist (equalization, after all, is not at issue here), the non-Russians— and Russians for that matter—have experienced broadly similar political, economic, social, and cultural processes since the 1920s as a result of Moscow's consistent pursuit of centrally directed policies of Sovietization in each of these spheres.[10]

The second exception concerns more narrowly bounded contexts, those affecting sets of individuals. As Williams suggests, modes of living or working serve as experiential sources of values and, as such, appear to correlate, in the aggregate of course, with certain value inclinations. Two such correlations, fairly well established in the social science literature, spring to mind. In modern times—and I stress the modifier—there appears to be a close empirical connection between rural life and religiosity: whether the connection is logical and necessary or contingent on the countryside's delayed exposure to modernity need not concern us. By the same token, nationalist and democratic sentiments tend to be associated most closely with educated individuals in intelligentsia professions.[11] As such locational and professional disparities unavoidably typify the USSR (along with every other country of the world), we do expect them, in contrast to the developmental trends discussed above, to influence the value inclinations of aggregates of individual members of non-Russian collectivities.

We are now well positioned to determine how collective values and individual life situations can interact under broadly similar developmental conditions to produce clusters of intensely held nationalist, religious, and democratic individual preferences. If we can isolate more or less bounded sets of preference holders, we should be able to ascertain where nationalist, religious, and democratic dissidents are most likely to be found. According to the logic outlined above, the pool of potential nationalist martyrs, fanatics, and true believers—the reader will recall that I do not use these words pejoratively—should be a function of the size of a nation's intelligentsia and of the intensity of collectively held national and nationalist values. Thus, nationalist nations with large intelligentsias should have most potential martyrs, fanatics, and true believers, while mere ethnic groups with small intelligentsias should have least. We can perform the same kind of exercise with religious and democratic martyrs, fanatics, and true believers. The religious pool should be a function of the size of a region's rural population and the intensity of its inhabitants' collectively held religious values. The democratic pool should be a function of the size of a nation or region's intelligentsia and of the intensity of its collectively held democratic values (in other words, of a democratic political culture).

We appear to have determined where, other things being equal, martyrs, fanatics, and true believers are most likely to congregate. Whether or not they will actually translate their values into dissent now depends on the severity and efficiency of sanctions. By definition, martyrs and fanatics will ignore them. True believers, however, who are much more numerous than martyrs and fanatics, will engage in dissent only if severity and efficiency are not too high.

We expect severity of sanctions to vary with the severity of the crime. Because nationalism is instrinsically threatening to the integrity of the country and of the Party, democracy is subversive only of Party rule, and religion undermines only the Party's ideological hegemony, we should not be surprised to learn that the variable length of sentences meted out to convicted dissidents, although a most imperfect measure, supports our expectations: the Soviet state has indeed dealt most severely with nationalists, less so with democratic activists, and least harshly with religious ones.[12] The variable severity of sanctions suggests that the religious dissident pool has the largest number of true believers and is largest and the nationalist pool has fewest true believers and is smallest.

Unlike severity, the efficiency of sanctions is a function of international exposure, official resources, and elite position. The watchful eye of the world generally discourages the Soviet authorities from cracking down immediately or at all: in this sense Moscow's dissidents enjoy immense advantages over their colleagues in the periphery. State resources, and therefore the capacity to enforce sanctions, are likely to be greatest in cities and least in the countryside. Finally, we may assume that peripheral officials anticipate central expectations and, perhaps, evince unnecessary zeal in carrying out orders. In general, it is probably easiest to be a dissident in Moscow or in some village, and hardest in a provincial or republican city.

The two strands of my analysis regarding value intensity and sanctions can now be combined. Invoking once again the ever valuable *ceteris paribus* clause, we conclude that nationalist dissidents will be fewest: they operate under the greatest constraints—most severe sanctions and highest enforcement—and will therefore be confined to martyrs and fanatics among intellectuals in republican cities. Religious dissidents will be most numerous, including martyrs, fanatics, and true believers, as the sanctions upon their activity are least severe and least likely to be well enforced in the countryside. Democratic dissidents occupy a middle position: centrally located dissidents will include more true believers than peripheral ones, as republican and provincial cities are subjected to greater enforcement. Overall, we expect the largest Soviet dissident population to be religious, the second largest to be democratic, and the smallest by far to be nationalist.

Cronid Lubarsky's estimate of the number of dissidents in the 1970s tentatively supports these conclusions. Basing his calculations on personal experience—that only every twentieth dissident generally received mention in the *samizdat Chronicle of Current Events*—Lubarsky arrived at a total figure of some 260,000 dissidents in the USSR. This number encompassed about 10,000 human and civil rights dissidents (who included the nationalists), 50,000 believers (Baptists, Pentacostals, Catholics, and others), and—incorrectly, according to my definition of dissent—100,000 Crimean Tatar petition-signers and 100,000 Jewish would-be emigrants.[13] If we consider only the first two categories as valid, the proportion of democrats to faithful seems about right.

Can we disaggregate nationalist, religious, and democratic dissidents by community or region? My analysis suggests that nationalists should be most numerous in ethnic groups that possessed both intensely nationalist or, minimally, national values *and* large intelligentsias in the 1950s, 1960s, and 1970s: Balts, Georgians, Armenians, Ukrainians, Russians, and Crimean Tatars fulfill both criteria to a greater or lesser extent. (I exclude Jews but include Tatars, because the desire to emigrate to a nation-state is not nationalism, whereas the goal of a reconstituted Crimean Tatar ASSR may be.) Belorussians, Azeris, Central Asians, and Kazakhs generally did not. Religious dissidents should congregate in intensely religious rural communities, among the Roman Catholics of Lithuania, the Uniates of the western Ukraine, the Baptists, Pentecostals, and other sectarian groups of Belorussia, the Ukraine, Moldavia, and Russia, and the Muslims of Azerbaidzhan, the North Caucasus, Central Asia, and Kazakhstan. Finally, democratic dissidents will appear wherever intellectuals are numerous, but most of all in open cities such as Moscow as well as among urban populations with democratic political cultures, such as those of the Balts and the Jews.

Three objections will have to be countered before we proceed any further. First of all, is my argument not circular? Am I not inferring collective values from individual behavior and then turning the tables by claiming that the values are in fact the cause of the behavior? There are several responses to this objection. I could deny that the argument is circular by pointing to evidence strongly suggesting that, say, nationalist values are an integral part of contemporary Baltic political culture, that national consciousness is strong among the Armenians, that religious sectarians pursue their faith more fervently than, say, the Orthodox, and that intellectuals are more concerned with rights than workers.[14] (I could also note that this passage was originally written well before the emergence in 1988 of popular movements in the Baltic states and Armenia.) Of course, none of this soft evidence is likely to convince a skeptic and at that point I could brandish my second argument: that rational choice theory or, more generally, theory as such gives us the analytical tools and thus the right to dissect values and behavior as we wish and then recombine them as is theoretically most appropriate. And if this argument does not work, I could say, as I already argued in chapter 2, that the search for causes is indistinguishable from the search for effects and that, as long as the facts fit, so much the better.

The second objection is historical. If the expected dissident distribution is valid, how are we to explain the fact that nationalists, religious activists, and democrats have appeared among the "wrong" groups in the past? Here, my answer is simple and, perhaps, more appealing to the skeptic. Although nationalist dissidents are nationalists, nationalists are not necessarily dissidents. Nationalist dissent is the conscious overstepping of official norms, and as such it requires the values of martyrs, fanatics, and true believers. Nationalist behavior *per se*, however, can and does easily occur whenever state sanctions are eliminated and the far more numerous believers of convenience can join in. Indeed, as we have seen in chapters 6 and 7, nationalists *malgré soi* can emerge if outside forces compel them to embark on nationalist behavior.

The final objection is evidential. Can we actually prove that the dissident population is distributed in the manner predicted above? The answer, fortunately, is no and yes. (I say fortunately, because uncertain evidence undermines the circularity objection.) The Achilles' heel of studies of dissent is that they rely on arrest statistics as an index of dissident activity, a maneuver that at first glance seems perfectly reasonable. In reality, however, arrests are a function only of the efficiency of sanctions, whereas dissent is a function of values *and* of the severity and efficiency of sanctions. Arrests tell us, not how many people are dissidents, but how many dissidents were caught. For arrests to be a true measure of dissent, we would have to assume, incorrectly I believe, that repression is applied equally to all kinds of dissidents in all regions and with equal effectiveness. We would also have to assume that true believers do not take efficiency into account in deciding whether or not to become dissidents. Still, despite these complications, all is not lost. Because arrests deter true believers from dissent, we may consider arrest data to be a very rough measure of the number of individuals who are undeterred by repression, that is, of martyrs and fanatics. Although they are only a subset of the total number of religious and democratic dissidents, martyrs and fanatics comprise well-nigh the entire nationalist cohort. Consequently, statistics of nationalist arrests may indeed tell us something of significance about the relative representation of nationalists in the Soviet population. At this point, alas, another problem rears its head.

The Soviet definition of nationalist dissent is very broad, encompassing a wide range of objectionable national behavior, including what I have defined as nationalist behavior—propagating the ideal of nationalism or organizing and accumulating the resources necessary to the pursuit of independence. As a result, existing data on arrested nationalist dissidents really only tell us who the Soviet authorities perceive as nationalists: probably far more people than the number of actual nationalist dissidents. In reality, many of the Soviet-defined nationalists are concerned only with national or human rights and therefore belong in the democratic dissident camp. These objections notwithstanding—and in the desire to escape this statistical maelstrom at all costs—I shall assume that arrests of so-called nationalists are a very rough measure of the nationalist dissent of martyrs and fanatics.

The available statistics, as compiled by Peter Reddaway for 1957–1983, support my expectations. According to his data, 291 Ukrainians, 170 Crimean Tatars, 110 Lithuanians, 63 Armenians, 61 Estonians, 41 Latvians, 36 Russians, 23 Georgians, and 7 Moldavians were arrested for so-called nationalist activity in those years.[15] If we divide a nationality's percentage of the total number of dissidents arrested, 802, by its percentage of the Soviet population in 1979—an admittedly brutish procedure that is sure to cause demographers sleepless nights—the resulting ratios should give us some idea of a nation's overall nationalist "weight": Crimean Tatars, 1050; Estonians, 160; Latvians, 100; Lithuanians, 14; Armenians, 4; Georgians, 3; Ukrainians, 2; Moldavians, 1; and Russians, 0.1. For what they are worth, the figures generally support our expectations regarding the distribution of nationalist dissent. There are three anomalies, however. The Tatars are surely overrepresented because their cohort contains people who desire only to return to the Crimea as well as those who wish to reestablish a Tatar autonomous republic: the former are likely to be far more numerous, but only the latter can qualify as *bona fide* nationalists. The second surprise is the Moldavians, who must have been far more nationally minded in the era of stagnation than Sovietologists generally believed.[16] More important, and most astounding, the Russians score abysmally low, both in absolute and in relative terms, a curiosity I shall return to and attempt to explain in chapter 11.

Let us now engage in some very questionable mathematics. The 802 nationalists represent about 22 percent of Reddaway's 3,650 total arrests. If Lubarsky's figure of 10,000 political dissidents in the 1970s is accepted as more or less reliable, then no more—and probably many fewer—than 22 percent, or 2,200, were nationalists. This, I submit, is not a lot in a country as large as the Soviet Union in the space of a decade or so. This number is the absolute upper limit, as Reddaway's definition of nationalist dissent is very broad and Lubarsky's estimates are based on uncertain techniques (if nothing else, they may be relevant only to Moscow). We do not have statistics on the number of national activists who were also intensely committed to independence for their nations, but my guess, based on readings of *samizdat*, is that they were a distinct minority, no more than a fifth of the national activists. If so, their number, based on Lubarsky's statistics, would be about 450 or so for the entire Soviet Union in the 1970s. Even if we inflate the percentage, they could not possibly constitute more than a third of national activists, or about 700 individuals. There is, then, no way we can speak of massive nationalist dissent in the USSR. There were, of course, some *bona fide* nationalist organizations in several of the republics. For instance, Helsinki Groups calling for either some form of independence or referenda on the issue existed in the Ukraine, Lithuania, Armenia, Georgia, and Latvia. But insofar as nationalist organizations all had few members—the Helsinki Groups appear to have done best—they can be explained best, not in terms of the collective choice of groups, but in terms of the personal choices of like-minded individuals.

Why have there been so few apparently genuine nationalist dissidents in the USSR in an age of nationalism? The answer, quite simply, is that the Soviet state has never failed to conceal its extreme hostility to non-Russian nationalism. Nor has it ever hesitated to apply the most violent means to eradicate its manifestations. Under such severe conditions, where survival is literally on the line, few rational nationalists, except for the martyrs and fanatics, may be expected to pursue their preferences and become dissidents. As the events of 1988–1989 in the Baltic republics, Armenia, and Azerbaidzhan suggest, there may be hundreds of thousands of passive nationalist believers in the Soviet Union. Yet, very few of these putative multitudes were obviously willing to translate their values into actions in pre-*glasnost* conditions. We should not condemn them for their hesitancy, which was a rational response to an imperfectly totalitarian state's structure of very severe and very effective sanctions.

In view of the fact that nationalist dissent in the USSR was so rare a phenomenon, it becomes immediately evident why the sociological theories of Karl W. Deutsch, Anthony Smith, Ernest Gellner, Mary McAuley, and others are inadequate to explain it.[17] Modernization, social mobilization, competition, and the like have little to tell us about the behavior of several hundred or several thousand individuals out of a population of some 275 million in the course of several decades. The initial conditions just do not apply. Moreover, even if we give the sociological theories the benefit of the doubt, what they lead us to expect is all wrong. First, nationalists are not frustrated social climbers, but well-adjusted and socially successful individuals.[18] Second, the non-Russians in general and the Balts, Ukrainians, Armenians, and Georgians in particular have been competing very favorably with the Russians—indeed, these groups generally enjoy living standards and educational attainments that are no worse than those of the Russians.[19] Third, sociological theories cannot account for timing—for the rise and fall of nationalist dissent—as modernization is a continuous process. Fourth, if anything, such theories would lead us to expect nationalist dissent to have been greatest during the 1930s, when modernization was at its peak, but dissent clearly was not. Finally, sociological theories would lead us to believe that nationalist dissent should have been substantial in the regions undergoing most modernization and competition with Russians of late, Belorussia and Central Asia.

How, then, can a rational actor approach account for the only thing that is still left to explain: the rise and fall of dissent in general and nationalist dissent in particular? As it would be circular to assume that collective national or nationalist values fluctuated wildly in the three decades after Stalin's death, we would do better to look to state sanctions for the key to the mystery. I propose that the emergence and demise of dissent can be explained best by the Soviet state's manipulation of the efficiency and severity of sanctions.

To engage in any kind of dissent under Stalin required the inclinations of a martyr: generally speaking, not even your rational, run-of-the-mill fanatic would willingly accept the certainty of torture, death, or a lengthy sentence in Siberia in exchange for the mere attempt to express a political opinion and the certainty that it would go unheard. Stalinist sanctions were extremely severe and enforcement so very efficient that even most fanatics were deterred from pursuing their goals. But Khrushchev changed the rules of the game, and de-Stalinization marked a major turning point in Soviet history. It expanded the realm of the permissible and curbed the secret police, thereby giving all rational individuals more room to pursue their preferences. Many Soviet citizens interpreted de-Stalinization as a permanent liberalization of the system and began engaging in what they believed to be perfectly legitimate behavior. The members of the Ukrainian Workers' and Peasants' Union, for example, sincerely believed that their discussions of Ukrainian independence were within the legal limits of de-Stalinization.[20] Consequently, even though they, and others like them, were soon arrested, their behavior cannot be termed dissident.

The genuine dissidents emerged only in the middle to late 1960s, after the boundaries of permitted behavior were narrowed and individuals decided to persist in or venture into the forbidden zone. Why did the dissidents make this choice? Because enforcement of sanctions had changed, and for good. Khrushchev's successors were unwilling to re-Stalinize, the USSR was opening up to the world, and the rapidly growing intelligentsia was becoming increasingly important to Soviet economic development. In a word, sanctions had become relatively less severe and far more inefficient, both overall and with respect to the carriers of democratic and nationalist dissent. Although still irrational for the vast majority of Soviet citizens, the permanent slackening of sanctions made dissent a viable and rational option for fanatics and, occasionally, even for true believers.

In the late 1970s and early 1980s, however, the state cracked down once again and this time with a ferocity that belies Brezhnev's current reputation for indecision. But, ironically, it was not Brezhnev, but Gorbachev, who eliminated dissent. Dissent can be destroyed completely and permanently only under two conditions: either a return to full Stalinism, which not even Brezhnev could contemplate, or a radical liberalization of state norms and a permanent slackening of sanctions, as Gorbachev may have initiated. The weakness of dissent under *perestroika* is thus due, on the one hand, to severe repression in the early 1980s and, on the other hand, to substantial liberalization in the late 1980s. Paradoxically, dissent can thrive only when there is a little bit of both.

Although *glasnost* has undercut formerly dissident behavior and appropriated it for the state, if openness fades, stricter behavioral limits are decreed, and sanctions are tightened, dissent will again emerge. More important, the next wave of nationalist dissent will sweep all the republics, and not just those noted above. Although the nationalist pool will expand as non-Russian educational levels continue to rise and modernization, urbanization, and industrialization reinforce national identity, the most important contributing factors will have been *glasnost* and democratization themselves. These two phenomena have legitimized national identity, permitted expressions of nationalism, and, in combination with the economic imperatives and failures of *perestroika*, transformed nationalism into a respectable, if not indeed the only viable, political vision of the USSR's future.[21] All these factors, their potency magnified by the drive for systemic decentralization, have given nationalism a boost that it is unlikely to lose any time soon, if at all. Indeed, judging from the popularity of nationalism in such completely unexpected republics as Belorussia, Moldavia, Azerbaidzhan, and Uzbekistan,[22] we may be justified in suggesting that a sea change is transpiring in the political cultures of ethnic groups that, until recently, were indifferent or even hostile to nationalism.[23]

The Soviet Union thus faces an unenviable, if richly deserved, dilemma. Reform creates nationalism, while reaction creates nationalist dissent. To pander to the non-Russians means to encourage centrifugal tendencies and threaten the empire; to crack down and accommodate the dominant nationality, the Russians, is to undermine reform and guarantee systemic backwardness. An analogy with Austria-Hungary suggests itself, but with one big difference. Although the Habsburg empire, like that of the Soviets, was in decline internationally, it was relatively stable domestically. The "iron ring" constrained Franz Josef and his ministers, but at least they had the luxury of time and could, to quote his prime minister, Eduard Taaffe, *fortwursteln* indefinitely. Not so the Soviet leadership: because Gorbachev pushed, wittingly or not, the imperfectly totalitarian Soviet state to the brink, the current Soviet leadership must formulate its policies under conditions of extreme time pressure and constraint. If the past is any guide to the future, reliance on the Russians will become an increasingly attractive option and perhaps the only alternative to willful decolonization or inevitable system breakdown.

— 11 —

The Myth of Russian Nationalism

It is high time to examine that which the non-Russians are not and to determine how the Russians fit into the ongoing analysis. As will shortly be evident, the best way to do this is to consider why there are so few Russian nationalists. My findings clearly go against most popular as well as scholarly notions of Russian nationalism as a widespread, indeed a rapidly burgeoning, phenomenon that appeals to simple muzhiks, loutish truckdrivers, sensitive painters, and cynical apparatchiks.[1] Which version is more accurate? Is Russian nationalism sweeping the USSR or is it a marginal force? My answer, that the marginality of Russian nationalism is inextricably related to the centrality of the Russians, rests, as always, on definitional exactness and involves closer examination of the relationship between the Russians and the Soviet state.

As I argued long ago, in chapter 3, culture, ideals, and behavior are fundamentally different concepts with different referents and should not be used as synonyms for one another. Yet precisely this cardinal conceptual sin is committed in the case of Russian nationalism, as specific variants of cultural identity, ideational beliefs, and behavioral patterns are all subsumed in the catchall category popularly known as Russian nationalism. Such conceptual stretching not only grossly overstates the importance of Russian nationalism, but it also obscures the nature of the Soviet state. On the one hand, undiscerning scholars, policy makers, and journalists see Russian nationalists in every nook and cranny; on the other, they fail to grasp that the Soviet multinational state is sufficiently imperial not to permit any nationalism, Russian or other, to flourish.

Some conceptual distinctions may again be in order. As I have already suggested, national consciousness should not be considered the equivalent of nationalism. Nationalism and chauvinism, which is an extreme version of cultural identity, are also quite different. They can and often do overlap, but there is no reason for someone who desires a state necessarily to have an overbearing attitude toward other nations or vice versa. By the same token, one can hate other ethnic groups without desiring a state for one's own. Chauvinism and imperialism are also very different things. One can consider one's nation to be superior and yet not share a political ideal that aspires to expand state influence into other areas. Finally, in contrast to both nationalism and imperialism, internationalism is a political ideal grounded in the conviction that many nations should coexist under an ethnically neutral state.

Significantly, nationalism and imperialism are polar types. They are diametrically opposed to each other: nationalists desire a state for their nation alone, whereas imperialists want a state to extend beyond their own nation. Imperialists accept the nation-state, but only to repudiate it. While nationalism and internationalism are logically incompatible, chauvinism, internationalism, and imperialism are not. A federation of nations need not exclude chauvinism, although such a system would function more smoothly if chauvinist attitudes were absent. The points of contact between imperialism and internationalism are far fewer, yet here, too, some overlap can exist, especially if we think of the two as degenerate forms of each other. Imperialism and internationalism are similar in that both argue for many nations to be ruled by one state. They differ as to the nature of the state— national or neutral—but we can easily imagine circumstances in which the ingathering of lands would be assigned primary importance and an alliance of internationalists and imperialists might appear the order of the day.

As a form of the larger phenomenon of nationalism, Russian nationalism must be defined as a political ideal that aspires to statehood for the Russians, and Russian nationalists must be individuals who share this ideal. Irrespective of the problem of exact national boundaries (some Russians consider Ukrainians and Belorussians to be Russians), Russian nationalists must actually want or be willing to countenance the dismemberment of the multinational Soviet state: there is no way to erect an independent Russian state without doing so. In this sense, Russian nationalism, like non-Russian nationalism, is a mortal enemy of the Soviet state. Given the state's extreme hostility to all forms of nationalism, we expect to find potential Russian nationalist dissidents among the martyr, fanatic, and, perhaps, true believer populations and, thus, to be small even in the best of circumstances. Based on what we know from Russian dissident writings, however, genuine nationalist sentiments are much rarer than what even my theoretical expectations lead us to believe. Indeed, known Russian nationalists from the era of stagnation probably can be counted on the fingers of two hands. Aleksandr Solzhenitsyn, for instance, is a nationalist in my sense of the term, as he supports (or at one time supported) Russian and non-Russian withdrawal from the Soviet state.[2] A. Amalrik, V. Bukovsky, A. Galich, N. Gorbanevskaia, V. Maksimov, and V. Nekrasov also qualify as Russian nationalists on the basis of their "Statement on the Ukrainian Question," which appeared in *Kontinent* in 1977:

In contrast to Tsarist Russia, the Soviet Union today is the world's last colonial empire, and sooner or later the universal wave of national liberation will hit its anachronistic existence. . . . In making this statement, we place three questions before society. First, the Ukrainian question as such. Second, the question of all the other "national minorities" (all of whom today represent a "national majority" in the USSR). And third and last, the question of the "imperial nation" itself, which would benefit from as rapid as possible an awareness of the fact that the liquidation of Soviet colonialism lies in its own interests: only that can stop the threat of a future fratricidal slaughter. With particular hope, we call upon the Russian participants in the civil rights movement in the USSR and on the Russian political emigration to consolidate and intensify their cooperation with the fighters for the Ukraine's independence.[3]

Finally, the little-known dissidents Sergei Soldatov and V. Gorskii have expressed genuinely nationalist sentiments. Gorskii, for example, has written: "One thing is indubitable: the collapse of the Soviet empire is neither humiliating nor unnatural for Russia. Bereft of its colonies, Russia will not grow economically poorer or lose its political importance. Freed of occupational and violent inclinations, she will be able to face her real problems: the construction of a free democratic society, religious rebirth, and the creation of a national culture."[4]

Those Russians who are commonly considered to be nationalists for the most part are either silent about, indifferent to, or hostile to the idea of non-Russian separation and the founding of a Russian state. Igor Shafarevich may have been right in arguing that "we must rid ourselves of certain habits of thought, of the unverifiable and undebatable conviction that breaking away from the Russians and creating one's own state is the automatic solution to all the problems of every nation,"[5] but such beliefs automatically deprived him of the nationalist label. The editors of *Veche* called themselves, but were not, nationalists, as they "do not share the centrifugal tendencies of some nationalistic movements directed at alienating peoples and territories from Russia."[6] Finally, although the national Bolsheviks and supporters of *Pamiat'* may evince chauvinist tendencies, they certainly are not nationalist in any but the most muddled sense of the word.[7] My point, of course, is that we should not take self-styled nationalists at their word, any more than we suspend our definitional judgment in the presence of self-styled democrats, revolutionaries, and Communists. No serious comparative study of socialism, for example, would include Hitler's National Socialism as a case study.

How, then, should we characterize all the disparate Russian types who are squeezed into the category of nationalists? Most are simply nationally conscious Russians: decent individuals who love their nation and their country, want to preserve its culture, monuments, environment, and language, and are concerned about its future—characteristics that should not surprise us in an age of nations and nationalism. Some, such as Valery Chalidze, are sincere internationalists, acknowledging all nations' right to self-determination but preferring that the state be reformed so as to accommodate most non-Russian and Russian national aspirations.[8] Many, alas, can be best labeled chauvinists and imperialists—individuals who hold over-bearing, supremacist ethnic attitudes or believe in a Russian empire.

There is substantial impressionistic evidence of widespread Russian chauvinist sentiments toward virtually all non-Russians—Jews, Central Asians, Siberians, Caucasians, Ukrainians, Belorussians, and Balts—at the level both of elites and masses.[9] No less abundant is similarly soft evidence of the continued popularity of Russian imperial ideals, such as those of Vladimir Osipov and the national Bolsheviks.[10] G. Pomerants conveys more or less exactly what I have in mind:

> The politics of pluralism clash, in part, with the traditional Russian blend of nationalism and imperialism. The Russian empire antedated Russian self-awareness, and therefore every territory that Russian soldiers set foot on is considered Russian. This can be seen in the national (not just the official) reaction to the Prague Spring and in other similar events (up to and including the problem of the Crimean Tatars). . . . Imperial arrogance has settled in deep.[11]

In light of such "imperial arrogance," it is all the more remarkable that, in contrast to the non-Russians, there are so few Russian national activists in jail: both in absolute terms (Peter Reddaway's sample of 802 arrested nationalists contains only 36 Russians—5 fewer than the Latvians!) and in relative terms (even the Moldavian "weight," 1, is ten times larger than the Russian weight). Indeed, inasmuch as about half of the thirty-six Russians were members of the All-Russian Social-Christian Union for the Liberation of the People, which advocated armed struggle (and had little to say about the non-Russians), the number of Russians who were repressed for specifically Russian national dissent becomes smaller still.

What conclusions are we to draw from these soft data? First, because the Russian propensity to generate martyrs, fanatics, and true believers is presumably no smaller than that of other nations; because the Russians have also undergone modernization and social mobilization and possess a sizable urban intelligentsia; and because the Soviet state anathematizes all nationalisms—the absence of Russian nationalist dissidents must in large measure be due to the absence of nationalist attitudes among the Russian population as a whole. To the contrary, chauvinism and imperialism appear to be the dominant mode of Russian self-assertiveness with regard to the non-Russians. And second, unlike their non-Russian counterparts, Russian chauvinism and imperialism are not only widespread, but are also tolerated, if not actually sanctioned, by the authorities.[12] In other words, the Soviet state's definition of non-Russian nationalism is far broader than its conceptually correct definition of Russian nationalism: the former includes patriotic activism, nationalism, chauvinism, and imperialism, while the latter includes only nationalism. As a consequence, genuine Russian nationalists are repressed, Russian chauvinists and imperialists tend to be encouraged, and devotees of Russia, patriots who love their country, are always tolerated. Clearly, we have here an exceptional phenomenon. While Russian nationalism is a myth, Russian chauvinism and imperialism are very much a reality that appears to have a peculiar relationship with an unusually tolerant Soviet state. As we shall see, the peculiarity of this relationship is a reflection of the peculiar nature of the Soviet state.

As I suggested in chapter 7, the expansion of Soviet power in 1917–1921 was, *de facto*, a form of Russian imperialism. The Civil War was primarily a conflict between Russian contenders for state power. The non-Russians were drawn against their will into that conflict, which ended in Bolshevik victory and penetration of the non-Russian borderlands. In addition, as Lenin recognized, many Bolsheviks were chauvinists and imperialists. At that time, the two tendencies could easily coexist with the officially proclaimed Bolshevik goal of internationalism, because the practical programs of both were identical: expansion of Soviet power into the periphery.

Success was exceedingly problematic for the Bolsheviks, however. They came to power via a Russian imperialist state, but their stated commitment to an internationalist resolution of the nationality question impelled them to try to square the circle by adopting Austro-Marxism. Non-Russian republics were created and granted a form of territorial-cultural autonomy, while political and economic power was concentrated in institutions that were located in Russia—various commissariats and ministries—or were in fact institutionally Russian, in particular, the secret police and the Party. In this manner, the levers of power in the imperfectly totalitarian Soviet state—bureaucracy, coercive apparatus, and strategic elite—have remained Russian since its inception, so much so that the state itself can but be termed Russian as well.

Although an institutional imbalance between Russians and non-Russians has persisted since the 1920s, the degree of imbalance has diminished. As the dynamics of totalitarian decay would lead us to expect, the republics have acquired a life and momentum of their own and have progressively, if undramatically, superseded their original status as mere concessions to local nationalism.[13] Even in the pre-Gorbachev period it was evident that republican Communist parties, government bureaucracies, and political-economic elites were pursuing their own interests as assiduously as they claimed to be following Moscow's dictates. More important, republican institutions acquired varying degrees of all the earmarks of what Samuel P. Huntington calls "institutionalization"—the "adaptability, complexity, autonomy, and coherence of . . . organizations and procedures."[14] As such, the republics gradually became *bona fide* political units: their sovereignty was still largely symbolic, and their powers were mostly administrative, but the form of their political status was gradually molding its content as well. The currently existing Soviet state is therefore a curious hybrid: the state cannot be called imperialist as it is impossible to argue, in light of the republics' institutionalization, that the political system consists solely of Russian rulers and non-Russian satraps. Yet, neither is the state internationalist, as it is not ethnically neutral: its leading institutions continue to be Russian. Let me borrow from the Trotskyites and call the Soviet state a degenerate Russian imperialist state or, better still, a Russian internationalist state. Both designations convey, quite usefully, the transitional nature of the contemporary Soviet state.

These conclusions suggest why the Soviet state's relationship with the Russians is special. Although Russian nationalism is deadly, Russian chauvinism, imperialism, and internationalism are permissible as they reinforce, other things being equal, the state's centralized Russian institutional structure. There thus exists the basis for a greater or lesser degree of accommodation between the Russian internationalist state on the one hand and nationally conscious Russians along with Russian chauvinists, imperialists, and internationalists on the other. The state utilizes the Russians as a pillar of support, while the Russians look to the state for policies that reinforce Russian language and culture, tolerate prejudicial attitudes, and encourage imperial visions, while being sufficiently evenhanded with respect to the non-Russians to assuage most internationalists.

Not surprisingly, the number of Russian nationalists actively committed to the destruction of the multinational state is small. Instead, as befits a nationality with a symbiotic relationship with an imperial state, the opposition of Russians generally involves the content of the state, rather than its form, its "Russian-ness." As Reddaway's data suggest, Russians become dissidents in order to oppose not the state as such, but its ideology and policies.[15] Russian dissent is, thus, an "in-system" phenomenon, focusing on political, social, and economic issues. It is similar to the dissent of most Jews, who resist, not the state, but its emigration policies. It is therefore a mistake to argue, as John Dunlop does, that the perception of Marxism-Leninism as foreign suffices to make nationalists of anti-Communist Russians.[16] Ideological struggles regarding the true sources of national traditions are commonplace within all states and empires, be they between liberals and conservatives, socialists and capitalists, or traditionalists and modernists. The *Smena vekh* group, General Andrei Vlasov, and Solzhenitsyn all rejected the ideology, but only the latter qualifies as a nationalist: the former two were quite content with existing Soviet boundaries.[17] By the same token, the All-Russian Social-Christian Union for the Liberation of the People accepted the state as is, wanting only to change its policies, ideology, and rulers—somewhat on the order of the American Christian Right.[18]

The distinction between opposition to form and opposition to content is particularly evident from the different manner in which non-Russians and Russians treat the state's cultural and language policies. What Russians legitimately decry as Sovietization non-Russians condemn as Russification.[19] The difference between these two positions is enormous. That of the non-Russians is an attack on the Russian basis of the Soviet state; that of the Russians is only a criticism of the state's cultural policies. Non-Russians see Soviet policies as undermining the very foundations of their national existence. Russian activists, on the other hand, claim that Soviet policies are insufficiently attuned to traditional Russian culture and values. Although their charge may not be unfounded, it is typical of all intellectual elites to accuse their leaders of insensitivity and boorishness toward national traditions: the French debates regarding foreign loan words are instructive. Similarly, the many Russians who accuse non-Russians of being the primary beneficiaries of the state's social and economic policies are not unlike Americans who oppose welfare and other redistributive policies on the grounds that they benefit supposedly undeserving ethnic groups. In both cases, it is dissatisfaction with the weight of the "white man's burden" and not the burden itself that is in question.

In contrast to the non-Russians, whose nationalism we had to explain, the nationalism of Russians is explained almost by definition. Here, too, in light of the fact that just a handful of individuals appear to be genuine Russian nationalists, we need have no recourse to sociological theories. There will always be fanatical believers who pursue their visions despite an unfavorable structure of incentives. The *absence* of Russian nationalism and the *presence* of chauvinism and imperialism, on the other hand, do require explanation. We may account for the absence of nationalism by pointing to the fact that the Soviet state is, after all, some sort of Russian state: being degenerate, it is not quite as Russian as purists may desire, but it is sufficiently Russian to accommodate the aspirations of potentially nationalist Russians, who tend to identify with it and its troubles.[20] Chauvinist attitudes and imperialist ideals, which are beyond the purview of this book, can probably be traced to several hundred years of empire and the *mission civilisatrice* that they engendered, particularly in the latter half of the nineteenth century.[21] No less important, for most of Soviet history such sentiments and behavior were encouraged by the state, which often rewarded them with positive sanctions and generally refused to forbid them by negative ones. Russian rational actors could indulge in such inclinations because they usually had nothing to lose and something to gain by doing so. In other words, chauvinists and imperialists could be found among martyrs, fanatics, and true believers, as well as among believers of convenience—that is, potentially among the entire Russian population.

The historical relationship between the Russian internationalist state and the Russians supports this interpretation. As early as the 1920s, the policy of nativization (*korenizatsiia*) and the promotion of non-Russian cultures and languages served as concessions to non-Russian national aspirations without effectively addressing the chauvinism of Russians. In other words, disincentives decreased for the non-Russians but did not increase for the Russians. To be sure, Lenin railed against Russian chauvinism and the Twelfth Party Congress obliged cadres "to wage a decisive struggle above all against the remnants of Great Russian chauvinism,"[22] but such exhortations were not translated into policies with real bite. Indeed, those non-Russians who tried to turn the tables on the Russians, such as the Ukrainian Commissar of Education Oleksandr Shums'kyi, were rebuked for nationalist excesses and purged.

The nativization of cadres, and the promulgation of language and culture, had inherent limits that were the product of the state's Austro-Marxist framework. Because culture and politics are ultimately inseparable, non-Russian efforts to advance their own cultures in the 1920s could go no further than the state's reliance on Russian chauvinism and imperialism permitted. For all its successes, *korenizatsiia* and the promotion of culture and language could not overstep the bounds of the state's Russocentric Austro-Marxism. Stalin's critical comments about Shums'kyi, made in 1926, show that he understood the political implications of culture and therefore the limitations to *korenizatsiia* quite well:

> While Shumski is perfectly correct in emphasizing the positive nature of the new movement in the Ukraine for a Ukrainian culture and public life, he does not, however, see the darker side of that movement. Shumski fails to realize that, in view of the weakness of the indigenous communist cadres in the Ukraine, this movement, which is very often led by the non-communist intelligentsia, may in some places assume the character of a fight for alienating Ukrainian culture and Ukrainian society from Soviet culture and society as a whole. He fails to realize that it may turn into a struggle against "Moscow" in general, against the Russians in general, against Russian culture and its supreme achievement—Leninism.[23]

From this perspective, Stalin's declaration in 1934 that non-Russian nationalism represented a greater threat to the USSR than Russian chauvinism was only a formal assertion of a long since evident reality—the prevalence of Russian chauvinism and imperialism. Austro-Marxism had misfired, and Stalin logically resorted to the imperialist and chauvinist part of the federal formula. Tsarist history was reclaimed for the Soviet state, Russian national symbols became ubiquitous, and even expressions of non-Russian national consciousness were frequently branded a form of nationalism. The Russian tendency got another boost during World War II, when the Russian Orthodox Church was permitted to operate with greater freedom, and almost exclusively Russian national slogans were used to mobilize the Russian populace in support of the regime.

World War II, however, did not, as is often argued, lead the state to legitimize Russian national feelings: they had already been legitimized in the 1930s (if not much earlier, with the founding of the USSR) and the war simply reinforced their status within the USSR. What the war did do, however, was to impel the state once again to make concessions to non-Russian national consciousness. Republican military formations were revived, national military awards and symbols were introduced, and fronts were named after the Belorussians and Ukrainians. Furthermore, in 1944–1945 the republics were granted their own ministries of foreign affairs and Stalin insisted on United Nations representation for the Ukraine and Belorussia.[24]

Seen in this light, Khrushchev's decision to create a Bureau for the RSFSR within the CPSU Central Committee was not, as some scholars insist, a concession to the Russians, because Russian national consciousness, chauvinism, and imperialism had consistently been tolerated.[25] Quite the contrary, insofar as it was not just an instance of bureaucratic reshuffling, Khrushchev's move was another concession to the non-Russians. It was a signal that the state was indeed becoming more internationalist: the first step seemed to have been taken toward transforming the Communist Party into a federation of national parties along the lines of the League of Communists of Yugoslavia. Such an interpretation is particularly persuasive in view of Khrushchev's genuine commitment to a greater degree of internationalism, as manifested in the 1961 Party Program's frequent references to republican sovereignty and his formulation of the notion of the "all-people's state."[26]

Brezhnev's abolition of the Bureau in the mid–1960s must therefore be seen as a reassertion of Russian institutional dominance, a move that was consistent with his active encouragement of Russian national consciousness, chauvinism, and imperialism. Indeed, Russian national consciousness took off in the mid-1960s. Concern for landmarks, churches, environment, language, culture, and peasant and village values boomed in that decade and remained strong into the 1970s and 1980s.[27] Naturally, the Russian national revival was, in part, a reaction to Khrushchev's animosity toward churches and monuments, but it was also fueled by state support of such attitudes. Most telling perhaps, while non-Russian defenders of culture and language could pursue their activity only as dissidents already in the 1960s, their Russian colleagues published openly in such journals as *Ogonek* and *Molodaia gvardiia* and organized in *Rodina* clubs until the early 1970s.[28] At that point, a mild slap on the fingers did take place, but not because of the sentiments involved, as these continued to be expressed in official forums, but because some Russian national activity evidently had become too autonomous for the state's taste.

Significantly, there was a remarkable degree of continuity in the kinds of Russian national sentiments that were voiced in the 1960s, 1970s, and 1980s. Official ideology continued to speak of the progressive character of tsarist expansion, the monolithic unity of the "Soviet people" (*sovetskii narod*), the primacy of the Russian language and culture, the greatness of the "great Russian people" (*velikii*

171

russkii narod, instead of *velikorusskii narod*), and the indissoluble "friendship of peoples."[29] Writers such as Valentin Rasputin continued to extol the Russian village; Mikhail Gorbachev confused the USSR with Russia in, of all places, Kiev; Ilia Glazunov could paint canvases with unabashedly Russian sentiments, exhibit them in Moscow, and attract huge and enthusiastic crowds that did not hide their Russian sympathies.[30] By and large, until 1988–1989, non-Russians with such views either kept them to themselves or voiced them openly only in concentration camps.

This dualism also characterized the official response to the many instances of national assertiveness that transpired in the early Gorbachev years. Although *Pamiat'*, like various non-Russian groups, was savagely excoriated in the press for its extremist program, the Russian movement was not accused of being a threat to state stability and its activists by and large were spared the administrative and KGB harassment that befell *Pamiat'*'s non-Russian counterparts.[31] By 1989, tolerance of non-Russian assertiveness reached new heights—indeed, as in the 1950s a Central Committee Bureau for the RSFSR Party organization was established—but, even so, traditional patterns of behavior persisted. As *Pamiat'* grew in strength, it receded from the policy and media agenda; other unabashedly Russian chauvinist organizations, such as the United Working People's Front of Russia, also escaped official ire.[32] In contrast, the Baltic popular fronts were the target of an unprecedented Central Committee statement issued in August 1989, while the nascent Ukrainian, Belorussian, and Moldavian fronts continued to receive negative coverage in the official press and were even the targets of substantial police repression.[33] Most telling perhaps was the manner in which the official Soviet line managed to manipulate the language of the debate surrounding the use by Russians of non-Russian languages. Despite many decades of Russian disregard for non-Russian languages and cultures, it was the non-Russian moderates demanding equal treatment who were branded "extremists," and the Russian extremists who were transformed into "victims." To be sure, Russians were encouraged to correct "past mistakes" and learn the languages of the non-Russians, but they were not reprimanded for having refrained from such elementary civility in all the years of their residence in the non-Russian republics.

The message was as clear as it was unsurprising: Russian chauvinists were wrong to go too far, while non-Russian nationalists were, quite simply, wrong. Although Gorbachev's encouragement of popular activism has translated into a certain ambiguity in state policy toward non-Russian national initiatives, this ambiguity will become untenable as independent non-Russian groups increasingly challenge the very foundations of the state and the supporters of *Pamiat'* (or of *Pamiat'*-type sentiments, such as the Leningrad school teacher, Nina Andreeva) prove themselves to be dedicated front-line defenders of the Russian internationalist state against assaults by radicalized non-Russians.[34]

There is a significant pattern to the Soviet state's policies toward Russian chauvinism and imperialism and to non-Russian national activism. Despite certain fluctuations—formal opposition to Russian chauvinism and imperialism in the 1920s, active support under Stalin, reduced support under Khrushchev, a revival of support under Brezhnev, reduced support under Gorbachev—there is a thread that runs throughout. Rarely incurring negative sanctions, Russian chauvinism and imperialism are never actively discouraged by the state. Instead, the positive incentives to convert such attitudes and ideals into behavior fluctuate—that is, state encouragement varies. Exactly the opposite set of policies holds for non-Russian national assertiveness. Positive encouragement is rare and therefore constant. Instead, negative discouragement fluctuates, and when it is low during times of real or perceived crisis, as in the early 1920s, during World War II, after Stalin's death, or in 1987–1990, the non-Russians can mobilize and press their demands.

Note the critical difference between Russian and non-Russian national assertiveness: the former is encouraged or not encouraged by the state; the latter is permitted or not permitted, but only if circumstances force the state's hand. The former is a policy tool of the state and is therefore permanent; the latter is a concession and therefore temporary. Usually Russian and non-Russian national assertiveness are inversely related: when one is strong, the other is weak, and vice versa. Indeed, as we have seen, when concessions to the non-Russians are necessary, chauvinism and imperialism tend to be downplayed. When non-Russian assertiveness tends to get out of line, and chapter 6 argued that it inevitably does, Russian chauvinism and imperialism are reactivated. This dynamic relationship is at the heart of the dilemma that Gorbachev faced in 1990: how to include the entire Soviet population—and that means Russians and non-Russians—in *perestroika* without undermining *perestroika*. Chapter 12 illustrates why Gorbachev's task was exceedingly difficult. The conclusion will then suggest that the unintended consequences of his efforts might even subvert Lenin's Austro-Marxist legacy.

— 12 —

Nationalist Movements in the
Era of Gorbachev

A remarkable thing happened in 1988: nationalist movements emerged in several Soviet republics and survived. For the first time in Soviet history vast numbers of people came together to make explicitly nationalist demands, while the Soviet authorities stood by and did not respond, as every Sovietologist expected, with coercion and violence. Quite clearly, the events of 1988 had a wondrous quality, not unlike that attributed by many to the Millenium of Christianity in the Ukraine, Belorussia, and Russia.

Movements belong to the semantic field of collective actions: that is, movements are special types of collective actions. As such, movements are *self-conscious* activities. We speak of *the* movement of commuters during rush hour, but we do not call these individuals *a* movement, because their activity is not self-consciously directed toward some collective end.[1] By the same token, the discrete actions of like-minded individuals do not constitute a movement, because movements are premised on self-consciously *collective* activity. Movements are also *mass* collective actions; this qualification precludes their being mere organizations, although they may, but need not, be centered on organizations.[2] Moverover, as "things" that are "on the move," movements cannot be stable institutions; but, as things that move over time, movements are too sustained to be mere outbursts, such as riots, marches, strikes, and the like. Movements, thus, are sustained, mass collective actions. Clearly, they are special phenomena, and we will not err in agreeing with Frances Fox Piven and Richard Cloward that movements can emerge in special circumstances only.[3]

I make the above conceptual distinctions for two reasons. The first, obviously, is to locate as exactly as possible the empirical referent of the concept of movement, and to do so in a manner that is neither overly redundant, nor overly ambiguous. The second is to emphasize, if indeed this point needs underlining, how different the current nationalist movements are from all that preceded them in Soviet history. We are in the presence of a completely new phenomenon, one that has overtones of, but is nevertheless completely distinct from, incipient states, guerrilla struggles, and individual dissent. Explaining such a phenomenon is not only a challenge for Sovietology but also, and especially, for collective choice theory.

It is unnecessary to describe the events of 1988 in great detail as the facts are well known to all students of the Soviet Union. These "events"—to use a favorite Soviet term for embarrassing instances of popular unrest—had been preceded in 1987 by such transitory collective actions as riots, strikes, marches, sit-ins, protests, and violent demonstrations by Balts, Kazakhs, Russians, Jews, Crimean Tatars, and Ukrainians.[4] The size, frequency, and radicalism of these outbursts were unusual by recent Soviet standards, but activities of this sort had been a constant feature of post-Stalinist Soviet politics and were therefore not wholly unexpected.[5] What happened in 1988, however, was. First, in the early months of that year, hundreds of thousands of Armenians—perhaps up to fifteen percent of the population—engaged in continuous demonstrations to press for the annexation of the Nagorno-Karabakh Autonomous Oblast (NKAO), an Armenian enclave just across the border in neighboring Azerbaidzhan.[6] These demonstrations persisted, more or less unabated, until December, when a massive earthquake stilled what turned out to be only the first, most massive phase of the Armenian protests.[7] Then, during the summer months of 1988, popular fronts boasting large followings and brandishing programs directly or indirectly pointing to separatism emerged in all three Baltic republics: the Independent

Popular Front of Estonia, the Latvian Popular Front, and the Lithuanian Movement in Support of *Perestroika*, Sajudis.[8] Proto-fronts arose in several other republics, but only in Latvia, Estonia, Lithuania, and Armenia did popular activity assume the distinct character of sustained mass collective actions. Moreover, in all four republics the movements were driven by distinctly nationalist aspirations: the Armenians desired to include an irredenta in the symbolic state they possessed, while the Balts sought to infuse their statehood with greater sovereign content.

In contrast, the tragic violence between Azeris and Armenians, like that between Kazakhs and non-Kazakhs in Novyi Uzen' and Uzbeks and Meskhetian Turks in the Fergana Valley, although mistakenly labeled nationalist by scholars and journalists, actually belongs to the semantic field of interethnic strife. Only in early 1990, after the Soviet Army's occupation of Baku transformed anti-Armenian collective actions into a fleeting national liberation struggle waged by nationalists *malgré soi*, did the Azerbaidzhani movement assume contextually nationalist overtones. Unless the Popular Front of Azerbaidzhan initiates an anti-Soviet armed resistance or follows in the footsteps of the Baltic fronts by mobilizing its multitudinous followers for strictly nationalist ends, its activity will not fall within the definitional parameters of this study.

I shall address three distinct analytical questions: Why did popular movements emerge? Why did they emerge in these republics, and not elsewhere? And why did these movements have nationalist programs? As we shall see, the collective choice framework I have utilized throughout this book provides compelling answers to each of these questions.

My starting point, now as in previous chapters, is of course the state, and the most striking aspect of the imperfectly totalitarian Soviet state in 1988 is that it was divided against itself, a condition that conceptually is not dissimilar to that which prevailed in 1917–1920. Whatever the reasons for Mikhail Gorbachev's decision to embark on a radical political reform that had the Party and government "bureaucracy" as its target—be they his belief that the state was the major obstacle to economic modernization or the greatest threat to his own position[9]—Gorbachev launched a two-pronged attack against the "forces of stagnation" in the Party-state apparatus sometime in 1987.[10] His immediate allies were located at the highest levels of the Party and government and, probably, within the secret police and army.[11] Gorbachev could also count on the active and passive support of the creative intelligentsia and of sectors of the broader population, which might be expected to turn their frustrations on inefficient and repressive apparatchiks. Personnel cuts, bureaucratic streamlining, the promotion of the soviets, and *glasnost* were the weapons Gorbachev used to undermine his opponents by means of assaults from above and from below. This tactic, perhaps not incidentally, bears uncanny resemblance to that pursued by Stalin in the late 1930s and by Mao Zedong during the Cultural Revolution.[12]

Mobilizing popular support through *glasnost* necessitated a certain liberalization of the system, and in its most practical terms this meant reducing the presence of the secret police. With the KGB out of the way, popular and elite initiative could be unleashed and mobilized, but, unavoidably, in ways that systemically were both functional as well as dysfunctional. Although the intended consequence of Gorbachev's efforts was only to reform what even Soviets now openly call the totalitarian Brezhnevite state, in drastically reducing its detailed, if inefficient, supervision of the public sphere, Gorbachev's reckless assault unwittingly created the political space necessary for political opposition—as well as civil society—to emerge.[13] It was as inevitable that anti-Soviet opposition groups should arise in the wake of Gorbachev's war against the state as it is impossible, in circumstances of liberalization, to channel popular energy in one direction only, that desired by a reforming elite. Confronted with the truism that liberalizing dictators the world over never fail to overlook, Gorbachev unhappily discovered not only that the entire *narod* did not share his preferences, but also that they were no longer fearful about registering their disagreements. Once the structure of incentives had been radically changed—negative incentives against public action had been largely eliminated, while positive incentives had to some degree been increased—it was no wonder that martyrs, fanatics, true believers, *and* believers of convenience (whom I posited as the vast majority of any population) should have begun engaging in the kind of systemically disruptive activities that are commonplace in most laissez-faire states.

The first analytical point of my argument is clear: as in 1917–1921, in the post-World War II period, or during Khrushchev's Thaw, it is the weakening of the state, whether imposed from outside or self-imposed, that is the necessary condition of the emergence of oppositional activity. Why the outbursts of 1987 evolved into the mass collective actions of 1988, however, is another question altogether. As I argued in chapters 2 and 3, the factors we must focus on now are

177

elites, resources, culture, and ideals: elites, like political space, are necessary conditions, while resources, culture, and ideals are sufficient ones.

It was one of the many unfortunate features of the late Brezhnev period that virtually all of the Soviet Union's dissident opposition had been effectively neutralized: either incarcerated or exiled, internally or to the West.[14] As a consequence, martyrs and fanatics had been removed from the scene, while true believers logically chose to remain silent as the structure of incentives was to their disadvantage. Political liberalization, which was the precondition of involving both intelligentsia and masses in Gorbachev's struggle with the state, radically changed the structure of incentives and made protest by true believers a viable option once again. That there were in fact many true believers became evident in 1987–1990, as heretofore conformist elites—official writers, artists, and intellectuals—vigorously began voicing opinions that they claimed to have held privately for many years. At the same time, Gorbachev's decision, arising partly from his desire to appeal to the intelligenstia and partly from human rights pressures from abroad, to release virtually all of the country's political prisoners suddenly flooded the USSR with tried and true anti-state elites, who had extensive political experience, enjoyed close contacts with their colleagues in all the republics, and possessed relatively well developed and coherent programs for addressing the Soviet Union's ills. Within the space of several months, Gorbachev had created two opposition elites, one official, the other unofficial, who were to play a crucial role in the formation and consolidation of the popular movements. On their own, however, the opposition elites were largely powerless: they lacked concrete resources and their demands, mostly regarding language, culture, and environment, would have remained only symbolic without the active backing of resource-endowed actors.

It is at this point of my analysis that national Communism enters the picture and, analytically, saves the day. As I argued in chapter 6, the national Communist inclination to pursue republican interests, even to the detriment of all-Union ones, is the inevitable consequence of the contradiction between a centralized Party-state and Austro-Marxism. National Communism rears its head whenever political and/ or economic decentralization takes place and the Party-state withdraws to the center, thereby giving republican cadres greater control over their own resources and providing them with the opportunity, as well as compelling them, to engage in distinctly political decision making. Seen from this perspective, the Gorbachev period represents an attempt both to enhance and to diminish national Communist tendencies.

On the one hand, Gorbachev and his colleagues understood that Brezhnev's policies—in particular, "stability of cadres" and central noninterference in the bailiwicks of republican Party bosses—had led to the creation of regional "mafias" and to the disintegration of the command structure of the Party and government. Gorbachev's first years in office witnessed a concerted effort to replace local bosses, as best typified by Kazakhstan's Dinmukhamed Kunaev, with men who shared Gorbachev's vision and priorities and who might have been expected to be more responsive to the needs of the center.[15] On the other hand, Gorbachev's determination to introduce economic and some political decentralization, which necessitates that central Party authority be diminished and the Austro-Marxist brand of federalism be converted into a more meaningful approximation of sovereignty, was precisely the lifeblood of national Communism. Paradoxically, Gorbachev's simultaneous curtailment *and* enhancement of republican authority functioned, not to negate each other, as we would expect, but to reinforce the latter. This was so because the conditions under which the center's assault on the republican mafias transpired were qualitatively different from those under which earlier attempts to replace corrupt republican leaders with Moscow's favorites had been undertaken. Gorbachev's task was immeasurably more difficult as he had to deal with entrenched "old-boy" networks that fiercely resisted encroachments on the authority they had enjoyed unchallenged for close to two decades.[16] Worse still, Gorbachev's decentralizing efforts provided local officials with just the ammunition they required to forestall what they accurately perceived as the center's intrusions into their affairs. The rioting that followed Kunaev's removal in December 1987 was, thus, not only an accurate barometer of the degree to which local Kazakhs viewed him as representing their interests, but also a symbol of national Communism's inherently adversarial relationship with the center.

In sum, Gorbachev created new opposition elites and he enraged and empowered entrenched republican elites. In addition, by legitimizing their opposition to the central state (after all, according to official discourse, the hypercentralized bureaucracy is at fault for interfering in the affairs of honest citizens and local clerks) and providing them with a rationale for their opposition (it is necessary if *perestroika* is to succeed), Gorbachev unwittingly impelled both

179

groups—the new, official and unofficial, opposition elites and the established Party elites—to collaborate against the center. As chapter
4 suggested, the reasons for doing so are powerful. Joining forces permitted the local Party at least partly to coopt the opposition elites
and thereby to pander to the center's ideological requirements; collaboration enabled the opposition elites to acquire legitimacy and resources; most important, working together was the most effective
means for pursuing both groups' agendas of reducing central authority. Logically, collaboration between the opposition elites and the
local parties was the order of the day and we should not be surprised
to learn that such cooperation did in fact emerge in several republics.
The relationship between Party and opposition varied, of course, being
closest, almost incestual, in Estonia and Armenia, and somewhat more
restrained in Latvia and Lithuania.[17] Nevertheless, all the local parties played a key role either in facilitating or in not preventing the
emergence, persistence, and popularity of the popular fronts.

The local parties' willingness to collaborate with opposition elites
had several important consequences for emergent movements. First,
the Party legitimized popular involvement in political affairs and
thereby transformed it into a viable option for even the most timid
of citizens. Second and more important, the Party provided the emergent movements with additional leaders, its own. And third and most
important, the Party endowed opposition elites and Party elites with
the resources necessary for mobilizing vast numbers of people for their
ends. I have already suggested why and how the accumulation of resources by national Communist elites takes place under conditions of
decentralization in chapters 4 and 5. The current situation is even
more volatile because the reinforcement of national Communist tendencies took place as opposition elites were mobilizing and as the
state was divided against itself.

Several kinds of resources came to play an important role in 1988.
Basically, the Party's acquiescence in opposition movements enormously facilitated the organization of mass marches and demonstrations. Not only did the police not interfere (indeed, in some instances,
as in Sumgait, it may actively have abetted the disturbances), but
officially controlled transportation, media, and organizational skills
also became available for staging mass events.[18] It is, for instance,
hard to imagine how half a million Armenians—or any other group,
for that matter—could have "spontaneously" descended on Erevan
in early 1988 without some assistance from the authorities.

No less important, Party backing of the opposition elites' demands for language and cultural concessions transformed language and culture from symbols of ethnic identity into potential political and economic resources that could mobilize believers of convenience for the nationalist cause. In all four republics, as in many other parts of the world, language and culture traditionally have served as a device for distinguishing between "us" and "them"—between Armenians and Azeris, and between Balts and immigrant Slavs, especially Russians. As during *korenizatsiia*, however, local Party support of native language and culture infused these ethnic markers with political content that promised the local populations what they valued: jobs, housing, and control over their own resources, in a word, greater national sovereignty. The fact that the Baltic Supreme Soviets granted Estonian, Latvian, and Lithuanian the status of state languages had far-reaching practical political and economic implications that were not lost on their popular constituencies. So exalted a position raised the possibility, on the one hand, of restricting employment opportunities in the republican state apparatus to representatives of the indigenous nationalities, and, on the other, of excluding the immigrant or non-eponymous populations, who by and large had no familiarity with these languages and cultures, from the local economies. Language and culture were transformed into zero-sum games, which the immigrant populations were slated to lose; it is no wonder that their resistance to the popular fronts was intense, both in the Baltic states and in those republics, such as Moldavia, the Ukraine, Kirgizia, and Uzbekistan, where similar language legislation had been discussed or passed.

In Armenia, meanwhile, official support of the Armenian identity of Nagorno-Karabakh transformed a symbol of—real or putative—Azeri tyranny into an incentive for enhancing Armenian political sovereignty and economic well-being. Secession from Azerbaidzhan and unification with Armenia may or may not have been the most expeditious means for defending the Armenian cultural heritage in Nagorno-Karabakh, but it unquestionably offered Armenians in the enclave and in the republic greater political and economic opportunities. Most important of these was that integrating Nagorno-Karabakh—economically one of the most advanced of Azerbaidzhan's provinces—into Armenia would create a larger Armenian market and richer productive base insulated from outside pressures by Armenian linguistic and cultural boundaries. An added attraction of a greater Armenia is that its viability would have required an immediate expansion of the republic's administrative apparatus. In Armenia, as in the Baltic republics, sovereignty—control of the territory and resources considered to be national—was the goal, and in all four republics sovereignty implied a rosier economic future than that suggested by a continuation of the status quo.

Finally, local Party support of environmental concerns, which became *de rigeur* after the Chernobyl catastrophe and Moscow's belated response to it, infused ecological symbols with practical content. Here, especially, the potential payoff for everyone—opposition elites, Party elites, and masses—from resisting central economic policies was both visible and immediate. In all four republics, as throughout the Soviet Union, ecology acquired patriotic overtones involving love of the soil and protection of the Motherland from rapacious central authorities and insensitive Russian bureaucrats. Although environmental initiatives rarely came from the local authorities, only they were in the position actually to do what they have done: to challenge the center effectively, cancel projects, or implement desired safeguards, as with nuclear power plants in Lithuania, Armenia, and the Ukraine. Popular movements were able to rally support around these goals, but it is the relative responsiveness of the authorities, which have their own national Communist agendas, that provided immediate gratification to impatient publics.

The active or passive support of local Party authorities was a necessary condition of both the emergence and the persistence of movements. Without that support (or, minimally, without their willingness not to repress popular initiatives), opposition elites would have remained isolated and, what is far more important, incapable of converting their symbolic appeals into policies that promised potential constituencies a variety of political and economic benefits. It was no surprise, therefore, that movements of the sort found in the Baltic states and Armenia were absent wherever the local Party authorities refused, for one reason or another, to collaborate with opposition elites. Most striking was, of course, the inability of the Ukrainian opposition elites to form a popular front, the *Rukh*, until the summer of 1989. There is much evidence to suggest that the *Rukh*'s belated emergence is directly attributable to the resistance of V. V. Shcherbyts'kyi, formerly the First Secretary of the Communist Party of the Ukraine, and his comrades. But why resist? According to my argument, lack of republican enthusiasm for *perestroika* is irrational in light of the logic of Austro-Marxism and of the opportunities for national Communist self-aggrandizement opened up by Gorbachev. By the same token, to ascribe this reluctance to engage in national Communism to the political culture of the respective elites is unconvincing: the Ukrainian

Party's long-standing national Communist inclinations and the empire building by Sharaf Rashidov and Kunaev in, respectively, Uzbekistan and Kazakhstan, militate against such a view.[19]

What, then, is left? The theory impels me to conclude that the rejection of popular initiative by the Ukrainian, Belorussian, and Central Asian authorities was due either to explicit restraints imposed by the center or to the still undiluted loyalty and lack of republican roots of Gorbachev's appointees to responsible republican positions, especially in Kazakhstan, the republics of Central Asia, and Azerbaidzhan, or to some combination of the two. The second interpretation appears eminently reasonable, as we would not expect "parachuted" apparatchiks, such as Kunaev's replacement Gennadii Kolbin, to identify immediately with their republics and begin to think and act as national Communists. The first interpretation, meanwhile, rests on the commonsense notion that the center views genuinely popular movements as too dangerous to be allowed in strategic republics, such as the Ukraine and Belorussia. None other than Gorbachev himself enhanced this argument's persuasiveness by drawing the following instructive comparison during his visit to the Ukraine in February 1989:

> You recall the events in Nagorno-Karabakh. A small autonomous oblast, but it is connected economically and cooperates with other regions. As soon as disruptions began there, they were immediately felt by the country. But imagine if similar disruptions were to begin in a republic such as the Ukraine, where there live and work more than 51 million people. Then the entire cause will become disorganized. And restructuring in the country will slow down. That is why we are interested that everything work out well in all respects in the Ukraine.[20]

We know now why movements *could* emerge—due to *perestroika* and the mobilization of elites—and why they emerged in the Baltic republics and Armenia—due to collusion between opposition elites and local leaders and the ready availability of resources. We are now in a position to determine why the popular movements that emerged in the Baltic states and Armenia were of a distinctly nationalist kind. Did they have to be nationalist movements only? The answer is, of course, no, as the formation of countermovements among the Slavic settler populations in the Baltic states and Moldavia testifies. Although the so-called internationalist fronts do not concern me directly, as they are not nationalist, the circumstances of their emergence are no different from those of the popular fronts. Here as there, Gorbachev provided the political space, while non-Party activists managed to forge coalitions with interested sectors of the local authorities, who were in a position effectively to protect the status of the settler populations by means of their access to Party resources. No less important, like the popular fronts, the Slavic movements could appeal to a variety of political and economic values, such as continued residence or employment in the republics, to overcome the free-rider problem.[21]

Nevertheless, the fact that the Baltic fronts and the Karabakh movement all adopted a distinctly nationalist perspective, as opposed to one that might have focused on general civil and human rights, is not accidental. The reasons are several. First, because language and culture are among the most important resources that the non-Russians possess, a national coloration, if not a nationalist direction, was probably inevitable. Second, the Balts and Armenians are highly homogeneous culturally, and culture, as we know, can spark collective action insofar as it overcomes the free-rider effect by providing for conventions and enhancing communication. Finally, and most important, nationalist ideals are an integral part of the political cultures of each of these nations. It is significant that my findings on nationalist dissent, in chapter 10, suggested as much. I attributed the high profile of nationalist dissent in these republics to the intensity of nationalist political culture: it should be no surprise that such ideals would have come to dominate the movements of 1988 once the structure of incentives had changed to the degree that involvement by the "silent majority," the true believers and believers of convenience, became a distinct possibility.

Nagorno-Karabakh, like the Genocide of 1915, is a deeply felt symbol of the sufferings of the Armenian nation: evidently, the symbol remains an important part of the system of meaning that Armenians possess and pass on from generation to generation. For the Balts, meanwhile, memories of interwar independence are very much alive among significant publics of all three republics, and interwar traditions, songs, symbols, and the like have been transmitted to generations of Lithuanians, Latvians, and Estonians growing up under Soviet conditions. Significantly, émigrés have played an important role in maintaining the intensity of all four nationalist political cultures. Since the 1960s, the Balts and the Armenians, like the Jews, have enjoyed unusually extensive contacts with their brethren abroad. In particular, the exchange of information, the mutual reinforcement of traditions, and the infusion of tourist money helped to convert the Baltic states and Armenia into outposts of the West in the era of stagnation and surely did much to propel them into the forefront of the mass movements of the *perestroika* era.

In light of these factors, resources, cultural homogeneity, and nationalist ideals, it was probably a foregone conclusion that *national* movements in these republics would have acquired a distinctly *nationalist* overtone. Significantly, however, the latter two factors, homogeneous national culture and intensely held nationalist ideals, militate against popular movements' developing in a nationalist direction in almost all the other republics—but only if other things are equal. The Belorussians lack both on a mass scale. The Ukrainians fare well in the western oblasts—which, not surprisingly, witnessed the closest approximation to a movement in mid–1988 and again in mid–1989—and rather less well in the more populous eastern oblasts, where Ukrainian cultural identity and nationalism are largely elite phenomena.[22] The Georgians, who engaged in large-scale nationalist demonstrations in April 1989, score high on both counts and, not unexpectedly, appear to have produced a dynamic protomovement in late 1989.[23] The Islamic peoples may have a strong sense of cultural-religious identity, but nationalist political ideals are, at best, a marginal phenomenon. The Russians, finally, lack a nationalist political culture, although their chauvinist inclinations have managed to spawn a movement of *Pamiat's* orientation. All of this sounds like good news for the Soviet leadership, were it not for the fact that, as I argued in chapter 10, *perestroika* and its many unintended consequences may be transforming republican political cultures and investing them with greater national and nationalist content. In time, and especially if the initial conditions that were associated with *perestroika* in 1988 continue, we may expect popular front activity to assume greater nationalist overtones in all the republics, excepting, perhaps, Russia.

Most worrisome for the Soviet center, however, should be the fact that systemic restructuring, in conjunction with Gorbachev's war against the Party-state, forced republican parties to go beyond mere collaboration with popular fronts and actually establish formal alliances as well as to seek maximal independence from Moscow. Relatively free elections to the Congress of People's Deputies in early 1989 proved disastrous for the Party in general and for republican organizations in particular. Subsequent elections to republican legislatures in 1990 proved no less catastrophic. Under such dismal conditions, republican parties have two options, and only one of them is realistic. They can seek legitimacy and succor from a discredited central Party that rejects their overtures anyway. Or they can embark on self-reform, join forces with local fronts, and strike out on their own—in the manner of the Lithuanian Communist Party. Seen in this light, Gorbachev's replacement in September 1989 of Shcherbyts'kyi, presumably because of his poor handling of the 1989 Donbass miners' strike and personal unpopularity with just about everyone in the Ukraine, with Volodymyr Ivashko will probably prove to have been another in a long series of strategic mistakes. Ivashko can neither be tougher than nor the same as Shcherbyts'kyi, lest his mentor, Gorbachev, be made to appear heavy-handed or incompetent. Instead, the new Ukrainian Party boss, or, for that matter, *his* successor, will have to identify with his republic's popular initiatives in general and with the *Rukh* in particular. We may expect Ivashko's inevitable turn to national Communism to redound to the *Rukh*'s favor by transforming what has, thus far, been largely an elite phenomenon into a mass movement of the sort found in the Baltic states.

All of this bodes exceedingly ill for the center. Popular fronts have sprouted everywhere, political culture may be becoming increasingly nationalist, and local republican parties are turning their backs on Moscow—and all three developments are the direct consequence of pell-mell *perestroika* in an imperfectly totalitarian state. Unless it transforms itself into a confederation or willingly grants republics independence, options that the special Central Committee Plenum on nationalities rejected in September 1989,[24] the Soviet state will face two options: repression, which spells the end of restructuring, or continued *perestroika*, which promises breakdown. Tienanmen Square or Wenceslaus Square—*tertium non datur?*

186

Conclusion: The Dilemmas of the Soviet State

Wherever human beings are concerned, trend is
never destiny.

— René Dubos

In 1985, when Mikhail Sergeevich Gorbachev came to power, the Soviet state was stable by any measure.[1] Party rule was perceived as legitimate, the economy sputtered along, the populace was quiescent and to a large degree satisfied, and open opposition was minimal. Problems abounded, of course, and totalitarian decay was well advanced, but there was no reason for the imperfectly totalitarian Soviet state not to have muddled through and survived indefinitely. As I have argued elsewhere, crisis was an inappropriate term to describe the USSR's pre-Gorbachev state of affairs.[2]

By 1990, five years after Gorbachev came to power, the Soviet state's condition had experienced a 180-degree turn. The Party was thoroughly delegitimized, the economy was virtually in shambles, the population was in the streets, and open opposition was the order of the day. The USSR seemed to be on the verge of collapse and crisis finally became an appropriate designation for its condition. This development was not inevitable.[3] Totalitarian *decay* was inevitable, but

187

Conclusion

collapse, as we know from chapter 4, can come about only in the wake of efforts at reform. Who or what pushed the USSR onto this slippery slope? The answer, quite simply, is Gorbachev. He created the crisis, he permitted the non-Russians to contemplate rebellion, he forced the Soviet state to the very brink of nonsurvival, and the forces he set in motion may actually push it over as well. *Glasnost*, *demokratizatsiia*, and *perestroika* are the intervening variables that transformed normal degeneration into a process that seems inexorably to lead either to breakdown or to a crackdown.

It is foolhardy to make any predictions about the future of the Soviet Union—not because predictions are foolhardy, and not because the country may have no future, but only because it is impossible to determine with any degree of certainty whether or not the initial conditions of any theory will hold. Even so, the logic of current changes raises an unprecedented and no longer completely fantastic question, that of state breakdown, in whole or in part due to non-Russian collective actions. Although even the most catastrophic of scenarios will, I suspect, founder on the Soviet state's coercive capacity to put down massive unrest—as evidenced by the January 1990 crackdown in Azerbaidzhan—it is at least possible now to envision a theoretically grounded sequence of events that might put this capacity into question. Stated simply, we can imagine the unimaginable: the emergence of a revolutionary situation in the Soviet Union.

Although *perestroika* may or may not be the "revolution from above" that Gorbachev wanted it to be, the process of change that he initiated could lay the grounds for a revolution from below. By dangerously raising expectations and falling far short of their fulfillment, by attacking traditional values almost recklessly, by encouraging mass participation and initiative, and by attempting to democratize an imperfectly totalitarian system, *perestroika* is creating the very conditions that a broad variety of scholars deem necessary to, and perhaps even sufficient for, revolution. As Ted Robert Gurr, Chalmers Johnson, Samuel P. Huntington, Charles Tilly, and Theda Skocpol suggest, the potential for revolution in the Soviet Union is growing, and the availability of political opposition groups capable of overcoming state resistance and converting that potential into an actuality is the key to the process.

Gurr's contribution to the study of revolutions is, of course, the concept of relative deprivation, or RD. Rebellions are most likely to occur when expectations greatly outstrip the capacity for attaining them. Frustration presumably results, and aggression then follows.

188

The greater the RD, the more widespread it is, the greater the frustration and the more likely the aggression. Relative deprivation alone will lead to little, however, unless, as Gurr insists, it is politicized by some revolutionary organization and channeled into antistate ends. Thus, revolution in Gurr's scheme of things is politicized aggression multiplied by a huge factor. Clearly, a Gurrian analyst would sense that a revolutionary situation might be brewing in the Soviet Union. On the one hand, Gorbachev is promising a significant improvement in life to all Soviet citizens; on the other hand, things clearly have not improved, and economically they have become even worse. A combination such as this both heralds a massive outbreak of relative deprivation and offers excellent opportunities for antistate entrepreneurs.[4]

Johnson, like Gurr, sees the main impetus for revolution in popular perceptions, more specifically, in what he terms value dyssynchronization. A "contradiction" such as this can, if unresolved, lead to a massive loss of elite legitimacy and, thus, requires reforms that aim to resynchronize values with environment. A bad situation turns worse only if elite intransigence or incompetence fails to produce the needed reforms and "power deflation" results, as authority is increasingly reliant on the threat or actual use of coercion. If, at that point, some triggering factor either so weakens the authorities or so emboldens the opposition, revolution may occur.[5]

The parallels with the contemporary USSR are striking. Soviet society suffers from what even Soviet authors admit is an extreme case of value dyssynchronization arising in part from the cognitive dissonance engendered by Brezhnevism and, far more perhaps, from Gorbachev's own efforts to rewrite Soviet history, discredit Stalinism, decisively break with the past, and thereby propel Soviet citizenry into the modern age.[6] So far, the elite has not been intransigent. Its competence, however, especially if measured by its ability to restructure the system successfully, is either low or declining or both. Worse still, blustering language, threats, and intimations of a harder line appear increasingly to characterize elite policy toward the "actual or potential leadership of a group of organized status protestors,"[7] who, thus far, have refused to be intimidated. As with Gurr, then, perceptual contradictions bring us to organized oppositions.

Both Huntington and Tilly have much to say about the conditions in which oppositionist groups emerge and mobilize against the polity. Huntington explains revolution in terms of the extent to which participation outstrips institutionalization. Regardless of why participation should come to increase rapidly—and Huntington attributes its growth to modernization—the key to stability is that popular activism be channeled into existing institutional structures and, thus, be converted into system-supportive and not system-disruptive behavior.[8]

Once again, the applicability of this scheme to the USSR seems apparent. The urge to participate, and participation itself, is very much on the rise in the Soviet Union, thanks in large part to the state's encouragement of mass initiative on the implicitly Huntingtonian rationale that social and economic modernization is impossible without participation. Much of this boom is taking place outside the bounds of existing institutions, and many of the emergent alternative institutions, the popular fronts being the most striking example, are acquiring, or already possess, distinctly political overtones. If participation continues to expand at the rate of 1987–1990, the expressly political component will grow. If unchecked, such a development could even result in a form of "praetorianism" that would represent a real danger for the state.[9]

Tilly's argument raises these same points, only in highlighted form. For Tilly, the mobilization by groups of popular support through resources and other incentives is the key to the emergence of revolutionary situations, which he defines as conditions of multiple sovereignty. If oppositionist groups and the polity both enjoy the loyalties of significant populations, revolutionary outcomes involving the seizure of full sovereignty by the challengers become possible.[10] Gorbachev's toleration of independent social groups, some of which already have assumed, and more of which inevitably will assume, an antistate stance, represents at least the first and probably most important necessary condition of group mobilization against the polity. As these groups mobilize resources to court constituencies and challenge the state, multiple sovereignty appears to be increasingly likely, not only in the Baltic republics, where parallel sovereignty arguably already existed in 1989, but in other regions as well. The Soviet state's continued decay and war against itself, the emergence of alliances between challengers and defecting national Communists, and their steady accumulation of resources all portend the possibility that multiple sovereignty could even translate into loss of sovereignty by the state.

What happens next on the road to revolution depends on whether or not the Party's insistence on maintaining its own primacy and the KGB's vigilance will eventually relegate such challenges to the status of abnormal political phenomena. It is at this point that Skocpol's discussion of state crisis becomes relevant. Although Skocpol's multiple visions of the revolutionary process offer mixed prognoses about the fate of the Soviet state, the constant elements in her shifting analysis are group autonomy on the one hand and a crisis of the state on the other.[11] The former has already emerged, while the latter may soon be at hand. The state's budgetary difficulties are severe and probably will grow in the foreseeable future. Its legitimacy appears to be increasingly thin, as evidenced by the elections to the Congress of People's Deputies in 1989. Its capacity to project military power may be declining, as the debacle in Afghanistan suggests, while its ability to sustain such huge armed forces may be waning.

Taken together as more or less distinct steps on a causal chain, all five theories foresee the growth of revolutionary potential in the USSR. Gurr and Johnson suggest why values are acquiring an increasingly antistate orientation; Huntington and Tilly explain the emergence of antistate popular activity in general and autonomous collective action in particular, while Skocpol suggests why the capacity of the state to meet these challenges may be declining. We have, in a word, all the ingredients that collective choice theory deems necessary to or facilitating of the emergence of elite and mass mobilization against the state: antistate values, opposition elites, and reduction of constraints or political space.[12] As I suggested in chapters 2 and 3, even such obvious advantages are rarely enough for a challenger to overcome a state's coercive apparatus. This may be a rule, but the logic of current trends suggests how an exception might arise and coercive obstacles be overcome in a manner that is fully consistent with the framework developed in this study.

How might this happen? If we extract from the above theories only those elements that meet the requirements of my theoretical framework, it is possible to construct a not implausible scenario of something like system breakdown. The key elements here, as of course elsewhere in this book, are elites, resources, values, beliefs, constraints, and the state. Socioeconomic factors are important only insofar as they structure resource availability, value orientations, and conflict possibilities. As will shortly be evident, although Gorbachev himself does not figure in the following scenario, his legacy may be in the process of validating collective choice theory's capacity to predict major instability.[13]

My assumptions are simple and premised on existing trends: the continuation of *glasnost*, the introduction of territorial economic decentralization, the introduction of elements of the market, continued weak economic performance, continued sociopolitical liberalization (or, minimally, no significant retrenchment), reform of the political system, growing political-economic rapprochement with the West, and growing republican sovereignty. It is not unreasonable to suggest that these assumptions may have, or will continue to have, the following consequences:

GLASNOST: ideological erosion, regime delegitimation, religious revival, politicization of elites and masses, enhancement of national consciousness, and environmental concern.

ECONOMIC DECENTRALIZATION: uneven development, regional economic decline, and intra-elite competition over the budget.

MARKETIZATION: inflation, unemployment, class and status differentiation, and immiseration.

POOR ECONOMIC PERFORMANCE: labor unrest, competition for scarce resources, ethnic tensions, and continued budgetary problems.

POLITICAL LIBERALIZATION: organizational autonomy, emergence of alternative leaders, group mobilization, intensification of popular demands on the state, development of inner-party factions, and continued curbing of the KGB and MVD.

POLITICAL REFORMS: divisive elections, heated constitutional debates, and reduced roles for the Party and the Komsomol.

RAPPROCHEMENT WITH THE WEST: dependence on the international economy, sensitivity to human rights criticism, partial opening of borders, and vulnerability to outside interference.

REPUBLICAN SOVEREIGNTY: acceleration of national Communism, intensification of popular anti-Sovietism, and growth of pro-Western tendencies.

With these premises as our starting points, we can now embark on the following scenario. As in all such exercises, the direction and logic of events are far more important than the actual events. The first step is the proliferation of ethnic, political, and class-based mass movements, which are led by former political prisoners, the creative intelligentsia, and local Party leaders. They attract increasingly dissatisfied, fearless citizens and respond to the state's promises of *perestroika* with unrealizable demands for republican sovereignty, Russian outmigration, political democracy, and economic security. In some republics they even seize control of local legislatures. The center rejects the most extreme demands as destabilizing, unconstitutional, or divisive and attempts to reassert control. But this move only widens already existing fissures in the Party elite, especially along center-periphery lines, enhances the disillusionment of radical Party and non-Party intelligentsias, and spurs the radicalization of the popular movements. Under such conditions, the popular movements, both those in power and those out of power, split into liberal and social-democratic accommodationist majorities and intransigent minorities, which include non-Russian nationalists, the political left (New Left internationalists and Greens), the political right (hard-core *Pamiat'* types), and Sufi brotherhoods and Muslim clans.

Next, the radicals mobilize support and build coalitions. The non-Russian nationalists draw on the creative intelligentsia, youth, and workers from regions with large immigrant populations; they also appeal to peasants. The political left recruits disaffected urban intellectuals, students, and workers; the political right mobilizes the Russian working class, creating a Peronist-type movement. In turn, the non-Russian nationalists, the political left, and Crimean Tatars form working coalitions in the Baltic states and the Ukraine, while the Sufi brotherhoods acquire support among peasants and town intellectuals of the North Caucasus and Central Asia. Resources are acquired in a manner akin to that discussed in chapter 12.

Zero-sum politics among radical groups is a likely consequence of the above alignments and realignments. As economic conditions remain unchanged or perhaps worsen, the state appears ineffective and the future seems bleak; radical political entrepreneurs turn to demagoguery and reject compromise; fringe elements of the accommodationist majorities are drawn into radical politics; urban ethnic conflict between Russians and non-Russians breaks out in the Baltic republics, the western Ukraine, Kazakhstan, and Central Asia; leftists and Peronists engage in street confrontations; and Russian workers stage strikes demanding greater state attention and law and order. Aghast at these developments, Western firms contemplate noninvolvement in the Soviet economy.

In such extreme circumstances, the center sides with the Peronists politically and supports them economically, as they represent the working class majority and the largest ethnic group and can bolster its flagging legitimacy. Thereupon, the Party elite splits along center-periphery lines, as non-Russian Communists object to the center's support of Peronism. The Russian elite also splits, as some Russian Communists object to the visible turn to the right, while disaffected Party elites take advantage of inner-party democracy and begin to forge left-national Communist coalitions against the center. Non-Russian nationalists, Muslims, and the political left are further radicalized, while the state's adoption of Peronist ideology leads to defections by more elements within the accommodationist majorities. Finally, the peasants express outrage at what they perceive as state betrayal: the non-Russians ally with the nationalists and Muslims, while the Russian peasants turn against state representatives in the countryside.

At this point, the radicalized minorities decide to go underground and engage in low-level sabotage, arson, and terrorism. They receive material assistance, weapons, and manpower—through the USSR's porous borders with Eastern Europe and the Middle East—from Russians and non-Russians living in the United States, Canada, Western and Eastern Europe, anti-Communist organizations such as the Anti-Bolshevik Bloc of Nations, left-wing organizations such as the Fourth International, Maoist groups, etc., and from Muslim factions in the Middle East and the Afghan mujahidin. In particular, émigré Russian rightists (NTS) funnel aid to the Peronists, urban Russian radicals form self-defense groups, and Russian and non-Russian peasants expropriate land and attack regime supporters, especially in regions struck by famine in 1932–1933.

Not surprisingly, there follows a harsh crackdown by the hitherto restrained MVD and KGB as well as ethnic violence and pogroms by Peronist death squads. These developments lead to the further delegitimation of the state, increased defections among accommodationists and intellectuals, widening splits within the Party and non-Party elites, and, last but not least, an international human rights outcry, led by Amnesty International, the Socialist International, West European Communist parties, the European Parliament, and Western Jewish groups, along with threats of economic sanctions by the United States and Great Britain, and protests by Soviet liberal intellectuals and accommodationist majorities. Worse still perhaps, some Western firms actually disinvest and Western banks become reluctant to extend loans. As the economy worsens sharply, the authorities feel trapped.

Pressured from within and without, the center halts the crackdown and makes minor political and economic concessions to the radical movements and major concessions to peasants regarding private-landholdings. The consequences are severalfold: the legitimation of the radical movements, the emergence of national Communist elites in all the republics, the remobilization of the accommodationist majorities, a drastic decline in agricultural production and reduced supplies of foodstuffs to cities, the incipient alienation of the Peronists, the enhancement of pro-independence tendencies in the republics, and the continued wariness of Western capital.

At this juncture, in light of the Soviet state's obvious weakness and inclination to back down in confrontations, some republics decide to secede. Fearful of the domino effect, Moscow sends in troops. Some republics are cowed by this action, but others decide to make use of the diversion to press their own demands. These national Communists forge alliances with and support the revived popular movements, coopt, win over, or neutralize local MVD and KGB forces, negotiate with the center about a radical devolution of political authority, demand United Nations intervention, appeal to human rights conventions, acquire lukewarm Western support, and, of course, greatly alarm the Peronists.

Most radical nationalists and Muslim brotherhoods reject the national Communists as moderate, accommodationist, and untrustworthy. Instead, they resolve to take advantage of the chaos and turn to armed struggle, continuing to receive outside assistance and finding sanctuary in neighboring states, Poland, Iran, Afghanistan, and in mountainous areas—the Carpathians and Tien Shan. Fringe elements initiate ethnic violence against Russian settlers and Jews, thereby alienating the radical left. The state responds uncertainly, as the MVD and the KGB are fragmented by the national Communists, demoralized due to regime indecision, and overextended as armed groups emerge along the entire periphery, especially in Lithuania, the western Ukraine, the Caucasus, and Central Asia. The army appears unreliable and fragmented along national lines. Worst of all, the Soviet state's financial resources are spread very thin and a financial collapse looms on the horizon.

Under such fluid conditions, political realignments take place, as the Peronists respond to state ineffectiveness and unresponsiveness by attempting to seize control of large cities, engaging in violence against non-Russians and the left, and confronting the state with an ultimatum on the reestablishment of law and order and pro-worker policies. Unwilling and unable to meet the Peronists' demands, the state searches for new allies. In turn, the left breaks with the non-Russian nationalists, establishes ties to the state, and the resulting left-state alliance breaks with the Peronists; indeed, the MVD, KGB, and military are now deployed against the recalcitrant Peronists, thereby further undermining army morale. Finally, the nationalists and Muslims forge links with or overthrow out-of-step national Communist moderates; Baltic, Ukrainian, Armenian, Azerbaidzhani, and Georgian nationalists declare independence; Crimean Tatars occupy the Crimea.

The streets become thoroughly chaotic. Left-right battles, mass worker protests, and demonstrations take place. The radical nationalists turn against one another over border disputes in the Caucasus, the Crimea, the western Ukraine, Lithuania, Belorussia, and Kaliningrad, while radical Muslims initiate a jihad against settler populations in Central Asia. The left-state coalition appeals to Kerensky-type liberals within the accommodationist majorities and to the ousted national Communists. In turn, Western states and the United Nations offer to mediate and send missions. Who exactly is in charge becomes difficult to determine. Whether or not such a condition is tantamount to breakdown is unclear, but surely it is an instance of a crisis that is unlikely to be resolved in the established authorities' favor.

Will the USSR follow the course outlined above? Any one factor might fall away and the hardly ironclad logic of the whole scheme might collapse. And yet, and yet. . . . *Perestroika*'s all too many unintended consequences and all too few intended ones suggest that the conditions that prevented non-Russians from rebelling may be changing. I still doubt that the non-Russians, who may increasingly want to rebel, will be able to do so successfully.[14] But the USSR is tempting fate, and that is serious. Worse still, it is tempting theory—and that may be hopeless.

Notes

Preface

1. Alexander J. Motyl, " 'Sovietology in One Country.' "
2. Gail Stokes, "The Undeveloped Theory of Nationalism."
3. Dick Howard, *Defining the Political*, p. 15.

Introduction

1. Throughout this study, the term *Sovietology* designates the study of Soviet domestic politics by political scientists and, where relevant, historians in the United States. I am not concerned with Soviet foreign policy or with demography, geography, and economics. Confining my enquiry to scholarly developments in the United States is valid, because the American versions of Sovietology and political science have dominated both fields since World War II, so that the connections, or lack thereof, between Sovietology and political science may be best comprehended in the American setting.

2. On the "comparative communism" debate, see John H. Kautsky,

"Comparative Communism Versus Comparative Politics," and S. N. Eisenstadt, "Change in Communist Systems and the Comparative Analysis of Modern Societies"; Rudolf L. Tökés, "Comparative Communism."

3. See Alfred G. Meyer, *The Soviet Political System*; H. Gordon Skilling and Franklyn Griffiths, *Interest Groups in Soviet Politics*; J. M. Montias, "Modernization in Communist Countries"; Robert C. Tucker, "Communist Revolutions, National Cultures, and the Divided Nation."

4. Joseph LaPalombara, "Monoliths or Plural Systems," p. 314.

5. Lawrence C. Mayer, *Redefining Comparative Politics: Promise Versus Performance*, pp. 234–268. Who are the "best Sovietologists"? As a rational actor who prefers to maximize utility *and* minimize risk, I suggest that readers answer this question for themselves.

6. See Roger Kanet, *The Behavioral Revolution and Communist Studies*, p. 2.

7. Jacques Barzun, "Doing Research—Should the Sport Be Regulated?" Of course, Sovietologists are not the only scholars who suffer from this affliction. Gore Vidal has written of "squirrel scholars," a somewhat harsh term for the type of academic who feels impelled to collect for the sake of collecting, a tendency that is all too manifest in the contemporary vogue for writing biographies of no fewer than one thousand pages.

8. Frederic J. Fleron, Jr., "Soviet Area Studies and the Social Sciences," pp. 313–317.

9. Thus, in 1909, James Bryce, the American Political Science Association's fourth president,

> called upon his colleagues to "stick close to the facts." Above all, he said, researchers should avoid losing themselves in "abstractions," meaning that the time had come to abandon the traditional search for wisdom on matters such as "sovereignty," "law," or the "state," via "efforts of thought" and "the methods of metaphysics." In the era of science, or so it seemed to Bryce, more empirical research was needed, to see "what forms the state has taken and which have proved best, what powers governments have enjoyed and how those powers have worked." Bryce did not advocate a complete disregard for "philosophical generalizations" about politics, but he did strongly insist that political inquiry needed a new approach to its subject, and that such generalizations would be justifiable only after the thoroughgoing examination of facts which political science could provide. (David M. Ricci, *The Tragedy of Political Science*, p. 67.)

10. Paul Hollander, *Political Pilgrims*.

11. Walter Laqueur, "In Search of Russia," p. 44.

12. Sidney and Beatrice Webb, *Soviet Communism: A New Civilization*.

13. Consider the bizarre Shul'gin affair, as depicted by Roland Gaucher in *Opposition in the U.S.S.R.: 1917–1967*, p. 147.

14. See Alexander J. Motyl, "Bringing the USSR Back In: Comparative

Notes

Research Agendas and the Necessity of a Totalitarian Type," unpublished paper, 1988.

15. Consider the following statement by Columbia University's Presidential Commission on the Future of the University:

Because it represents the creation of knowledge and extends the influence and activity of the university beyond its walls, the publication of important and original work is the best, and indispensable, measure of the productivity of both the junior and senior faculty of a research university and of how the university itself is known and judged. Publications provide the primary evidence of the quality of individuals and programs, particularly when they appear in influential refereed journals or take the form of books and monographs under a distinguished imprint. Reviews by professional peers and prizes for outstanding works in a given field or category provide further external evidence. In some fields the number of citations to original work is an important indicator. The writing of a widely-used textbook can add to professional standing as well as to visibility. A long publication list is not synonymous with quality, but at least it indicates drive and activity. (*Strategies of Renewal: Report of the President's Commission on the Future of the University* [New York: Columbia University, May 1987], pp. 129–130.)

16. Ricci, pp. 221–222.

17. Laqueur, "In Search of Russia," p. 44.

18. See John N. Hazard, *Recollections of a Pioneering Sovietologist.*

19. See Arnold Buchholz, *Soviet and East European Studies in the International Framework*, pp. 11–31.

20. Stephen F. Cohen, *Rethinking the Soviet Experience*, p. 12.

21. Ibid., pp. 11–12.

22. Surely, there is no logical reason why moral condemnation of the USSR should imply acceptance of a conservative agenda. That it has done so over time is due to the peculiar nature of American politics and not to any logical connection between opposition to Stalinism and conservatism.

23. See L. G. Ionin, " . . . I vozzovet proshedshee (razmyshleniia sotsiologa o novom fil'me T. Abuladze."

24. See Alexander J. Motyl, " 'Sovietology in One Country.' "

25. Harley Balzer, "Can We Survive Glasnost?," pp. 1–2.

26. On the conceptual confusion surrounding the term crisis, see Alexander J. Motyl, "Reassessing the Soviet Crisis."

27. Vernon Van Dyke, *Political Science: A Philosophical Analysis*, p. 96.

28. Stephen Gaukroger, *Explanatory Structures*, p. 45.

29. How, then, are theories generated? Popper's comments regarding ideas are instructive:

There is no such thing as a logical method of having new ideas, or a logical reconstruction of this process. My view may be expressed by saying that every discovery contains 'an irrational element,' or 'a creative intuition,' in Bergson's sense. In a similar way Einstein speaks of the 'search for those highly universal laws . . . from which a picture of the world can be obtained by pure deduction. There is no logical path,' he says, 'leading us to these . . . laws. They can only be reached by intuition, based upon something like an intellectual love (*Einfühlung*) of the objects of experience.' (Karl Popper, *The Logic of Scientific Discovery*, p. 32.)

30. Alexander Rabinowitch, *The Bolsheviks Come to Power*, p. xxi.

31. For example, see John L. H. Keep, *The Russian Revolution: A Study in Mass Mobilization.*

32. Sheila Fitzpatrick, *The Russian Revolution: 1917–1932.*

33. J. Arch Getty, *Origins of the Great Purges.*

34. Clifford Geertz, *The Interpretation of Cultures*, pp. 21–22.

1. The Labyrinth of Theory

1. Throughout this chapter I am concerned only with social science theory. I draw on philosophers of science when what they say of natural science theory may also apply to social science theory, but I make no pretense of addressing the theoretical issues of interest to natural scientists.

2. Giovanni Sartori, "Guidelines for Concept Analysis," in *Social Science Concepts*, p. 84.

3. George Caspar Homans, "Contemporary Theory in Sociology," p. 53.

4. Johan Galtung, *Theory and Methods of Social Research*, p. 451.

5. Gaukroger, *Explanatory Structures*, pp. 39, 14, 68, 15.

6. Imre Lakatos, "Falsification and the Methodology of Scientific Research Programmes," in *Criticism and the Growth of Knowledge*

7. Sovietologists are notoriously prone to miss this point. It seems that every second review in professional journals tediously disputes some book's premises as "false," "incorrect," "questionable," or "debatable."

8. Popper, *The Logic of Scientific Discovery*, pp. 71–72.

9. Sartori, p. 74.

10. Walter Carlsnaes, *The Concept of Ideology and Political Analysis*, p. 5.

11. Gaukroger, p. 244.

12. Ibid., pp. 77, 74.

13. Ernst Nagel, *The Structure of Science*, p. 31. Here, again, Sovietologists are inclined to ignore the importance of initial conditions and to assume that a theory that may have held under, say, Brezhnevite conditions is proven "wrong" under Gorbachevian ones.

14. Galtung, p. 334.

15. Thomas A. Spragens, Jr., *The Dilemma of Contemporary Political Theory*, p. 155.

Notes

16. W. V. Quine, *Theories and Things*, pp. 71–72.

17. Paul A. Roth, *Meaning and Method in the Social Sciences*, p. 19.

18. Ibid., pp. 4–8.

19. Ibid., pp. 44–72.

20. See, for example, Ronald H. Chilcote, *Theories of Comparative Politics*.

21. Galtung, pp. 23–25.

22. Jack Snyder, "Richness, Rigor, and Relevance in the Study of Soviet Foreign Policy"; "Science and Sovietology: Bridging the Methods Gap in Soviet Foreign Policy Studies."

23. More specifically, according to Chalmers, all such "interpretive frameworks" consist of a "macro-theory" based on a conceptual and historical macrostructure, valued dimensions, and explanations of structural change; a "problematic" that identifies crises, problems, tensions, or contradictions within the macrostructure; and a "model for explaining and interpreting the significance of particular events." (Douglas A. Chalmers, "Interpretive Frameworks," pp. 29, 31.)

24. Ibid., p. 56.

25. Spragens, pp. 165–166.

26. See Paul Feyerabend, *Against Method*.

27. Chalmers, p. 45.

28. See Alan C. Isaak, *Scope and Methods of Political Science*.

29. Nagel, pp. 79–88.

30. Galtung, p. 458. *Modus tollens* is the "argument that if a conditional statement is true but its consequent is false, then its antecedent is false, e.g., 'If this, then that. But not that. Therefore not this.' " (A. R. Lacey, *A Dictionary of Philosophy*, p. 137.)

31. W. V. Quine, *From a Logical Point of View*, p. 43, as quoted in Galtung, p. 458.

32. Lakatos, p. 116. For a discussion of Lakatos' approach to theory-building, see Terence Ball, "From Paradigms to Research Programs."

33. Quine, *Theories and Things*, pp. 24–30; Roth, p. 7.

34. Thomas S. Kuhn, *The Structure of Scientific Revolutions*.

35. Chalmers, p. 51.

36. Theda Skocpol, *States and Social Revolutions*; Peter B. Evans et al., *Bringing the State Back In*.

37. On the utility of the totalitarianism concept, see Giovanni Sartori, "Soviet Studies: A Scheme for Analysis"; Edward W. Walker, "Totalitarianism, Comparative Politics, and Sovietology."

38. Peter Bachrach and Morton Baratz, "Decisions and Nondecisions."

39. See Alfred G. Meyer, "Coming to Terms with the Past . . . And with One's Older Colleagues."

40. For example, see Jerry F. Hough, *Russia and the West*.

41. Karl Marx, "The German Ideology," in Robert C. Tucker, *The Marx-Engels Reader*, p. 172.

42. Anthony Giddens, *The Nation-State and Violence*, p. 301.

43. The following comments, by prominent scholars whose names—mercifully—will go unmentioned, illustrate exactly the lack of civility I have in mind: (1) "I doubt he [a scholar whose academic interests the scholar disagrees with] could have gotten a real academic job. . . . If he hadn't hopped on this political cause, he would be running research for a bank, or running an export-import business." (2) "This [Robert Conquest's book, *Harvest of Sorrow*] is crap, rubbish" ("In Search of a Soviet Holocaust: A 55-Year-Old Famine Feeds the Right," in *The Village Voice*, January 12, 1988, pp. 31–32). The ultimate irony is, of course, that some of Conquest's work on the famine and the terror currently is being published by the Soviets.

44. Fleron, "Soviet Area Studies and the Social Sciences."

45. C. Wright Mills, *The Sociological Imagination*, p. 147.

46. Motyl, " 'Sovietology in One Country.' "

2. Rationality, Resources, and the State

1. For a devastating critique of the underpinnings of rational actor theory, see Alexander Rosenberg, *Philosophy of Social Science*, pp. 22–49, 65–74.

2. Robin M. Williams, Jr., "Change and Stability in Values and Value Systems," in Milton Rokeach, *Understanding Human Values*, p. 23.

3. Others disagree, citing common sense and the theoretical difficulties that utility maximization engenders. Instead, they suggest that minimizing loss, or risk-loss aversion, is the key. Both premises are perfectly reasonable, but there are two excellent reasons for retaining the former. First, the classical rational choice literature, which I greatly respect, shares this assumption. And second, as will shortly become evident, I must accept utility maximization, because I want to insist that there are individuals, whom I call martyrs and fanatics, who value things unequivocally and who will sacrifice everything for these ends. Risk aversion contravenes the conceptual framework I wish to construct and therefore it is an assumption I choose to reject. For an analysis of these two approaches, see George A. Quattrone and Amos Tversky, "Contrasting Rational and Psychological Analyses of Political Choice."

4. Robert E. Goodin, *The Politics of Rational Man*, pp. 9–10.

5. Herbert A. Simon, "Human Nature in Politics."

6. Jon Elster, "Introduction," in Elster, *Rational Choice*, p. 1.

7. Geertz, *The Interpretation of Cultures*, pp. 1–30.

8. Henry D. Aiken, *Hume's Moral and Political Philosophy*, p. 25.

9. Elster, pp. 13–14.

10. Richard A. Schweder, "Anthropology's Romantic Rebellion Against the Enlightenment," in Richard A. Schweder and Robert A. LeVine, *Culture Theory*, p. 43.

11. Geertz, pp. 10–11.

12. Richard A. Schweder, "Divergent Rationalities," in Donald W. Fiske and Richard A. Schweder, *Metatheory in Social Science*. For a fascinating anthropological study of just this issue, see David Lan, *Guns and Rain*. See also Thomas Merton, *The Seven Storey Mountain*.

13. Leszek Kolakowski, *The Presence of Myth*.

14. Ernest Gellner, *Relativism and the Social Sciences*, pp. 68–82. For other critiques of rational choice theory, see Adam Przeworski, "Marxism and Rational Choice"; Richard Kimber, "Collective Action and the Fallacy of the Liberal Fallacy."

15. On "organizing ideas," see Chalmers, "Interpretive Frameworks."

16. Rosenberg (pp. 87–91) argues that such "folk psychology," which seems to make so much common sense, actually is irreconcilable with rational actor theory's pretensions to explaining individual behavior in causal terms. Instead, folk psychology is far more compatible with approaches that attempt to interpret rule-governed behavior.

17. Cicero's classic essay, *On Duties*, for example, is replete with the kind of conundrums that rational choice theorists have faced throughout the ages. Consider the following passage:

But there is also a fourth division, relating to the problems that arise when one expediency has to be weighed against another. Panaetius said nothing about this type of issue either; yet assessments of such a kind frequently have to be attempted. To take one example, it is often necessary to measure expediencies or advantages of a physical nature against those of an external or accidental character, derived from outward circumstances. Furthermore, if you consider these two categories separately, each of them includes, within itself, potential advantages which have to be measured against others in one and the same category. (Cicero, *On the Good Life*, p. 170.)

My suggestion, that scholars seek the approbation of the classics, is, of course, an implicit rejection of positivist approaches to normal science. See Jeffrey C. Alexander, "The Centrality of the Classics."

18. Goodin, pp. 118–136.

19. According to this argument, therefore, the "voter's paradox" is really just a conceptual misunderstanding.

20. Aiken, p. 101.

21. Mancur Olson, *The Rise and Decline of Nations*, p. 18.

22. Barbara Salert, *Revolutions and Revolutionaries*, pp. 46–47.

23. Olson, p. 21.

24. Two facilitating factors involving the homogeneity of a group and the size of the required contribution also can come into play. The more uniform a group, the more likely is it to "agree on the exact nature of whatever collective good is at issue or on how much of it is worth buying." In other words, the greater the consensus, the greater the likelihood

of coordinating collective action and maintaining group cohesiveness. I elaborate on this point later in the chapter. Finally: "If the individual knows the costs of a contribution to collective action in the interest of a group of which he is a part are trivially small, he may rationally not take the trouble to consider whether the gains are smaller still." Oddly enough, the last point suggests that the disincentive to contribute will decrease once the number of contributors becomes immense (Olson, pp. 24, 28).

25. Edward M. Muller and Karl-Dieter Opp, "Rational Choice and Rebellious Collective Action," p. 484.

26. George Klosko, "Rebellious Collective Action Revisited."

27. Mark N. Hagopian, *Ideals and Ideologies of Modern Politics*, pp. 1–4. An ideal, according to Hagopian, is "a vague symbol that is positively evaluated by large numbers of different people for somewhat different reasons" (p. 2). See also Carlsnaes, *The Concept of Ideology*; Raymond Boudon, *The Analysis of Ideology*.

28. See Lenin's classic essay, *What Is to Be Done?*, for the quintessential statement of this elitist position. Lenin's views regarding vanguard parties are, incidentally, eerily reminiscent of Hitler's; see *Mein Kampf* (Boston: Houghton Mifflin, 1971), pp. 579–595.

29. This terminoloy is drawn from, among others, Mark Hagopian, *The Phenomenon of Revolution*, pp. 314–315, and Charles Tilly, *From Mobilization to Revolution*, pp. 88–89.

30. Russell Hardin, *Collective Action*, p. 158.

31. Ibid., p. 3.

32. Ibid., p. 172.

33. David K. Lewis, *Convention*, p. 78.

34. Geertz, pp. 49, 46.

35. John Walton, *Reluctant Rebels*.

36. The following authors have also utilized variants of rational actor theory in their work on ethnicity: Michael Hechter, "Nationalism as Group Solidarity"; Susan Olzak, "Ethnicity and Theories of Ethnic Collective Behavior"; Michael Banton, "Ethnic Bargaining"; Francois Nielsen, "Toward a Theory of Ethnic Solidarity in Modern Societies"; Michael Banton, *Racial and Ethnic Competition*; David D. Laitin, "Language Games"; Edward A. Tiryakian and Ronald Rogowski, *New Nationalisms of the Developed West*; Hudson Meadwell, "Ethnic Nationalism and Collective Choice Theory"; Michael Hechter, *Principles of Group Solidarity*.

37. Anthony Oberschall, *Social Conflict and Social Movements*, pp. 28–29. As we know, sanctions are of two kinds—positive and negative, material and coercive. The sanctions groups can impose may be considered roughly proportionate to the amount of resources they possess. Strictly speaking, of course, such resources as guns and butter are not yet sanctions: they become sanctions only if groups manage to convert them into, say, violence and bribes. Although there is no guarantee that a group with resources will actually convert them into sanctions, we may as-

sume—not too injudiciously I believe—that the respective resource endowments of states and serious contenders for state power, which purposefully accumulate resources for the sole purpose of winning the zero-sum game with the state, can be treated as roughly equivalent to sanction availability.

38. Douglass North, "A Neoclassical Theory of the State," in Elster, p. 254.

39. Giddens, p. 20.

40. Oberschall, *Social Conflict and Social Movements*; Tilly, *From Mobilization to Revolution*.

41. See Gabriel A. Almond, "Review Article: The International-National Connection."

42. On the international sources of revolutions, see Hagopian, *The Phenomenon of Revolution*, pp. 106–116.

43. See, in particular, Jan T. Gross, *Revolution from Abroad*.

3. Nations, States, and Nationalism

1. W. V. Quine is critical of the concept of *idea*. See *Quiddities*, pp. 87–89.

2. Giovanni Sartori, "Guidelines for Concept Analysis," pp. 35–44.

3. Ibid., p. 74.

4. See Jonathan Culler, *Ferdinand de Saussure*.

5. To argue in this manner is, obviously, to flirt with deconstruction. See Jonathan Culler, *On Deconstruction*. For a realist interpretation of concepts, see William Outhwaite, *Concept Formation in Social Science*.

6. On semantic fields, see Sartori, pp. 51–54.

7. Friedrich Nietzsche, *On the Genealogy of Morals and Ecce Homo*, p. 80.

8. Feyerabend, *Against Method*.

9. Skocpol, *States and Social Revolutions*, p. 4.

10. Konstantin Symmons-Symonolewicz, *Modern Nationalism: Towards a Consensus in Theory*, p. 26.

11. John Breuilly, *Nationalism and the State*, p. 3. Consider also the following, not too dissimilar, definition by Anthony D. Smith:

I shall define nationalism as an ideological movement for the attainment and maintenance of autonomy, cohesion and individuality for a social group deemed by some of its members to constitute an actual or potential nation. In other words, nationalism is both an ideology and a movement, usually a minority one, which aspires to 'nationhood' for the chosen group; and 'nationhood' in turn comprises three basic ideals, autonomy and self-government for the group, often but not always in a sovereign state, solidarity and fraternity of the group in a recognized territory or 'home', and third, a distinctive, and preferably unique, culture and history peculiar to the group in question. (Anthony D. Smith, "Introduction" in *Nationalist Movements*, pp. 1–2.)

12. Symmons-Symonolewicz, pp. 27–28.

13. Marco Carynnyk, *Alexander Dovzhenko*, pp. 113–114.

14. Anthony D. Smith, *Theories of Nationalism*, p. 3.

15. Breuilly, p. 4.

16. On the question of intentions and their determinacy, see Rosenberg, *Philosophy of Social Science*, pp. 22–50.

17. Hagopian, *Ideals and Ideologies*, pp. 2, 70.

18. Ernest Gellner and Elie Kedourie define nationalism in similar, though in somewhat more elaborate, terms. According to Gellner, "Thus the doctrine of nationalism can be split into three principal components. One is a piece of philosophical anthropology: men have a 'nationality' as they have a nose and two eyes, and this is a central part of their being. The second is a psychological contention: they wish to live with those of the same nationality, and above all resent being ruled by those of another one. The third is an evaluative contention, and adds that this is rightly so." (Ernest Gellner, *Thought and Change*, p. 150.) Kedourie, meanwhile, states: "Briefly, the doctrine [nationalism] holds that humanity is naturally divided into nations, that nations are known by certain characteristics which can be ascertained, and that the only legitimate type of government is national self-government." (Elie Kedourie, *Nationalism*, p. 9.)

19. For a contrary view, see Walker Connor, *The National Question in Marxist-Leninist Theory and Strategy*, p. 5.

20. Carlton J. H. Hayes, *Essays on Nationalism*; E. J. Hobsbawm, *The Age of Revolution, 1789–1848*; Gellner, *Nations and Nationalism*.

21. David D. Laitin, *Hegemony and Culture*, p. 19.

22. Walker Connor, "The Politics of Ethnonationalism."

23. Gellner, *Thought and Change*, p. 154.

24. See Anthony D. Smith, *The Ethnic Origins of Nations*; John Armstrong, *Nations Before Nationalism*.

25. Benedict Anderson, *Imagined Communities*.

26. See note 18 for the quotation by Gellner. Clifford Geertz, *The Interpretation of Cultures*, p. 46.

27. Elster, *Rational Choice*, pp. 12–14.

28. Frantz Fanon, *The Wretched of the Earth*.

29. Karl W. Deutsch, *Nationalism and Social Communication*, pp. 102–103. Smith's argument is remarkably similar to Deutsch's:

When the educated professionals find themselves unable to gain admission to posts commensurate with their degrees and talents, they tend to turn away also from the metropolitan culture of the dominant ethnic group and return to their 'own' culture, the culture of the once despised subject ethnic group. Exclusion breeds 'failed assimilation', and reawakens an ethnic consciousness among the professional elites, at exactly the moment when the intellectuals are beginning to explore the historic roots of the community. Alternatively, there may be a gap of several decades between this initial historicist exploration and the rejection and reawakening of the broader intelligentsia. Only when the two processes, historicism and reawakening, are conjoined, can the ethnic revival blossom and assume full political form. (Anthony D. Smith, "Nationalism, Ethnic Separatism and the Intelligentsia," pp. 32–33.)

30. Breuilly, pp. 352, 370. Joseph Rothschild's comments, which represent a synthesis of Deutsch and Breuilly, also bear citing:

Whereas ethnicity is not necessarily or inevitably politicized in all historical eras and under all social conditions, it is likely to become so (1) if the patterned correlation among ethnic categories, socioeconomic categories, and political-power distributions is such as to generate systems of structured interethnic inequality and (2) if those with a conscious interest in maintaining or changing these existing patterns, distributions, and structures determine that it would be instrumentally useful to them to mobilize ethnicity from a psychological or cultural or social datum into a political resource and lever of action. (Joseph Rothschild, *Ethnopolitics*, p. 248.)

31. Barrington Moore, Jr., *Injustice: The Social Bases of Obedience and Revolt*, p. 90.

32. Even Theda Skocpol has recognized the importance of ideas in revolutionary processes. See her "Rentier State and Shi'a Islam in the Iranian Revolution." For a critique of Skocpol's reluctance to acknowledge the importance of ideology and culture, see Said Amir Arjomand, "Iran's Islamic Revolution in Comparative Perspective."

33. See Rothschild, *Ethnopolitics*; Tilly, *From Mobilization to Revolution*; Mostafa Rejai with Kay Phillips, *Leaders of Revolution*.

4. The Withering Away of the Totalitarian State

1. The pitfalls of assuming that behavior and values always coincide, especially under conditions of maximal constraint, are most evident in the literature that ascribes East European passivity in the face of the Holocaust to anti-Semitism. For an illustration of this fallacy, see Helen Fein's otherwise excellent *Accounting for Genocide*.

2. St. Augustine, *Confessions*; Merton, *The Seven Storey Mountain* and *The Sign of Jonas*.

3. On the costs of maintaining extreme forms of compliance, see Ian Lustick, "Stability in Deeply Divided Societies."

4. The "political system" is too diffuse, too benign, to serve as the unit of analysis in maximally constraining conditions. As I suggested in chapter 3, concepts "hang together," regardless of whether or not we want

them to. For a similar instance of how one concept draws others in its wake, see Motyl, *Will the Non-Russians Rebel?*, pp. 1–19.

5. Obviously, nothing is ever quite total in human affairs. This fact, however, which is incessantly intoned by opponents of the totalitarian model, is irrelevant, as it is the point of ideal types to be ideal.

6. Recent defenders of the concept include Leonard Schapiro, *Totalitarianism*; Laqueur, *The Fate of the Revolution*; Z, "To the Stalin Mausoleum"; Sartori, "Soviet Studies: A Scheme for Analysis"; Edward W. Walker, "Totalitarianism, Comparative Politics, and Sovietology"; Motyl, "Bringing the USSR Back In." Detractors of the concept are legion. Examples are Michael Curtis, *Totalitarianism*; Benjamin R. Barber, "Conceptual Foundations of Totalitarianism"; Abbott Gleason, " 'Totalitarianism' in 1984"; Cohen, *Rethinking the Soviet Experience*.

7. Carl J. Friedrich and Zbigniew K. Brzezinski, *Totalitarian Dictatorship and Autocracy*, p. 22.

8. The Soviet experience in World War II supports the view that totalitarian states are well equipped to resist military onslaughts. The Nazi experience, meanwhile, suggests that totalitarian states are also capable of launching devastating wars.

9. Chalmers Johnson also argues along these lines. See "Comparing Communist Nations" in *Change in Communist Systems*, pp. 16–17.

10. See Deutsch's brilliant and unjustly forgotten essay, "Cracks in the Monolith," p. 502.

11. The terminology is inspired by Kenneth Jowitt's remarks at the Columbia University Seminar on Communism, December 1, 1988.

12. As Anthony Downs has written, "No one can control the behavior of a large organization; any attempt to control one large organization tends to generate another; each official tends to distort the information he passes upward in the hierarchy, exaggerating those data favorable to himself and minimizing those unfavorable to himself; each official is biased in favor of those policies or actions that advance his own interests or the programs he advocates, and against those that injure or simply fail to advance those interests or programs." (Anthony Downs, *Inside Bureaucracy* [Boston: Little, Brown, 1967], pp. 262, 266. As quoted in Johnson, *Change in Communist Systems*, p. 17.)

13. For a similar argument, see Bartlomiej Kaminski, "The Anatomy of the Directive Capacity of the Socialist State," pp. 76–77.

14. It is noteworthy that Soviet and East European dissidents, even those who were not nationalists, generally viewed themselves as representing "the people," their "soul," "identity," and "cultural authenticity" against the brutish state. See Jeffrey C. Goldfarb, *Beyond Glasnost: The Post-Totalitarian Mind*.

15. Johnson, p. 21. See also Mary McAuley, "Soviet Political Reform in a Comparative Context."

16. Johnson, p. 17.

17. My use of this term is, of course, intentionally ironic.

18. The explosion in popular intiative in Czechoslovakia in 1968, in Poland in 1980, in the USSR in 1987–1989, and in Bulgaria and East Germany in 1989 appears to validate this proposition.

19. On civil society, see John Keane, ed., *Civil Society and the State*. For a recent Soviet discussion of a formerly taboo concept, see "Butenko on Charting the New Socialism," *Current Digest of the Soviet Press*, vol. 41, no. 32 (September 6, 1989), pp. 5–6.

20. See G. Arbatov and E. Batalov, "Politicheskaia reforma i evoliutsiia sovetskogo gosudarstva"; V. Tishkov, "Narody i gosudarstvo," p. 59; Agdas Burganov, "Giving Up Totalitarian Rule," *News from Ukraine*, p. 3; A. Migranyan, "The Long Road to the European Home."

21. Readers who recoil at my use of the term *totalitarianism* may prefer some euphemism—say, the administrative-command system, monism, or the like. There is, I submit, no essential difference between these terms and totalitarianism as I have defined it. The taboo on totalitarianism, even on discussion of the term, seems wholly unwarranted, surely now if not in the past. Such a totalitarian mentality, to quote Douglas Chalmers, must be rejected for reasoned discourse regarding regime or state types to return to Sovietology.

5. The Contradictions of the Soviet State

1. Peter Zwick, *National Communism*, p. 1. See also Roman Szporluk, *Nationalism and Communism*; Hans Kohn, "Soviet Communism and Nationalism."

2. Walker Connor, *The National Question in Marxist-Leninist Theory and Strategy*, pp. 5–9. For other discussions of the relationship between Marxism and nationalism, see Michael Löwy, "Marxism and the National Question"; Horace B. Davis, *Nationalism and Socialism*.

3. Richard Pipes, *The Formation of the Soviet Union*, p. 21.

4. My tripartite approach to nationalism is similar to Connor's, pp. 6–20.

5. Tucker, *The Marx-Engels Reader*, p. 473.

6. Ibid., pp. 160–161.

7. Ibid., pp. 488–489.

8. Ian Cummins, *Marx, Engels and National Movements*, p. 114.

9. Ibid., pp. 42–44.

10. Tucker, *The Marx-Engels Reader*, p. 488.

11. Ibid., pp. 26–52, 653–664.

12. Frederick Engels, *Germany: Revolution and Counter-Revolution*, pp. 54–61. See also Charles C. Herod, *The Nation in the History of Marxian Thought*.

13. See George Liber, "Ukrainian Nationalism and the 1918 Law on National-Personal Autonomy."

Notes

14. Horace B. Davis, *The National Question*, p. 105.
15. Tom Bottomore and Patrick Goode, *Austro-Marxism*, p. 116.
16. Ibid., pp. 106–107.
17. Ernest Gellner, *Nations and Nationalism*.
18. Taras Hunchak and Roman Sol'chanyk, *Ukrains'ka suspil'no-politychna dumka v 20 stolitti*, vol. 1, p. 154.
19. Davis, *The National Question*, p. 111.
20. Ibid., p. 297.
21. Luxemburg's self-defeating myopia and remarkable inability to comprehend the times she was living in are particularly evident from the following passage, written in 1918, which requires no comment:

> Ukrainian nationalism in Russia was something quite different from, let us say, Czech, Polish, or Finnish nationalism, in that the former was a mere whim, a folly of a few dozen petit bourgeois intellectuals, without the slightest roots in the economic, political, or psychological relationships of the country; it was without any historical tradition, since the Ukraine never formed a nation or government, was without any national culture, except for the reactionary romantic poems of Shevchenko. It is exactly as if, one fine day, the people living in the *Wasserkante* should want to found a new Low-German [*Plattdeutsche*] nation and government! And this ridiculous pose of a few university professors and students was inflated into a political force by Lenin and his comrades through their doctrinaire agitation concerning the "right of self-determination including, etc." To what was at first a mere farce they lent such importance that the farce became a matter of the most deadly seriousness— not as a serious national movement for which, afterward as before, there are no roots at all, but as a shingle and rallying flag of counter-revolution! At Brest, out of this addled egg crept the German bayonets. (Davis, *The National Question*, p. 298.)

22. Lenin's analogy of Bolshevik support of the right to self-determination with their support of the right to divorce is, on closer inspection, merely a subterfuge. To be sure, to support the right to divorce (or the right to self-determination) is not to insist that all marriages end in divorce (or that all multinational states break up). To support the right to divorce must mean supporting unconditionally the right of married and unmarried persons to self-determination, that is, to choose or not to choose to have a divorce without outside interference. But permitting nations alone to choose or not to choose to separate from some state is precisely what Lenin is not willing to concede.
23. Lenin, *Selected Works*, pp. 163–164. See also Alfred D. Low, *Lenin on the Question of Nationality; Leninism and the National Question*.
24. Lenin, *Selected Works*, p. 165.
25. On Galicia, see John-Paul Himka, *Socialism in Galicia*.
26. L. Rybalka [Lev Iurkevych], "The Russian Social Democrats and

the National Question"; Robert C. Tucker, *The Lenin Anthology*, p. 166.

27. Serhii Mazlakh and Vasyl' Shakhrai, *On the Current Situation in the Ukraine*, pp. 150–151. See also M. S. Sultan-Galiev, *Stat'i*.

28. Alexandre A. Bennigsen and S. Enders Wimbush, *Muslim National Communism in the Soviet Union*, p. 47.

29. See Jurij Borys, *The Sovietization of Ukraine, 1917–1923*; Iwan Majstrenko, *Borot'bism: A Chapter in the History of Ukrainian Communism*.

30. For an elaboration of this argument, see Motyl, *Will the Non-Russians Rebel?*, pp. 36–52.

31. Aleksandr Solzhenitsyn, "Misconceptions About Russia Are a Threat to America."

32. For a Soviet interpretation of these events, see V. Zotov, "Natsional'nyi vopros: deformatsii proshlogo."

6. The Inevitability of National Communism

1. On national Communism, see Bennigsen and Wimbush, *Muslim National Communism in the Soviet Union*; Michael Rywkin, *Moscow's Muslim Challenge*; Yaroslav Bilinsky, "Mykola Skrypnyk and Petro Shclcst"; Gregory Gleason, "Prefect or Palladin? Centrist and Nationalist Leaders in Soviet Central Asia," and "Sharaf Rashidov and the Dilemmas of National Leadership"; James E. Mace, *Communism and the Dilemmas of National Liberation*.

2. Of Alec Nove's many writings on this theme, see in particular *Political Economy and Soviet Socialism*. For excellent discussions of related issues, see Hans-Hermann Höhmann et al,, *Economics and Politics in the USSR*; George R. Feiwell, *The Soviet Quest for Economic Efficiency*; James R. Millar, *The ABC's of Soviet Socialism*.

3. For a balanced view of the Soviet economy's strengths and weaknesses, see Ed A. Hewett, *Reforming the Soviet Economy*.

4. See Robert Campbell, "The Soviet Economic Model"; Radoslav Selucky, *Economic Reforms in Eastern Europe*; Jan Marczewski, *Crisis in Socialist Planning*; Richard E. Ericson, "The New Enterprise Law"; Abel G. Aganbegyan, "Economic Reforms," in *Perestroika 1989*; Gertrude E. Schroeder, "The State-run Economy." Some economists suggest that partial decentralization is untenable over the long run and that the only logically coherent alternatives are complete centralization or complete decentralization. Whether or not this is the case need not concern us, insofar as all economists seem to agree that decentralization of some kind is the best antidote to overcentralization.

5. Franz Schurmann, "Politics and Economics in Russia and China," pp. 310–311. Current Soviet plans appear to involve a combination of both. See the draft of the "Obshchie printsipy perestroiki rukovodstva ekonomikoi i sotsial'noi sferoi v soiuznykh respublikakh na osnove ras-

shireniia ikh suverennykh prav, samoupravleniia i samofinansirovaniia," *Pravda*, March 14, 1989, pp. 2–3.

6. The republics have acquired a life of their own now. See Seweryn Bialer, *Stalin's Successors*, pp. 207–226; Motyl, "The Sobering of Gorbachev: Nationality, Restructuring, and the West."

7. Charles Lindblom, *Politics and Markets*, p. 133.

8. For a similar argument, see Robert A. Dahl, *Polyarchy*.

9. Lindblom, p. 165.

10. Wlodzimierz Brus, "Political Pluralism and Markets in Communist Systems," pp. 126–129. See also Brus, *The Economics and Politics of Socialism* and *The Market in a Socialist Economy*.

11. Brus, in Solomon, p. 128.

12. Ibid., p. 122.

13. This section is drawn from Motyl, "The Sobering of Gorbachev," pp. 166–169.

14. For a similar argument, see Donna Bahry, "*Perestroika* and the Debate over Territorial Economic Decentralization."

15. On the confusion surrounding the word *crisis*, see Motyl, "Reassessing the Soviet Crisis: Big Problems, Muddling Through, Business as Usual."

7. State Building, States, and Incipient States

1. The concept of dual sovereignty is, of course, borrowed from Leon Trotsky, *The Russian Revolution*. For a scholarly elaboration of the concept's significance for understanding revolutions, see Tilly's *From Mobilization to Revolution*.

2. Hannah Arendt, *On Revolution*, pp. 11–20; Skocpol, *States and Social Revolutions*.

3. Tilly, "Reflections on the History of European State-Making," p. 42.

4. See Evan Mawdsley, *The Russian Civil War*, pp. 272–290. See also Skocpol, pp. 210–220.

5. On Russia's borderlands, see Edward C. Thaden, *Russia's Western Borderlands, 1710–1870*; Zenon E. Kohut, *Russian Centralism and Ukrainian Autonomy*; Richard A. Pierce, *Russian Central Asia, 1867–1917*; Michael Rywkin, *Russian Colonial Expansion to 1917*; Pipes, *The Formation of the Soviet Union*; Ronald Grigor Suny, *Transcaucasia: Nationalism and Social Change*.

6. See Robert A. Kann, *Das Nationalitätenproblem der Habsburgermonarchie*.

7. See John A. Armstrong, "Mobilized Diaspora in Tsarist Russia: The Case of the Baltic Germans."

8. Seymour Becker, *Russia's Protectorates in Central Asia: Bukhara and Khiva, 1865–1924*.

9. Steven Guthier, "The Popular Base of Ukrainian Nationalism in 1917."

10. See Bohdan Krawchenko, "The Social Structure of the Ukraine at the Turn of the Twentieth Century."

11. Eric R. Wolf, *Peasant Wars of the Twentieth Century*.

12. Georg von Rauch, *The Baltic States*, pp. 34–36.

13. On Menshevism in Georgia, see Ronald Grigor Suny, *The Making of the Georgian Nation*, pp. 144–181.

14. On the Ukrainian Galician Army, see Motyl, *The Turn to the Right*, pp. 17–21.

15. Von Rauch, pp. 53; Pipes, p. 162; Mawdsley, pp. 116–118; *Estonian War of Independence, 1918–1920*, pp. 21–27; Edward Allworth, *Central Asia: A Century of Russian Rule*, pp. 236–250.

16. For the best account of Pilsudski's campaign, see Norman Davies, *White Eagle, Red Star*.

17. See Arthur E. Adams, *Bolsheviks in the Ukraine*; Allworth, *Central Asia*, pp. 224–253.

18. Joseph Rothschild, *East Central Europe Between the Two World Wars*, pp. 368–381.

19. M. K. Dziewanowski, *Poland in the Twentieth Century*, pp. 61, 70.

20. Ibid., pp. 72–73.

21. John H. Wuorinen, *A History of Finland*, p. 221. See also D. G. Kirby, *Finland in the Twentieth Century*; Risto Alapuro, *State and Revolution in Finland*; Mawdsley, p. 117.

22. Mawdsley, p. 118.

23. Nicholas Vakar's criticism of Belorussian nationalists—"the argument that Belorussia was not prepared for statehood is waved away"—betrays a curiously romantic understanding of state building and if applied consistently today would result in the immediate depopulation of the United Nations General Assembly. (Vakar, *Belorussia: The Making of a Nation*, p. 106.)

24. Alan W. Fisher, *The Crimean Tatars*, pp. 122–126.

25. John Reshetar, *The Ukrainian Revolution, 1917–1920*, pp. 163–168.

26. Pipes, pp. 193–195.

27. David Marshall Lang, *A Modern History of Soviet Georgia*, p. 211. The behavior of non-nationalists acting in a nationalist manner and attaining nationalist outcomes is not just ironic. It is also testimony to the fact that values and behavior generally cannot be conflated, because rational actors make their choices in response to the structure of incentives and disincentives in the environment. Neither modernization, social mobilization, social frustration, the decline of religion, or the rise of the scientific state made the Transcaucasians choose independence. Rather, their behavior was a rational response to conditions of extreme constraint—which only goes to show that both nationalists and nonnationalists respond to the positive and negative sanctions about them. Nationalism as ideal is, as I argued, neither sufficient nor even necessary for nationalist outcomes.

28. On the Alash Orda, see Allworth, *Central Asia*, pp. 236–241; Martha Brill Olcott, *The Kazakhs*, pp. 137–156.

29. Allworth, *Central Asia*, p. 227.

30. See Motyl, *Turn to the Right*, pp. 18–19.

31. Fisher, pp. 127–129.

32. This unfortunate term is not mine. See Arvids Ziedonis et al., *Problems of Mininations: Baltic Perspectives*.

33. See Pipes, pp. 221–241.

34. On the Polish occupation of Belorussia and the Ukraine, see Vakar, pp. 107–118; Reshetar, pp. 299–316.

35. The vast literature on modern ethnic movements makes this point persuasively. For example, see Raymond L. Hall, *Ethnic Autonomy—Comparative Dynamics*; Crawford Young, *The Politics of Cultural Pluralism*.

36. Gellner, *Thought and Change*, p. 174.

8. Guerrilla Struggles Against the Soviet State

1. A fine historical survey of guerrilla warfare is provided by Walter Laqueur, *Guerrilla*.

2. For a related argument, see Theda Skocpol, "What Makes Peasants Revolutionary?"

3. Joel S. Migdal, *Peasants, Politics, and Revolution*, p. 254. For an explicitly rational-choice analysis of peasant revolutionary activity, see Samuel Popkin, *The Rational Peasant: The Political Economy of Revolution in Vietnam*. For an alternative perspective, see James C. Scott, *The Moral Economy of the Peasant*.

4. Strictly speaking, only the Ukrainians and Balts were nationalists, but I am extending my analysis to the Basmachi and Daghestanis because the dynamics of their struggles were very similar to those of the nationalists and can be explained in similar collective-choice terms.

5. On the wartime resistance movements in the Baltic states, see Romuald J. Misiunas and Rein Taagepera, *The Baltic States: Years of Dependence, 1940–1980*, pp. 62–68; Zenonas Ivinskis, "Lithuania During the War: Resistance Against the Soviet and Nazi Occupants." See also Rein Taagepera, "Soviet Documentation on the Estonian Pro-Independence Guerrilla Movement, 1945–1952."

6. On Nazi policies in occupied Eastern Europe and the Soviet Union, see Alexander Dallin, *German Rule in Russia, 1941–1945*.

7. See Motyl, *The Turn to the Right*. See also Motyl, "Ukrainian Nationalist Political Violence in Inter-War Poland, 1921–1939," and "The Rural Origins of the Communist and Nationalist Movements in Wolyn Wojewodztwo, 1921–1939."

8. John A. Armstrong, *Ukrainian Nationalism*. See also Yaroslav Bil-

Notes

insky, *The Second Soviet Republic: The Ukraine After World War II*. Especially valuable are the two volumes of German documents on the Ukrainian nationalist underground contained in Taras Hunchak, *UPA v svitli nimets'kykh dokumentiv*. See also Luba Fajfer, "The Ukrainian Insurgent Army in Documents."

9. Alexandre Bennigsen, "Muslim Guerrilla Warfare in the Caucasus (1918–1928)," pp. 49–51.

10. Marie Broxup, "The Basmachi," p. 58. See also Martha B. Olcott, "The Basmachi or Freemen's Revolt in Turkestan, 1918–24"; William S. Ritter, "The Final Phase in the Liquidation of Anti-Soviet Resistance in Tadzhikistan: Ibrahim Bek and the *Basmachi*, 1924–1931."

11. E. J. Hobsbawm, *Primitive Rebels*. For an interesting application of Hobsbawm's scheme, see Linda Gordon, *Cossack Rebellions: Social Turmoil in the Sixteenth-Century Ukraine*.

12. Misiunas and Taagepera, pp. 81, 277; "Mynule nam potribne zarady maibut'noho," *Lenins'ka molod'*, December 19, 1988, as reprinted in *Svoboda*, February 9, 1989, p. 1; Bennigsen, p. 50; Broxup, p. 61.

13. Broxup, p. 68; Bennigsen, p. 52; Misiunas and Taagepera, p. 277; Yuriy Tys-Krokhmaliuk, *UPA Warfare in Ukraine*, p. 308.

14. See Ilya Dzhirkvelov, *Secret Servant: My Life with the KGB and the Soviet Elite*, pp. 36–39, for an account of NKVD anti-guerrilla campaigns in Latvia.

15. Misiunas and Taagepera, p. 278.

16. M. Bohor, "Dva taktychni periody UPA," *Do Zbroi*, no. 13 (November 1951), p. 6; Stepan Danyliuk, "Balians boiovykh dosiahnen' UPA i zbroinoho pidpillia," *Do Zbroi*, no. 19 (June 1953), p. 9.

17. *Lenins'ka molod'*, December 19, 1988.

18. Ritter, p. 487; E. H. Cookridge, *Gehlen: Spy of the Century*, pp. 237–264; Bruce Page et al., *The Philby Conspiracy*, pp. 185–189.

19. On the Soviet terror of 1940–1941, see Gross, *Revolution from Abroad*.

20. Misiunas and Taagepera, p. 279; *Ukraine: A Concise Encyclopedia*, vol. 1, p. 902. See also Alfreds Berzins, *The Unpunished Crime*.

21. Broxup, p. 70.

22. On collectivization, see Kestutis K. Girnius, "The Collectivization of Lithuanian Agriculture, 1944–1950"; Rein Taagepera, "Soviet Collectivization of Estonian Agriculture: The Taxation Phase," and "Soviet Collectivization of Estonian Agriculture: The Deportation Phase"; David R. Marples, "Western Ukraine and Western Belorussia under Soviet Occupation: The Development of Socialist Farming, 1939–1941," and "The Soviet Collectivization of Western Ukraine, 1948–1949."

23. *UHVR v svitli postanov Velykoho Zboru ta inshykh dokumentiv z dial'nosty 1944–1951 rr.*

24. K. V. Tauras, *Guerrilla Warfare on the Amber Coast*, p. 38.

25. Olcott, "The Basmachi or Freemen's Revolt," p. 362.

26. This fact probably explains why the notion of an urban guerrilla

strikes us as being an oxymoron. See Carlos Marighella, "Minimanual of the Urban Guerrilla."

27. Roy Hofheinz makes a persuasive case for this argument in "The Ecology of Chinese Communist Success: Rural Influence Patterns, 1923–1945."

28. On nationalist hopes for a third world war, see Tauras, pp. 89–92; P. Poltava, "Preparatory Steps Toward the Third World War and the Tasks of the Ukrainian People."

9. The Triumph of the Émigrés

1. Scholarly books on émigrés are few. See Robert C. Williams, *Culture in Exile: Russian Émigrés in Germany, 1881– 1941*; Symon Narizhnyi, *Ukrains'ka emigratsiia*; Motyl, *The Turn to the Right*. By *émigrés* and *émigré community* I mean, not just those individuals who actually emigrated, but also those of their acculturated children who still retain ties to the community. In this sense, the terms are admittedly somewhat of a misnomer, but they may be less awkward than the alternatives: *exile, immigrant, refugee,* etc.

2. Sovietologists, especially those trained in the 1960s and 1970s, are most prone to treat East European émigrés with a contempt that borders on chauvinism and racism. Remarkably, some scholars do not shy away from the offensive generalizations, hoary stereotypes, and demeaning witticisms they would immediately denounce as racist if they were applied to American ethnic groups. Not only are such attitudes repugnant, but they also inhibit scholarly understanding of East European politics and societies, especially in light of the fact that émigré analyses of Soviet politics have, arguably, proved to be closer to the mark than those of academics.

3. Michail Heller and Alexander Nekrich, *Geschichte der Sowjetunion*.

4. See N. S. Stashkevich, *Prigovor revoliutsii: Krushenie antisovetskogo dvizheniia v Belorussii 1917–1925*; D. L. Golinkov, *Krushenie antisovetskogo podpol'ia v SSSR*, vols. 1–2.

5. Émigrés are particularly active in counterrevolutions. See Arno J. Mayer, *Dynamics of Counterrevolution in Europe, 1870–1956*; Hagopian, *The Phenomenon of Revolution*, pp. 341–362.

6. Albert O. Hirschman, *Exit, Voice, and Loyalty*.

7. Sidney Hook, *The Hero in History*, pp. 184–228.

8. Martin Gilbert, *Imperial Russian History Atlas*, p. 70.

9. Martin Gilbert, *Soviet History Atlas*, p. 27.

10. Roman Ilnytzkyj, *The Free Press of the Suppressed Nations*, p. 44.

11. Laurie Salitan, "Soviet Emigration Policy: The Case of Jews and Germans," p. 2. For recent figures, see John Stavis and Julia Wishnevsky, "The Impact of *Glasnost'* on Soviet Emigration Policy," *Report on the USSR*, October 6, 1989, pp. 3–6.

12. The following very incomplete list gives some indication of the cornucopia of émigré groupings that have concerned and still worry the Soviet authorities.

Among the Russians: the monarchist Russian All-Military Union, founded by General Wrangel in 1923; the radical right People's Labor Union (NTS), established in 1930 as the National Union of Russian Youth; the Group of Russian Anarchist-Communists Abroad, under Petr Arshinov's guidance; the Menshevik Foreign Delegation, established in Berlin in 1921; the Young Russia movement under Aleksandr Kazem-Bek; the Supreme Monarchist Council and its rival, the Russian Legitimist-Monarchist Union, both active in Germany in the 1920s; Pavel Miliukov's followers grouped about the Paris-based *Poslednie novosti*; the Russian National Socialist Movement, founded in 1933; the Social Revolutionaries; the followers of Trotsky; the dissidents grouped about Valery Chalidze's Khronika Press and Vladimir Maksimov's *Kontinent*.

Among the Ukrainians: the Ukrainian People's Republic government in exile under Symon Petliura; the West Ukrainian People's Republic government in exile under Ievhen Petrushevych; the Ukrainian Military Organization, established in 1920; Hetman Skoropads'kyi's supporters, the Ukrainian Union of Landholding Statebuilders, founded in 1920 in Vienna; Volodymyr Vynnychenko's Vienna-based Foreign Group of the Ukrainian Communist Party; Mykyta Shapoval's Prague-based Foreign Delegation of the Ukrainian Party of Social Revolutionaries; the Organization of Ukrainian Nationalists (OUN) under Colonel Ievhen Konovalets'; the OUN's three splinter groups under Stepan Bandera, Andrii Mel'nyk, and Lev Rebet; the World Congress of Free Ukrainians, established in New York City in 1967.

Among the Belorussians and Balts: the Belorussian People's Republic government in exile; the Supreme Committee for the Liberation of Lithuania, originally founded in Lithuania in 1943 and reestablished in Germany after the war; the Lithuanian-American Council, founded in 1940; the Latvian Social-Democratic Party in exile under Bruno Kalniņš; the Estonian-American National Council; the Estonian World Council; the consulates general of all three countries.

13. See Dallin, *German Rule in Russia, 1941–1945*; Peter J. Potichnyj, "Ukrainians in World War II Military Formations: An Overview," and Myroslav Yurkevych, "Galician Ukrainians in German Military Formations and in the German Administration."

14. See Bruce Page et al., *The Philby Conspiracy*; Jonathan Adelman, "Soviet Secret Police," in Jonathan Adelman et al., *Terror and Communist Politics*, pp. 120–121; Philip Knightley, *The Master Spy: The Story of Kim Philby*.

15. Gaucher, *Opposition in the U.S.S.R., 1917–1967*, p. 430; *Ukraina: Suchasne i maibutnie: Zbirnyk stattei*, p. 75.

16. See R. E. Parta, "RFE/RL's Audience in the USSR. January–De-

cember 1984," *Soviet Area Audience and Opinion Research. Trend Report,* AR 2–85, April 1985, p. 6.

17. Motyl, *Turn to the Right,* pp. 54–55.

18. Stephen A. Garrett, "Eastern European Ethnic Groups and American Foreign Policy"; D. G. Dovgopolyi, "Etnicheskie gruppy SShA vostochnoevropeiskogo proiskhozhdeniia i formirovanie politiki Soedinennykh Shtatov v otnoshenii sotsialisticheskikh stran."

19. Anatol' Kamins'kyi, *Krai, emigratsiia i mizhnarodni zakulisy,* p. 132.

20. Motyl, *Will the Non-Russians Rebel?,* p. 110.

21. Gaucher, pp. 151, 426; *Survey* (Autumn-Winter 1983), 27(118/119):49–87.

22. See *Moskovs'ki vbyvtsi Bandery pered sudom.*

23. Tönu Parming, "The Soviet Union and the Émigré Communities," p. 310.

24. See Imants Lesinskis, "Cultural Relations or Ethnic Espionage: An Insider's View."

25. Ibid., pp. 324–328; Boshyk, pp. 121–144.

26. A favorite Soviet tactic used to be to brand all émigrés as nationalists, all nationalists as collaborators, and thus to be able to pin war crimes on both real and imagined criminals. Amazingly, such allegations of collective guilt not only cast suspicion on entire communities but also found resonance among liberal circles.

27. For a sampling of the Soviet literature, see Mykola Horlenko, *Fake Patriots*; Yevhen Sheremet, *Ukrainians by Profession*; V. Styrkul, *The SS Werewolves*, and *Up a Blind Alley*. Interestingly, the terminology, logic, and accusations made by Soviet writers against Ukrainian, Baltic, and Russian émigrés are virtually identical to those found in the Soviet anti-Zionist literature.

28. Policies similar to this were also pursued in the 1960s. What is especially distinctive about current bridge building is the scope of Soviet efforts and, most striking perhaps, the fact that visiting Soviet delegations are meeting with émigré political groups that never hid, and do not hide, their anti-Communist and anti-Soviet views. See Liutas Mockunas, "The Dynamics of Lithuanian Émigré-Homeland Relations."

29. See the OUN's call for support, "Do Ukrains'koho Hromadianstva v Diiaspori!," *Amerika,* October 24, 1989, p. 1.

30. G. Berzins and N. Morley-Fletcher, "Our Interaction with Our Homelands," pp. 32–34.

31. "Soviet Poll Finds Deep Pessimism Over Gorbachev's Economic Plan," *New York Times,* November 5, 1989, pp. 1, 18.

10. Rational Nationalist Dissent

1. Groups and organizations also existed, of course, but they were far too small and much too informal to qualify as collective actions. The

Notes

subtitle of Ludmilla Alexeyeva's *Soviet Dissent: Contemporary Movements for National, Religious, and Human Rights* suggests otherwise, although the content of the book actually supports my contention.

2. See Wsevolod Isajiw, "Urban Migration and Social Change in Contemporary Soviet Ukraine"; Walter D. Connor, "Dissent in a Complex Society"; Jaroslaw Bilocerkowicz, *Soviet Ukrainian Dissent: A Study of Political Alienation*. In this sense, dissent is like crime. The two differ, however, in terms of their ends: crime violates norms for the purpose of personal material gain or nonideologically motivated physical harm, whereas dissent violates given norms for the purpose of asserting different norms. Clearly, there will always be a grey area, in all countries, where dissent and crime overlap.

3. How these signals are conveyed is suggested by Michael E. Urban in "Political Language and Political Change in the USSR: Notes on the Gorbachev Leadership" and in Alexandre Bourmeyster, "Soviet Political Discourse, Narrative Program and the *Skaz* Theory"; and Rachel Walker, "Marxism-Leninism as Discourse: The Politics of the Empty Signifier and the Double Bind."

4. For an anlysis of the manner in which such signs regarding language use are conveyed, see Motyl, *Will the Non-Russians Rebel?*, pp. 88–106.

5. Robert Conquest, "Dissent in the Soviet Union," p. 95.

6. Valentyn Moroz, *Report from the Beria Reserve*, p. 89. Lesia Ukrainka is the *nom de plume* of a Ukrainian woman poet (1871–1913) generally considered to be third in importance after Taras Shevchenko and Ivan Franko. One such inspired individual appears to have been another Ukrainian dissident, Levko Luk'ianenko, who said, "Even if I were the only Ukrainian on earth, I would still continue to fight for Ukraine" (Moroz, p. 95). See also the *Chronicle of the Catholic Church in Lithuania* for numerous examples of inspired dissidents challenging the Soviet authorities in what they realize is a hopeless struggle.

7. Geertz, *The Interpretation of Cultures*, p. 49.

8. Milton Rokeach, "From Individual Values to Institutional Values: With Special Reference to the Values of Science," in *Understanding Human Values*, pp. 51–52.

9. Robin M. Williams, Jr., "Change and Stability in Values and Value Systems: A Sociological Perspective," pp. 31–32.

10. See Ellen Jones and Fred W. Grupp, "Modernisation and Ethnic Equalisation in the USSR"; *Present-Day Ethnic Processes in the USSR*

11. Seymour Martin Lipset, *Political Man: The Social Bases of Politics*, pp. 27–63; Basile Kerblay, *Modern Soviet Society*, p. 282; Chester L. Hunt, "The Sociology of Religion"; Rothschild, *Ethnopolitics*, pp. 137–171.

12. Cronid Lubarsky, "Soziale Basis und Umfang des sowjetischen Dissententums," p. 928.

13. Ibid., p. 927.

14. Misiunas and Taagepera, *The Baltic States*; Mary Kilbourne Ma-

tossian, "Communist Rule and the Changing Armenian Cultural Pattern"; Alexeyeva, pp. 201–266.

15. Peter Reddaway, "Soviet Policies on Dissent and Emigration: The Radical Change of Course since 1979," pp. 40–52. These figures, Professor Reddaway cautions, are somewhat out of date. Since writing this paper, he has gathered information on many more political arrests. Although he has not yet had the time to complete the research, Professor Reddaway's impression is that the new data do not greatly change any of the patterns. (Private communication to author, April 19, 1988.)

16. On the remarkable upsurge of Moldavian national activism in 1988–1989, see Bill Keller, "Confession in Moldavia: They Speak Rumanian," *New York Times*, February 25, 1989; "Nationale Bewegungen auch in Sowjetmoldawien," *Neue Zürcher Zeitung*, January 15/16, 1989, p. 5; Bohdan Nahaylo, "National Ferment in Moldavia," *The Ukrainian Weekly*, February 21, 1988, pp. 2, 14.

17. Deutsch, *Nationalism and Social Communication*; Anthony D. Smith, *Theories of Nationalism*; Gellner, *Nations and Nationalism*; Mary McAuley, "Nationalism and the Soviet Multi-ethnic State."

18. See David Kowalewski and Cheryl Johnson, "The Ukrainian Dissident: A Statistical Profile," pp. 52–53; Bohdan Krawchenko, *Social Change and National Consciousness in Twentieth-Century Ukraine*, pp. 252–253; Bilocerkowycz, pp. 108–130.

19. Jones and Grupp, pp. 159–184; Motyl, *Will the Non-Russians Rebel?*, pp. 53–70.

20. See Michael Browne, *Ferment in the Ukraine*, pp. 31–93.

21. See Ernest Gellner, "Nationalism in a Vacuum."

22. On Belorussia, see "A Letter to Gorbachev from 28 Belorussian Cultural Figures," *Soviet Nationality Survey*, vol. 4, no. 5 (May 1987), p. 8; Roman Solchanyk, "An open letter to Gorbachev sent by Byelorussian workers, intellectuals," *The Ukrainian Weekly*, August 30, 1987, p. 2; Kathleen Mihalisko, "Belorussian Notebook," *Report on the USSR*, February 17, 1989, pp. 23–25; Kathleen Mihalisko, "Belorussian Popular Front off to a Good Start," *Radio Liberty Resaerch*, RL 560/88, December 12, 1988; Bohdan Nahaylo, "Political Demonstration in Minsk Attests to Belorussian National Assertiveness," *Radio Liberty Research*, RL 481/87, November 26, 1987. On Azerbaidzhan, see Tadeusz Swietochowski, "Soviet Azerbaijan Today: The Problems of Group Identity"; David B. Nissman, *The Soviet Union and Iranian Azerbaijan*; Mirza Michaeli and William Reese, "The Popular Front in Azerbaijan and Its Program," *Report on the USSR*, August 25, 1989, pp. 29–32. On Uzbekistan, see Annette Bohr and Timur Kocaoglu, " 'Birlik' Stages Another Demonstration in Tashkent," Annette Bohr, "Violence Erupts in Uzbekistan," *Report on the USSR*, June 16, 1989, pp. 16–17, 23–25; Timur Kocaoglu, "Demonstrations by Uzbek Popular Front," *Report on the USSR*, April 28, 1989, pp. 13–15.

Notes

23. On the political culture literature, see Archie Brown and Jack Gray, *Political Culture and Political Change in Communist States*; Robert C. Tucker, *Political Culture and Leadership in the Soviet Union: From Lenin to Gorbachev*; Stephen White, *Political Culture and Soviet Politics*; Archie Brown, *Political Culture and Communist Studies*; Harry Eckstein, "A Culturalist Theory of Political Change."

11. The Myth of Russian Nationalism

1. Unfortunately, in this instance as in many others, Sovietologists have simply appropriated popular terminology without considering the methodological and theoretical consequences of such a procedure. As I argued in the introduction, such disregard for conceptual subtleties is not surprising, but it is nevertheless unfortunate. Consider, for example, the recent publication, *Russian Nationalism Today*.

2. Aleksandr Solzhenitsyn, *Pis'mo vozhdiam Sovetskogo Soiuza*.

3. "Zaiavlenie po ukrainskomu voprosu," *Kontinent*.

4. V. Gorskii, "Russkii messianizm i novoe natsional'noe soznanie," *Vestnik RSKhD*, no. 97 (1970), pp. 67–68.

5. Igor Shafarevich, "Separation or Reconciliation? The Nationalities Question in the USSR," p. 98.

6. John B. Dunlop, *The Faces of Contemporary Russian Nationalism*, p. 300.

7. On national Bolshevism, see Mikhail Agursky, *The Third Rome: National Bolshevism in the USSR*.

8. Valerii Chalidze, "O prave natsii na samoopredelenie." According to non-Russian intellectuals, there appear to be many such Russians, especially in Moscow.

9. See Viacheslav Chornovil, "O mezhnatsional'nykh konfliktakh v Iakutii"; Frederick C. Barghoorn, "Russian Nationalism and Soviet Politics: Official and Unofficial Perspectives"; Hedrick Smith, *The Russians*, pp 477–480; Toomas Ilves, "Estonian Press Breaks Nationality Discord Taboo," *Radio Free Europe Research*, Baltic Area SR/1, January 28, 1987; Elizabeth Pond, *From the Yaroslavsky Station*.

10. Dunlop, pp. 295–353; Mikhail Agursky, "The Prospects of National Bolshevism," in Robert Conquest, *The Last Empire*, pp. 87–106.

11. G. Pomerants, "Pluralism or Empire?," p. 6.

12. See Frederick C. Barghoorn, *Soviet Russian Nationalism*.

13. See Bialer, *Stalin's Successors*, pp. 207–225.

14. Samuel P. Huntington, *Political Order in Changing Societies*, p. 12.

15. Peter Reddaway, "Soviet Policies on Dissent and Emigration: The Radical Change of Course since 1979," pp. 40–52.

16. Dunlop, p. 275.

17. See Agursky, pp. 257–262; Dallin, *German Rule in Russia, 1941–1945*, pp. 553–580.

18. Dunlop, p. 247; Alexeyeva, *Soviet Dissent*, p. 436.

19. The classic statement of this position is found in Ivan Dzyuba, *Internationalism or Russification?*

20. Kathleen Mihalisko, "Poll of Soviet Citizens' Attitudes towards Ethnic Unrest," *Report on the USSR*, March 10, 1989, pp. 36–37.

21. On Russian imperial attitudes, see Taras Hunczak, "Pan-Slavism or Pan-Russianism," in *Russian Imperialism from Ivan the Great to the Revolution*; Marc Raeff, "Patterns of Russian Imperial Policy Toward the Nationalities."

22. V. I. Lenin, *KPSS o sovetskom mnogonatsional'nom gosudarstve*, p. 123.

23. Rudolf Schlesinger, *The Nationality Problem and Soviet Administration*, p. 80. On Shums'kyi and the struggle against "Moscow," see Mace, *Communism and the Dilemmas of National Liberation*, pp. 86–160.

24. Vernon V. Aspaturian, *The Union Republics in Soviet Diplomacy*. See also Konstantyn Sawczuk, *The Ukraine in the United Nations Organization*; Motyl, "The Foreign Relations of the Ukrainian SSR."

25. Dunlop, p. 34; Vadim Medish, "Special Status of the RSFSR," p. 192.

26. Roger E. Kanet, "The Rise and Fall of the 'All-People's State': Recent Changes in the Soviet Theory of the State."

27. Dunlop, pp. 35–41.

28. See Peter J. S. Duncan, "The Party and Russian Nationalism in the USSR: From Brezhnev to Gorbachev."

29. On the Soviet people, the friendship of peoples, and other such concepts, see Motyl, *Will the Non-Russians Rebel?*, pp. 71–82; Yaroslav Bilinsky, "The Concept of the Soviet People and Its Implications for Soviet Nationality Policy"; Oleh S. Fedyshyn, "The Role of Russians Among the New, Unified 'Soviet People'," and Ruslan O. Rasiak, " 'The Soviet People': Multiethnic Alternative or Ruse?," in Allworth, *Ethnic Russia in the USSR*; Borys Lewytzkyj, *"Sovetskij narod"—"Das Sowjetvolk."*

30. See Vladislav Krasnov, "Russian National Feeling: An Informal Poll."

31. For Soviet press criticism of *Pamiat'*, see "Ultranationalist Russian Group Denounced," *Current Digest of the Soviet Press*, vol. 39, no. 21 (June 24, 1987), pp. 1–7. On the organization's favorable relations with Party authorities, see Julia Wishnevsky, "The Emergence of 'Pamyat" and 'Otechestvo'," *Radio Liberty Research*, RL 342/87, August 26, 1987; Darrell P. Hammer, *"Glasnost'* and 'The Russian Idea' "; G. Anishchenko, "Who Is Guilty?," p. 58; Bill Keller, "Russian Nationalists: Yearning for an Iron Hand," *New York Times Magazine*, January 28, 1990, pp. 18–20, 46–50.

32. See Vera Tolz, "The United Front of Workers of Russia: Further Consolidation of Antireform Forces," *Report on the USSR*, September 29, 1989, pp. 11–13; " 'Labor' Front Girds for Political Battle," *Current Digest of the Soviet Press*, vol. 41, no. 43 (November 22, 1989), pp. 6–10.

33. See "Ukrainian 'Front' Stirs Media Furor," *Current Digest of the*

Soviet Press, vol. 41, no. 37 (October 11, 1989), pp. 1–5; "Zaiavlenie TsK KPSS o polozhenii v respublikakh Sovetskoi Pribaltiki," *Pravda*, August 27, 1989, p. 1; V. Tomal' and E. Naidenov, "Istina vsegda konkretna," *Vechernii Minsk*, August 5, 1989, p. 2.

34. On the controversy surrounding Andreeva's conservative manifesto, see "A Manifesto Against Restructuring?," *Current Digest of the Soviet Press*, vol. 40, no. 13 (April 27, 1988), pp. 1–6; "Pravda Rebuts 'Antirestructuring Manifesto'," *Current Digest of the Soviet Press*, vol. 40, no. 14 (May 4, 1988), pp. 1–5, 12, 20.

12. Nationalist Movements in the Era of Gorbachev

1. My definition is not unlike Paul Wilkinson's: "A social movement is a deliberate collective endeavor to promote change in any direction and by any means, not excluding violence, illegality, revolution or withdrawal into 'utopian' community" (*Social Movement*, p. 27). See also J. A. Banks, *The Sociology of Social Movements*.

2. Frances Fox Piven and Richard A. Cloward, *Poor People's Movements: Why They Succeed, How They Fail*, pp. xx–xxii.

3. Ibid., p. 14.

4. Motyl, "The Sobering of Gorbachev."

5. Ludmilla Alexeyeva and Valery Chalidze, *Mass Rioting in the USSR*.

6. *Chislennost' i sostav naseleniia SSSR* (Moscow: Finansy i statistika, 1984), p. 7.

7. It is interesting to speculate about the impact of the 1988 earthquake on the Armenian movement: Did it trigger additional discontent, as in Nicaragua after the 1972 earthquake, or will the Soviet authorities eventually win the hearts and minds of Armenians by efficiently rebuilding the country?

8. On the Baltic fronts, see Rein Taagepera, "Estonia Under Gorbachev: Stalinists, Autonomists, and Nationalists"; Aleksandras Shtromas, "On the Current Situation in Lithuania"; Janis Penikis, "Activism in Latvia 1988"; Ojars J. Rozitis, "The Rise of Latvian Nationalism," *Swiss Review of World Affairs*, vol. 38, no. 11 (February 1989), pp. 24–26; Marianna Butenschon, "Baltikum: Nur ein Wunder kann helfen," *Die Zeit*, December 9, 1988, p. 6. On the protofronts, see "USSR: Georgia," *Eastern Europe Newsletter*, vol. 3, no. 6 (March 22, 1989), pp. 5–6; Bohdan Nahaylo, "Confrontation Over Creation of Ukrainian Popular Front," *Report on the USSR*, March 3, 1989, pp. 13–17; Bohdan Nahaylo, "Inaugural Conference of Ukrainian Language Society Turns into Major Political Demonstration," *Report on the USSR*, March 3, 1989, pp. 20–22; Kathleen Mihalisko, "Belorussian Popular Front Off to a Good Start," *Radio Liberty Research*, RL 560/88, December 12, 1988; Mirza Michaeli, "Formation of Popular Front in Azerbaijan," *Radio Liberty Research*, RL 558/88, December 9, 1988.

9. Seweryn Bialer, "The Changing Soviet Political System: The Nineteenth Party Conference and After," in *Politics, Society, and Nationality*, pp. 193–241. The struggle against "bureaucracy" is based on a misnomer: bureaucracies characterize all modern states and Gorbachev, surely, is not interested in dismantling the Soviet state. Rather, the term *bureaucracy* really appears to mean something like "insensitive and inefficient administration."

10. John M. Battle, "Uskorenie, Glasnost' and Perestroika: The Pattern of Reform Under Gorbachev."

11. On Gorbachev's allies, see Condoleeza Rice, "Gorbachev and the Military: A Revolution in Security Policy, Too?"; Alexander Rahr, "Restructuring in the KGB," *Radio Liberty Research*, RL 226/87, June 15, 1987; Amy W. Knight, "The KGB and Soviet Reform"; Motyl, "Policing Perestroika: The Indispensable KGB"; Astrid von Borcke, *Unsichtbare Macht KGB*.

12. See Barry Sautman, "Retreat from Revolution: Why Communist Systems Deradicalize."

13. A striking example of the growing use even by official Soviet spokesmen of the term *totalitarianism* occurred on March 10, 1989, at a session of the Harriman Institute Seminar on Soviet Republics and Regional Issues, which heard a presentation on "Human Rights and the Nationalities" by Aleksandr Khodakov, the Second Secretary of the USSR Mission to the United Nations.

14. See Peter Reddaway, "Policy Towards Dissent Since Khrushchev."

15. On the scale of Gorbachev's early purges, see Timothy J. Colton, *The Dilemma of Reform in the Soviet Union*, pp. 87–97.

16. Gleason, "Prefect or Palladin?"

17. "Die Kundgebungen in Sowjetarmenien," *Neue Zürcher Zeitung*, February 26, 1988, p. 3; Taagepera, Shtromas, Penikis, *Occasional Papers on Baltic Political Action*.

18. On charges that the local militia abetted the Sumgait pogroms, see "Refugees Tell Their Stories," *Glasnost*, nos. 16–18 (January 1989), pp. 16, 21, 26, 31.

19. On Ukrainian national Communism, see Bilinsky, "Mykola Skrypnyk and Petro Shelest." See also Gleason, "Prefect or Palladin?"

20. "Rabochaia garantiia perestroiki," *Pravda*, February 24, 1989, p. 3. Significantly, Shcherbyts'kyi's electoral speech, delivered just after Gorbachev's departure, exuded self-confidence, if not indeed self-satisfaction. ("Bol'she vesomykh prakticheskikh del," *Pravda*, March 4, 1989, p. 2.) It is, of course, quite possible that Gorbachev desired to remove Shcherbyts'kyi but could not because of the latter's resistance, up through 1987–1988, when nationalist disturbances rocked the USSR. Thereafter, it seems plausible to suggest that Gorbachev's views of Shcherbyts'kyi may have changed and that he then came to consider him more of an asset than a liability.

Notes

21. On the internationalist fronts, see "Ethnic Russians March in Estonia," *New York Times*, March 15, 1989; "Latvians Take Steps Against 'Migrants'," *Current Digest of the Soviet Press*, vol. 41, no. 8 (March 22, 1989), pp. 7–10.

22. A series of mass demonstrations, similar to those that occurred in the Baltic states, took place in the West Ukrainian city of L'viv in the summers of 1988 and 1989.

23. "Soldiers Patrolling Soviet Georgia Amid Wave of Nationalist Protests," *New York Times*, April 8, 1989, pp. 1, 6; Esther B. Fein, "Soviet Georgians Continue Protests for More Autonomy," *New York Times*, April 9, 1989, p. 20; Esther B. Fein, "At Least 16 Killed as Protesters Battle the Police in Soviet Georgia," *New York Times*, April 10, 1989, pp. 1, 6.

24. "Natsional'naia politika partii v sovremennykh usloviiakh (platforma KPSS). Priniata Plenumom TsK KPSS 20 sentiabria 1989 goda," *Pravda*, September 24, 1989, pp. 1–2.

Conclusion

1. For an extended discussion of stability, see Motyl, *Will the Non-Russians Rebel?*

2. Crises, I submit, are immediately life-threatening conditions and, as such, are modes of being that verge on nonbeing. What most scholars really mean by the term are merely big problems. See Motyl, "Reassessing the Soviet Crisis."

3. See Zbigniew Brzezinski, *The Grand Failure: The Birth and Death of Communism in the Twentieth Century.*

4. Ted Robert Gurr, *Why Men Rebel.*

5. Chalmers Johnson, *Revolutionary Change*, pp. 91–121.

6. On the ongoing historical debates, see Mark von Hagen, "History and Politics under Gorbachev: Professional Autonomy and Democratization"; Thomas Sherlock, "Politics and History Under Gorbachev."

7. Johnson, p. 98.

8. Huntington, *Political Order in Changing Societies*, pp. 264–278.

9. Ibid., pp. 78–82.

10. Charles Tilly, *From Mobilization to Revolution*. See also his "Does Modernization Breed Revolution?"

11. Skocpol, *States and Social Revolutions*, "What Makes Peasants Revolutionary?," and "Rentier State and Shi'a Islam in the Iranian Revolution."

12. I develop a like argument in *Will the Non-Russians Rebel?*, pp. 15–19.

13. Parts of this scenario were originally presented at a Seminar on Prospects for Instability in the Soviet Union, held at Airlie House, Virginia, on December 12–13, 1988. For similar exercises of the imagination, see Alexander Shtromas, "How the End of the Soviet System May Come

Notes

About: Historical Precedents and Possible Scenarios"; Peter Reddaway, "Is the Soviet Union Drifting towards Anarchy?"; Peter Hauslohner, "The Soviet Transition to Democracy." For a more optimistic view, see Dawn Mann, "The Challenges Facing Gorbachev," *Report on the USSR*, September 1, 1989, pp. 15–19.

14. See the argument in Motyl, *Will the Non-Russians Rebel?*, especially pp. 155–170.

Selected Bibliography

Adamovich, Anthony. *Opposition to Sovietization in Belorussian Literature (1917–1957)*. Munich: Institute for the Study of the USSR, 1958.

Adams, Arthur E. *Bolsheviks in the Ukraine.* New Haven: Yale University Press, 1963.

Adelman, Jonathan R., ed. *Terror and Communist Politics: The Role of the Secret Police in Communist States*. Boulder, Colo.: Westview, 1984.

Aganbegyan, Abel G., ed. *Perestroika 1989*. New York: Scribner's, 1988.

Agursky, Mikhail. *The Third Rome: National Bolshevism in the USSR*. Boulder, Colo.: Westview, 1987.

Aiken, Henry D., ed. *Hume's Moral and Political Philosophy*. New York: Hafner, 1948.

Alapuro, Risto. *State and Revolution in Finland*. Berkeley: University of California Press, 1988.

Alexander, Jeffrey C. "The Centrality of the Classics." In Anthony Giddens and Jonathan H. Turner, eds., *Social Theory Today*, pp. 11–57. Cambridge: Polity Press, 1987.

Alexeyeva, Ludmilla and Valery Chalidze. *Mass Rioting in the USSR*. Silver Spring, Maryland: Foundation for Soviet Studies, 1985.

Selected Bibliography

Alexeyeva, Ludmilla. *Soviet Dissent: Contemporary Movements for National, Religious, and Human Rights*. Middletown, Conn.: Wesleyan University Press, 1985.

Allworth, Edward, ed. *Central Asia: A Century of Russian Rule*. New York: Columbia University Press, 1967.

Allworth, Edward, ed. *Ethnic Russia in the USSR*. New York: Pergamon Press, 1980.

Allworth, Edward, ed. *Soviet Nationality Problems*. New York: Columbia University Press, 1971.

Almond, Gabriel A. and Sidney Verba. *The Civic Culture*. Boston: Little, Brown, 1965.

Almond, Gabriel A. "Review Article: The International-National Connection." *British Journal of Political Science* (April 1989), 19(2):237–259.

Altstadt, Audrey L. "Azerbaijani Turks' Response to Russian Conquest." *Studies in Comparative Communism* (Autumn/Winter 1986), 19(3/4):267–286.

Amalrik, Andrei. *Will the Soviet Union Survive Until 1984?* New York: Harper & Row, 1980.

Anderson, Barbara A. and Brian D. Silver. "Equality, Efficiency, and Politics in Soviet Bilingual Education Policy: 1934–1980." *American Political Science Review* (December 1984), 78(4):1019–1039.

Anderson, Benedict. *Imagined Communities: Reflections on the Origin and Spread of Nationalism*. London: Verso, 1983.

Anishchenko, G. "Who Is Guilty?" *Glasnost* (October 1988), nos. 13–15, pp. 55–61.

Arbatov, G. and E. Batalov. "Politicheskaia reforma i evoliutsiia sovetskogo gosudarstva." *Kommunist* (March 1989), no. 4, pp. 35–46.

Arendt, Hannah. *On Revolution*. New York: Penguin Books, 1987.

Arjomand, Said Amir. "Iran's Islamic Revolution in Comparative Perspective." *World Politics* (April 1986), 38(3):383–414.

Armstrong, John A. "Mobilized Diaspora in Tsarist Russia: The Case of the Baltic Germans." In Jeremy R. Azrael, ed., *Soviet Nationality Policies and Practices*, pp. 63–104. New York: Praeger, 1978.

Armstrong, John A. *Nations Before Nationalism*. Chapel Hill: University of North Carolina Press, 1982.

Armstrong, John A. *Ukrainian Nationalism*. 2d ed. Littleton, Colo.: Ukrainian Academic Press, 1980.

Arslanian, Artin H. and Robert L. Nichols. "Nationalism and the Russian Civil War: The Case of Volunteer Army-Armenian Relations, 1918–20." *Soviet Studies* (October 1979), 31(4):559–573.

Aspaturian, Vernon V. *The Union Republics in Soviet Diplomacy*. Geneva: E. Droz, 1960.

Atkin, Muriel. *The Subtlest Battle: Islam in Soviet Tajikistan*. Philadelphia: Foreign Policy Research Institute, 1989.

Selected Bibliography

Azrael, Jeremy, ed. *Soviet Nationality Policies and Practices*. New York: Praeger, 1978.

Azrael, Jeremy. "The 'Nationality Problem' in the USSR: Domestic Pressures and Foreign Policy Constraints." In Seweryn Bialer, ed., *The Domestic Context of Soviet Foreign Policy*, pp. 139–153. Boulder, Colo.: Westview, 1981.

Bachrach, Peter and Morton Baratz. "Decisions and Nondecisions: An Analytical Framework." *American Political Science Review* (September 1963), 57(3):632–642.

Bahry, Donna and Carol Nechemias. "Half Full or Half Empty?: The Debate over Soviet Regional Equality." *Slavic Review* (Fall 1981), 40(3):366–383.

Bahry, Donna. *Outside Moscow: Power, Politics, and Budgetary Policy in the Soviet Republics*. New York: Columbia University Press, 1987.

Bahry, Donna. "*Perestroika* and the Debate over Territorial Economic Decentralization." *Harriman Institute Forum* (May 1989), 2(5):1–8.

Ball, Terence. "From Paradigms to Research Programs: Toward a Post-Kuhnian Political Science." In Herbert B. Asher et al., eds., *Theory-Building and Data Analysis in the Social Sciences*, pp. 23–49. Knoxville: University of Tennessee Press, 1984.

Balzer, Harley. "Can We Survive Glasnost?" *AAASS Newsletter* (January 1989), 29(1):1–2.

Banks, J. A. *The Sociology of Social Movements*. London: Macmillan, 1972.

Banton, Michael. "Ethnic Bargaining." In Dennis L. Thompson and Dov Ronen, eds., *Ethnicity, Politics, and Development*, pp. 11–24. Boulder, Colo.: Lynne Rienner, 1986.

Banton, Michael. *Racial and Ethnic Competition*. Cambridge: Cambridge University Press, 1983.

Barber, Benjamin R. "Conceptual Foundations of Totalitarianism." In Carl J. Friedrich et al., *Totalitarianism in Perspective: Three Views*, pp. 3–52. New York: Praeger, 1969.

Barghoorn, Frederick C. "Russian Nationalism and Soviet Politics: Official and Unofficial Perspectives." In Robert Conquest, ed., *The Last Empire: Nationality and the Soviet Future*, pp. 30–77. Stanford: Hoover Institution Press, 1986.

Barghoorn, Frederick C. *Soviet Russian Nationalism*. New York: Oxford University Press, 1956.

Barzun, Jacques. "Doing Research—Should the Sport Be Regulated?" *Columbia* (February 1987), 12(4):18–22.

Battle, John M. "Uskorenie, Glasnost' and Perestroika: The Pattern of Reform under Gorbachev." *Soviet Studies* (July 1988), 40(3):367–384.

Becker, Seymour. *Russia's Protectorates in Central Asia: Bukhara and Khiva, 1865–1924*. Cambridge: Harvard University Press, 1968.

Beissinger, Mark. "Ethnicity, the Personnel Weapon, and Neo-imperial

Selected Bibliography

Integration." *Studies in Comparative Communism* (Spring 1988), 21(1):71–85,
Belotserkovskii, Vadim, ed. *SSSR—Demokraticheskie al'ternativy*. West Germany: Achberg, 1976.
Bennigsen, Alexandre A. and S. Enders Wimbush. *Muslim National Communism in the Soviet Union*. Chicago: University of Chicago Press, 1979.
Bennigsen, Alexandre and Marie Broxup. *The Islamic Threat to the Soviet State*. London: Croom Helm, 1983.
Bennigsen, Alexandre. "Muslim Guerrilla Warfare in the Caucasus (1918–1928)." *Central Asian Survey* (July 1983), 2(1):45–56.
Bernstein, Thomas P. "Stalinism, Famine, and Chinese Peasants." *Theory and Society* (May 1984), 13(3):339–377.
Berzins, Alfreds. *The Unpunished Crime*. New York: Robert Speller, 1963.
Berzins, G. and N. Morley-Fletcher. "Our Interaction with Our Homelands." *Occasional Papers on Baltic Political Action* (September 1988), no. 2/3, pp. 32–34.
Bialer, Seweryn and Michael Mandelbaum, eds. *Gorbachev's Russia and American Foreign Policy*. Boulder, Colo.: Westview, 1988.
Bialer, Seweryn, ed. *Politics, Society, and Nationality Inside Gorbachev's Russia*. Boulder, Colo.: Westview, 1989.
Bialer, Seweryn. *Stalin's Successors: Leadership, Stability, and Change in the Soviet Union*. Cambridge: Cambridge University Press, 1980.
Bilinsky, Yaroslav. "Mykola Skrypnyk and Petro Shelest: An Essay on the Persistence and Limits of Ukrainian National Communism." In Jeremy R. Azrael, ed., *Soviet Nationality Policies and Practices*, pp. 105–143. New York: Praeger, 1978.
Bilinsky, Yaroslav. "The Concept of the Soviet People and Its Implications for Soviet Nationality Policy." *Annals of the Ukrainian Academy of Arts and Sciences in the United States* (1978–1980), 14(37–38):87–133.
Bilinsky, Yaroslav. *The Second Soviet Republic: The Ukraine After World War II*. New Brunswick, N.J.: Rutgers University Press, 1964.
Bilocerkowicz, Jaroslaw. *Soviet Ukrainian Dissent: A Study of Political Alienation*. Boulder, Colo.: Westview, 1988.
Borys, Jurij. *The Sovietization of Ukraine, 1917–1923*. 2d ed. Edmonton, Alta.: Canadian Institute of Ukrainian Studies, 1980.
Boshyk, Yury, ed. *Ukraine During World War II*. Edmonton, Alta.: Canadian Institute of Ukrainian Studies, 1986.
Bottomore, Tom and Patrick Goode, eds. *Austro-Marxism*. Oxford: Clarendon Press, 1978.
Boudon, Raymond. *The Analysis of Ideology*. Chicago: University of Chicago Press, 1989.
Bourmeyster, Alexandre. "Soviet Political Discourse, Narrative Program and the *Skaz* Theory." In Peter J. Potichnyj, ed., *The Soviet Union: Party and Society*, pp. 87–120. Cambridge: Cambridge University Press, 1988.
Breslauer, George W. "Provincial Party Leaders' Demand Articulation and

230

the Nature of Center-Periphery Relations in the USSR." *Slavic Review* (Winter 1986), 45(4):650–672.

Breuilly, John. *Nationalism and the State*. Manchester: Manchester University Press, 1985.

Brown, Archie and Jack Gray, eds. *Political Culture and Political Change in Communist States*. London: Macmillan, 1977.

Brown, Archie, ed. *Political Culture and Communist Studies*. London: Macmillan, 1984.

Browne, Michael, ed. *Ferment in the Ukraine*. New York: Praeger, 1971.

Brown, Michael and Amy Goldin. *Collective Behavior*. Pacific Palisades, Calif.: Goodyear, 1973.

Broxup, Marie. "The Basmachi." *Central Asian Survey* (July 1983), 2(1):57–82.

Bruchis, Michael. *Nations—Nationalities—Peoples: A Study of the Nationalities Policy of the Communist Party in Soviet Moldavia*. Boulder, Colo.: East European Monographs, 1984.

Brumberg, Abraham, ed. *In Quest of Justice*. New York: Praeger, 1970.

Brunner, Georg and Boris Meissner, eds. *Nationalitätenprobleme in der Sowjetunion und Osteuropa*. Cologne: Markus Verlag, 1982.

Brus, Wlodzimierz. "Political Pluralism and Markets in Communist Systems." In Susan Gross Solomon, ed., *Pluralism in the Soviet Union*, pp. 108-130. New York: St. Martin's Press, 1982.

Brus, Wlodzimierz. *The Economics and Politics of Socialism*. London: Routledge & Kegan Paul, 1973.

Brus, Wlodzimierz. *The Market in a Socialist Economy*. London: Routledge & Kegan Paul, 1972.

Brzezinski, Zbigniew. *The Grand Failure: The Birth and Death of Communism in the Twentieth Century*. New York: Scribner's, 1989.

Buchholz, Arnold, ed. *Soviet and East European Studies in the International Framework: Organization, Financing and Political Relevance*. Dobbs Ferry, N.Y.: Transnational, 1982.

Bunce, Valerie and John M. Echolls, III. "From Soviet Studies to Comparative Politics: The Unfinished Revolution." *Soviet Studies* (January 1979), 31(1):43–55.

Burganov, Agdas. "Giving Up Totalitarian Rule." *News from Ukraine* (September 1988), no. 36, p. 3.

Byrnes, Robert F. "USA: Work at the Universities." *Survey* (January 1964), no. 50, pp. 62–68.

Campbell, Robert. "The Soviet Economic Model." In Seweryn Bialer and Michael Mandelbaum, eds., *Gorbachev's Russia and American Foreign Policy*, pp. 65–96. Boulder, Colo.: Westview, 1988.

Carlsnaes, Walter. *The Concept of Ideology and Political Analysis*. Westport, Conn.: Greenwood Press, 1981.

Carrère d'Encausse, Hélène. *Decline of an Empire: The Soviet Socialist Republics in Revolt*. New York: Newsweek Books, 1979.

Selected Bibliography

Carrère d'Encausse, Hélène. *Islam and the Russian Empire.* Berkeley: University of California Press, 1988.

Carynnyk, Marco, ed. *Alexander Dovzhenko: The Poet as Filmmaker.* Cambridge: MIT Press, 1973.

Chalidze, Valerii. "O prave natsii na samoopredelenie." *SSSR: Vnutrennie protivorechiia* (1981), no. 1, pp. 121–139.

Chalmers, Douglas A. "Interpretive Frameworks: A Structure of Theory in Political Science." Unpublished paper, 1987.

Chilcote, Ronald H. *Theories of Comparative Politics: The Search for a Paradigm.* Boulder, Colo.: Westview, 1981.

Chislennost' i sostav naseleniia SSSR. Moscow: Finansy i statistika, 1984.

Chornovil, Viacheslav. "O mezhnatsional'nykh konfliktakh v Iakutii." *SSSR: Vnutrennie protivorechiia* (1981), no. 1, pp. 269–275.

Chornovil, Vyacheslav. *The Chornovil Papers.* New York: McGraw-Hill, 1968.

Cicero. *On the Good Life.* Harmondsworth, Middlesex: Penguin, 1971.

Cohen, Stephen F. et al., eds. *The Soviet Union Since Stalin.* Bloomington: Indiana University Press, 1980.

Cohen, Stephen F. *Rethinking the Soviet Experience: Politics and History since 1917.* New York: Oxford University Press, 1985.

Colton, Timothy J. *The Dilemma of Reform in the Soviet Union.* New York: Council on Foreign Relations, 1986.

Connor, Walker. "Nationalism and Political Illegitimacy." *Canadian Review of Studies in Nationalism* (Fall 1981), 8(2):201–228.

Connor, Walker. "Nation-Building or Nation-Destroying?" *World Politics* (April 1972), 24(3):319–355.

Connor, Walker. *The National Question in Marxist-Leninist Theory and Strategy.* Princeton: Princeton University Press, 1984.

Connor, Walker. "The Politics of Ethnonationalism." *Journal of International Affairs* (1973), 27(1):1–21.

Connor, Walter D. "Dissent in a Complex Society." *Problems of Communism* (March–April 1973), 22(2):40–52.

Connor, Walter D. *Socialism's Dilemmas: State and Society in the Soviet Bloc.* New York: Columbia University Press, 1988.

Conquest, Robert. "Dissent in the Soviet Union." In Alexander Dallin and Condoleeza Rice, eds., *The Gorbachev Era*, pp. 95–106. Stanford: Stanford Alumni Association, 1986.

Conquest, Robert, ed. *The Last Empire: Nationality and the Soviet Future.* Stanford: Hoover Institution Press, 1986.

Conquest, Robert. *The Harvest of Sorrow: Soviet Collectivization and the Terror-Famine.* Oxford: Oxford University Press, 1986.

Contemporary Soviet Propaganda and Disinformation. Washington, D.C.: Department of State, 1987.

Cookridge, E. H. *Gehlen: Spy of the Century.* New York: Random House, 1971.

Selected Bibliography

Culler, Jonathan. *Ferdinand de Saussure*. Ithaca, N.Y.: Cornell University Press, 1986.

Culler, Jonathan. *On Deconstruction: Theory and Criticism After Structuralism*. Ithaca, N.Y.: Cornell University Press, 1982.

Cummins, Ian. *Marx, Engels and National Movements*. New York: St. Martin's Press, 1980.

Curtis, Michael. *Totalitarianism*. New Brunswick, N.J.: Transaction, 1979.

Dahl, Robert A. *Polyarchy*. New Haven: Yale University Press, 1971.

Dallin, Alexander. *German Rule in Russia, 1941–1945*. London: Macmillan, 1957.

Davies, Norman. *White Eagle, Red Star*. New York: St. Martin's Press, 1972.

Davis, Horace B., ed. *The National Question: Selected Writings by Rosa Luxemburg*. New York: Monthly Review, 1976.

Davis, Horace B. *Nationalism and Socialism*. New York: Monthly Review, 1967.

Denzin, Norman K., ed. *Sociological Methods*. Chicago: Aldine, 1970.

Deutsch, Karl W. "Cracks in the Monolith: Possibilities and Patterns of Disintegration in Totalitarian Systems." In Harry Eckstein and David E. Apter, eds., *Comparative Politics: A Reader*, pp. 497–507. New York: Free Press, 1963.

Deutsch, Karl W. *Nationalism and Social Communication*. Cambridge: MIT Press, 1962.

Dima, Nicholas. *Bessarabia and Bukovina: The Soviet-Romanian Territorial Dispute*. Boulder, Colo.: East European Monographs, 1982.

Dovgopolyi, D. G. "Etnicheskie gruppy SShA vostochnoevropeiskogo proiskhozhdeniia i formirovanie politiki Soedinennykh Shtatov v otnoshenii do sotsialisticheskikh stran." *Vestnik Kievskogo universiteta* (Summer 1978), no. 2, pp. 50–54.

Duncan, Peter J. S. "The Party and Russian Nationalism in the USSR: From Brezhnev to Gorbachev." In Peter J. Potichnyj, ed., *The Soviet Union: Party and Society*, pp. 230–235. Cambridge: Cambridge University Press, 1988.

Dunlop, John B. *The Faces of Contemporary Russian Nationalism*. Princeton: Princeton University Press, 1983.

Dzhirkvelov, Ilya. *Secret Servant: My Life with the KGB and the Soviet Elite*. New York: Harper & Row, 1987.

Dziewanowski, M. K. *Poland in the Twentieth Century*. New York: Columbia University Press, 1977.

Dzyuba, Ivan. *Internationalism or Russification?* New York: Monad Press, 1974.

Easton, David. "The New Revolution in Political Science." *American Political Science Review* (December 1969), 63(4):1051–1061.

Eckstein, Harry. "A Culturalist Theory of Political Change." *American Political Science Review* (September 1988), 82(3):789–804.

Eisenstadt, S. N. "Change in Communist Systems and the Comparative

Analysis of Modern Societies." *Studies in Comparative Communism* (Spring/Summer 1973), 6(1–2):171–183.

Elster, Jon, ed. *Rational Choice*. New York: New York University Press, 1986.

Elster, Jon. *Nuts and Bolts for the Social Sciences*. Cambridge: Cambridge University Press, 1989.

Engels, Frederick. *Germany: Revolution and Counter-Revolution*. New York: International Publishers, 1969.

Ericson, Richard E. "The New Enterprise Law." *Harriman Institute Forum* (February 1988), 1(2):1–8.

Estonian War of Independence, 1918–1920. New York: Eesti Vabadusvoitlejate Liit, 1968.

Evans, Peter B. et al., eds. *Bringing the State Back In*. Cambridge: Cambridge University Press, 1985.

Ezergailis, Andrew. *The Latvian Impact on the Bolshevik Revolution*. Boulder, Colo.: East European Monographs, 1983.

Fajfer, Luba. "The Ukrainian Insurgent Army in Documents." *Problems of Communism* (September–October 1988), 37(5):77–84.

Fanon, Frantz. *The Wretched of the Earth*. New York: Grove Press, 1977.

Farmer, Kenneth C. *Ukrainian Nationalism in the Post-Stalin Era*. The Hague: Martinus Nijhoff, 1980.

Fedyshyn, Oleh S. "The Role of Russians Among the New, Unified 'Soviet People.' " In Edward Allworth, ed., *Ethnic Russia in the USSR*, pp. 149–158. New York: Pergamon Press, 1980.

Fein, Helen. *Accounting for Genocide*. Chicago: University of Chicago Press, 1979.

Feiwell, George R. *The Soviet Quest for Economic Efficiency*. New York: Praeger, 1967.

Feyerabend, Paul. *Against Method*. London: Verso, 1988.

Fisher, Alan W. *The Crimean Tatars*. Stanford: Hoover Institution Press, 1987.

Fiske, Donald W. and Richard A. Schweder, eds. *Metatheory in Social Science*. Chicago: University of Chicago Press, 1986.

Fitzpatrick, Sheila. *The Russian Revolution, 1917–1932*. Oxford: Oxford University Press, 1984.

Fleron, Frederic J., Jr. ed. *Communist Studies and the Social Sciences*. Chicago: Rand McNally, 1969.

Fleron, Frederic J., Jr. "Soviet Area Studies and the Social Sciences: Some Methodological Problems in Communist Studies." *Soviet Studies* (January 1968), 20(3):313–339.

Friedrich, Carl J. and Zbigniew K. Brzezinski. *Totalitarian Dictatorship and Autocracy*. 2d ed. Cambridge: Harvard University Press, 1965.

Galtung, Johan. *Theory and Methods of Social Research*. New York: Columbia University Press, 1969.

Garrett, Stephen A. "Eastern European Ethnic Groups and American

Selected Bibliography

Foreign Policy." *Political Science Quarterly* (Summer 1978), 93(2):301–323.

Gaucher, Roland. *Opposition in the U.S.S.R., 1917–1967*. New York: Funk & Wagnalls, 1969.

Gaukroger, Stephen. *Explanatory Structures*. Hassocks, Sussex: Harvester Press, 1978.

Geertz, Clifford. *Negara. The Theatre State in Nineteenth-Century Bali*. Princeton: Princeton University Press, 1980.

Geertz, Clifford. *The Interpretation of Cultures*. New York: Basic Books, 1973.

Gellner, Ernest. "Nationalism in a Vacuum." In Alexander J. Motyl, ed., *Building Bridges: Soviet Nationalities in Comparative Perspective*, forthcoming.

Gellner, Ernest. *Nations and Nationalism*. Ithaca, N.Y.: Cornell University Press, 1983.

Gellner, Ernest. *Relativism and the Social Sciences*. Cambridge: Cambridge University Press, 1985.

Gellner, Ernest. *Thought and Change*. Chicago: University of Chicago Press, 1964.

Getty, J. Arch. *Origins of the Great Purges: The Soviet Communist Party Reconsidered, 1933–1938*. Cambridge: Cambridge University Press, 1985.

Giddens, Anthony and Jonathan H. Turner, eds. *Social Theory Today*. Cambridge: Polity Press, 1987.

Giddens, Anthony. *The Nation-State and Violence*. Berkeley: University of California Press, 1987.

Gilbert, Martin. *Imperial Russian History Atlas*. London: Routledge & Kegan Paul, 1978.

Gilbert, Martin. *Soviet History Atlas*. London: Routledge & Kegan Paul, 1979.

Girnius, Kestutis K. "The Collectivization of Lithuanian Agriculture, 1944–1950." *Soviet Studies* (July 1988), 40(3):460–478.

Gitelman, Zvi. *Jewish Nationality and Soviet Politics: The Jewish Sections of the CPSU, 1917–1930*. Princeton: Princeton University Press, 1972.

Glazer, Nathan and Daniel P. Moynihan, eds. *Ethnicity. Theory and Experience*. Cambridge: Harvard University Press, 1975.

Gleason, Abbott. "'Totalitarianism' in 1984." *The Russian Review* (April 1984), 43(2):145–159.

Gleason, Gregory. "Prefect or Palladin? Centrist and Nationalist Leaders in Soviet Central Asia." Unpublished paper, November 1987.

Gleason, Gregory. "Sharaf Rashidov and the Dilemmas of National Leadership." *Central Asian Survey* (1986), 5(3/4):133–160.

Goldfarb, Jeffrey C. *Beyond Glasnost: The Post-Totalitarian Mind*. Chicago: University of Chicago Press, 1989.

Goldhagen, Erich, ed. *Ethnic Minorities in the Soviet Union*. New York: Praeger, 1968.

Selected Bibliography

Golinkov, D. L. *Krushenie antisovetskogo podpol'ia v SSSR*. Moscow: Izdatel'stvo politicheskoi literatury, 1978.

Goodin, Robert E. *The Politics of Rational Man*. London: Wiley, 1976.

Gordon, Linda. *Cossack Rebellions: Social Turmoil in the Sixteenth-Century Ukraine*. Albany: State University of New York Press, 1983.

Gouldner, Alvin. "Stalinism: A Study of Internal Colonialism." *Telos* (Winter 1977), no. 34, pp. 5–48.

Grigorenko, Petro G. *Memoirs*. New York: Norton, 1982.

Gross, Jan T. *Revolution from Abroad: The Soviet Conquest of Poland's Western Ukraine and Western Belorussia*. Princeton: Princeton University Press, 1988.

Gunnell, John G. "Deduction, Explanation, and Social Scientific Inquiry." *American Political Science Review* (December 1969), 63(4):1233–1246.

Gurr, Ted Robert. *Why Men Rebel*. Princeton: Princeton University Press, 1970.

Guthier, Steven. "The Popular Base of Ukrainian Nationalism in 1917." *Slavic Review* (March 1979), 38(1):30–47.

Habermas, Jürgen. *Legitimation Crisis*. Boston: Beacon Press, 1975.

Hagopian, Mark N. *Ideals and Ideologies of Modern Politics*. New York: Longman, 1985.

Hagopian, Mark N. *The Phenomenon of Revolution*. New York: Harper & Row, 1974.

Hall, Raymond L. ed. *Ethnic Autonomy—Comparative Dynamics*. New York: Pergamon Press, 1979.

Hammer, Darrell P. "*Glasnost'* and 'The Russian Idea.' " *Russian Nationalism Today*. Radio Liberty Research Bulletin, Special Edition, December 19, 1988, pp. 19–20.

Hammer, Darrell P. *Russian Nationalism and Soviet Politics*. Boulder, Colo.: Westview, 1987.

Hardin, Russell. *Collective Action*. Baltimore: Johns Hopkins University Press, 1982.

Hauslohner, Peter. "The Soviet Transition to Democracy." Unpublished paper, December 1988.

Hayes, Carlton J. H. *Essays on Nationalism*. New York: Russell & Russell, 1966.

Hazard, John N. *Recollections of a Pioneering Sovietologist*. New York: Oceana, 1984.

Hechter, Michael. "Nationalism as Group Solidarity." *Ethnic and Racial Studies* (October 1987), 10(4):415–426.

Hechter, Michael. *Principles of Group Solidarity*. Berkeley: University of California Press, 1988.

Heller, Michail and Alexander Nekrich. *Geschichte der Sowjetunion*. Frankfurt: Fischer Taschenbuch Verlag, 1985.

Selected Bibliography

Herod, Charles C. *The Nation in the History of Marxian Thought*. The Hague: Martinus Nijhoff, 1976.

Hewett, Ed A. *Reforming the Soviet Economy*. Washington, D.C.: Brookings Institution, 1988.

Himka, John-Paul. *Socialism in Galicia*. Cambridge: Harvard Ukrainian Research Institute, 1983.

Hinsley, F. H. *Nationalism and the International System*. London: Hodder and Stoughton, 1973.

Hirschman, Albert O. *Exit, Voice, and Loyalty*. Cambridge: Harvard University Press, 1970.

Hobsbawm, E. J. *Primitive Rebels*. New York: Norton, 1959.

Hobsbawm, E. J. *The Age of Revolution, 1789–1848*. New York: New American Library, 1962.

Hodnett, Grey. *Leadership in the Soviet National Republics*. Oakville, Ontario: Mosaic Press, 1980.

Hofheinz, Roy. "The Ecology of Chinese Communist Success: Rural Influence Patterns, 1923–1945." In A. Doak Barnett, ed., *Chinese Communist Politics in Action*, pp. 3–78. Seattle: University of Washington Press, 1969.

Höhmann, Hans-Hermann et al., eds. *Economics and Politics in the USSR*. Boulder, Colo.: Westview, 1986.

Hollander, Paul. *Political Pilgrims: Travels of Western Intellectuals to the Soviet Union, China, and Cuba*. New York: Harper & Row, 1983.

Homans, George Caspar. "Contemporary Theory in Sociology." In Norman K. Denzin, ed., *Sociological Methods*, pp. 51–69. Chicago: Aldine, 1970.

Hook, Sidney. *Revolution, Reform, and Social Justice*. New York: New York University Press, 1975.

Hook, Sidney. *The Hero in History*. Boston: Beacon Press, 1955.

Horlenko, Mykola. *Fake Patriots*. Odessa: Mayak, 1983.

Horowitz, Donald L. *Ethnic Groups in Conflict*. Berkeley: University of California Press, 1985.

Hough, Jerry F. and Merle Fainsod. *How the Soviet Union Is Governed*. Cambridge: Harvard University Press, 1979.

Hough, Jerry F. *Russia and the West: Gorbachev and the Politics of Reform*. New York: Simon & Schuster, 1988.

Hough, Jerry F. *The Soviet Prefects*. Cambridge: Harvard University Press, 1969.

Hovannisian, Richard G. *The Republic of Armenia*. Vol. 1. Berkeley: University of California Press, 1971.

Howard, Dick. *Defining the Political*. Minneapolis: University of Minnesota Press, 1989.

Hunchak, Taras and Roman Sol'chanyk, eds. *Ukrains'ka suspil'no-politychna dumka v 20 stolitti*. Vol. 1. New York: Suchasnist, 1983.

237

Selected Bibliography

Hunchak, Taras, ed. *UPA v svitli nimets'kykh dokumentiv*. Toronto: Litopys UPA, 1983.

Hunczak, Taras, ed. *Russian Imperialism from Ivan the Great to the Revolution*. New Brunswick, N.J.: Rutgers University Press, 1974.

Hunczak, Taras, ed. *The Ukraine, 1917–1921: A Study in Revolution*. Cambridge: Harvard Ukrainian Research Institute, 1977.

Hunt, Chester L. "The Sociology of Religion." In Joseph S. Roucek, ed., *Contemporary Sociology*, pp. 539–555. New York: Philosophical Library, 1958.

Huntington, Samuel P. *Political Order in Changing Societies*. New Haven: Yale University Press, 1968.

Ilnytzkyj, Roman. *The Free Press of the Suppressed Nations*. Augsburg, West Germany: Association of the Free Press, 1950.

Investigation of the Ukrainian Famine, 1932–1933. Washington, D.C.: Government Printing Office, 1988.

Ionin, L. G. " . . . I vozzovet proshedshee (razmyshleniia sotsiologa o novom fil'me T. Abuladze." *Sotsiologicheskie issledovaniia* (May–June 1987), no. 3, pp. 62–72.

Isaak, Alan C. *Scope and Methods of Political Science*. Homewood, Ill.: Dorsey Press, 1985.

Isajiw, Wsevolod. "Urban Migration and Social Change in Contemporary Soviet Ukraine." *Canadian Slavonic Papers* (March 1980), 22(1):56–66.

Ivinskis, Zenonas. "Lithuania During the War: Resistance Against the Soviet and Nazi Occupants." In V. Stanley Vardys, ed., *Lithuania Under the Soviets*, pp. 61–84. New York: Praeger, 1965.

Johnson, Chalmers, ed. *Change in Communist Systems*. Stanford: Stanford University Press, 1970.

Johnson, Chalmers. *Revolutionary Change*. 2d ed. Stanford: Stanford University Press, 1982.

Jones, Ellen and Fred W. Grupp. "Modernisation and Ethnic Equalisation in the USSR." *Soviet Studies* (April 1984), 36(2):159–184.

Jones, Stephen. "The Establishment of Soviet Power in Transcaucasia: The Case of Georgia, 1921–1928." *Soviet Studies* (October 1988), 40(4):616–639.

Jowitt, Kenneth. "Soviet Neo-Traditionalism: The Political Corruption of a Leninist Regime." *Soviet Studies* (July 1983), 35(3):275–297.

Kamenetsky, Ihor, ed. *Nationalism and Human Rights*. Littleton, Colo.: Libraries Unlimited, 1977.

Kaminski, Bartlomiej. "The Anatomy of the Directive Capacity of the Socialist State." *Comparative Political Studies* (April 1989), 22(1):66–92.

Kamins'kyi, Anatol'. *Krai, emigratsiia i mizhnarodni zakulisy*. Manchester: Politychna Rada OUNz, 1982.

Kanet, Roger E., ed. *The Behavioral Revolution and Communist Studies*. New York: Free Press, 1971.

Kanet, Roger E. "The Rise and Fall of the 'All-People's State': Recent

Selected Bibliography

Changes in the Soviet Theory of the State." *Soviet Studies* (July 1968), 20(1):81–93.

Kann, Robert A. *Das Nationalitätenproblem der Habsburgermonarchie*. Vienna: Bohlaus Nachfolger, 1964.

Karklins, Rasma. *Ethnic Relations in the USSR*. Boston: Allen & Unwin, 1986.

Katz, Zev, ed. *Handbook of Major Soviet Nationalities*. New York: Free Press, 1975.

Kautsky, John H. "Comparative Communism Versus Comparative Politics." *Studies in Comparative Communism* (Spring/Summer 1973), 6(1–2):135–170.

Keane, John, ed. *Civil Society and the State*. London: Verso, 1988.

Kedourie, Elie. *Nationalism*. London: Hutchinson, 1979.

Keep, John L. H. *The Russian Revolution: A Study in Mass Mobilization*. New York: Norton, 1976.

Kerblay, Basile. *Modern Soviet Society*. New York: Pantheon, 1983.

Kimber, Richard. "Collective Action and the Fallacy of the Liberal Fallacy." *World Politics* (January 1981), 33(2):178–196.

Kirby, D. G. *Finland in the Twentieth Century*. London: C. Hurst, 1979.

Klosko, George. "Rebellious Collective Action Revisited." *American Political Science Review* (June 1987), 81(2):557–560.

Knight, Amy W. "The KGB and Soviet Reform." *Problems of Communism* (September–October 1988), 37(5):61–70.

Knight, Amy W. *The KGB*. Boston: Allen & Unwin, 1988.

Knightley, Philip. *The Master Spy: The Story of Kim Philby*. New York: Knopf, 1989.

Kohn, Hans. "Soviet Communism and Nationalism: Three Stages of a Historical Development." In Edward Allworth, ed., *Soviet Nationality Problems*, pp. 43–71. New York: Columbia University Press, 1971.

Kohut, Zenon E. *Russian Centralism and Ukrainian Autonomy*. Cambridge: Harvard Ukrainian Research Institute, 1988.

Kolakowski, Leszek. *The Presence of Myth*. Chicago: University of Chicago Press, 1989.

Kolarz, Walter. *Russia and Her Colonies*. New York: Praeger, 1952.

Kostiuk, Hryhory. *Stalinist Rule in the Ukraine*. New York: Praeger, 1960.

Kowalewski, David and Cheryl Johnson. "The Ukrainian Dissident: A Statistical Profile." *Ukrainian Quarterly* (Spring 1984), 40(1):50–65.

Krasnov, Vladislav. "Russian National Feeling: An Informal Poll." In Robert Conquest, ed., *The Last Empire: Nationality and the Soviet Future*, pp. 109–130. Stanford: Hoover Institution Press, 1986.

Krawchenko, Bohdan. *Social Change and National Consciousness in Twentieth-Century Ukraine*. New York: St. Martin's Press, 1985.

Krawchenko, Bohdan. "The Social Structure of the Ukraine at the Turn of the 20th Century." *East European Quarterly* (June 1982), 16(2):171–181.

Selected Bibliography

Kuhn, Thomas S. *The Structure of Scientific Revolutions*. 2d ed. Chicago: University of Chicago Press, 1970.

Lacey, A. R. *A Dictionary of Philosophy*. New York: Scribner's, 1976.

Laitin, David D. *Hegemony and Culture*. Chicago: University of Chicago Press, 1986.

Laitin, David D. "Language Games." *Comparative Politics* (April 1988), 20(3):289–302.

Lakatos, Imre. "Falsification and the Methodology of Scientific Research Programmes." In Imre Lakatos and Alan Musgrave, eds., *Criticism and the Growth of Knowledge*, pp. 91–196. Cambridge: Cambridge University Press, 1970.

Landau, Martin. *Political Theory and Political Science*. New York: Macmillan, 1972.

Lan, David. *Guns and Rain: Guerrillas and Spirit Mediums in Zimbabwe*. London: James Currey, 1985.

Lane, David. *Politics and Society in the USSR*. 2d ed. New York: New York University Press, 1978.

Lang, David Marshall. *A Modern History of Soviet Georgia*. New York: Grove Press, 1962.

LaPalombara, Joseph. "Monoliths or Plural Systems: Through Conceptual Lens Darkly." *Studies in Comparative Communism* (Autumn 1975), 8(3):305–332.

Laqueur, Walter. *Guerrilla*. London: Weidenfeld & Nicolson, 1977.

Laqueur, Walter. "In Search of Russia." *Survey* (January 1964), no. 50, pp. 41–52.

Laqueur, Walter. *The Fate of the Revolution*. New York: Collier Books, 1987.

Leninism and the National Question. Moscow: Progress, 1977.

Lenin, V. I. *Selected Works*. New York: International Publishers, 1976.

Lesinskis, Imants. "Cultural Relations or Ethnic Espionage: An Insider's View." *Baltic Forum* (Spring 1985), 2(1):1–29.

Letter to a Russian Friend: A Samizdat Publication from Soviet Byelorussia. London: Association of Byelorussians in Great Britain, 1979.

Lewin, Moshe. *The Making of the Soviet System*. New York: Pantheon, 1985.

Lewis, David K. *Convention*. Cambridge: Harvard University Press, 1969.

Lewis, E. Glyn. *Multilingualism in the Soviet Union*. The Hague: Mouton, 1972.

Lewis, Robert A. and Richard H. Rowland. *Population Redistribution in the USSR*. New York: Praeger, 1979.

Lewytzkyj, Borys. *Die sowjetische Nationalitätenpolitik nach Stalins Tod (1953–1970)*. Munich: Ukrainische Freie Universität, 1970.

Lewytzkyj, Borys. *Politics and Society in Soviet Ukraine, 1953–1980*. Edmonton, Alta.: Canadian Institute of Ukrainian Studies, 1984.

Lewytzkyj, Borys. *"Sovetskij narod"—"Das Sowjetvolk."* Hamburg: Hoffmann und Campe, 1983.

Selected Bibliography

Liber, George. "Ukrainian Nationalism and the 1918 Law on National-Personal Autonomy." *Nationalities Papers* (Spring 1987), 15(1):22–42.

Lindblom, Charles. *Politics and Markets*. New York: Basic Books, 1977.

Linden, Carl A. et al., eds. *Nationalities and Nationalism in the USSR: A Soviet Dilemma*. Washington, D.C.: Center for Strategic and International Studies, 1977.

Linz, Juan. *Crisis, Breakdown, and Reequilibration*. Baltimore: Johns Hopkins University Press, 1978.

Linz, Juan. "Totalitarian and Authoritarian Regimes." In Fred Greenstein and Nelson Polsby, eds., *Handbook of Political Science*, vol. 3, pp. 175–411. Reading, Penn.: Addison-Wesley, 1975.

Lipset, Seymour Martin. *Political Man: The Social Bases of Politics*. Garden City, N.Y.: Anchor Books, 1963.

Low, Alfred D. *Lenin on the Question of Nationality*. New York: Bookman, 1958.

Löwy, Michael. "Marxism and the National Question." In Robin Blackburn, ed., *Revolution and Class Struggle*, pp. 136–160. Hassocks, Sussex: Harvester Press, 1978.

Lubachko, Ivan S. *Belorussia Under Soviet Rule, 1917–1957*. Lexington: University of Kentucky Press, 1972.

Lubarsky, Cronid. "Soziale Basis und Umfang des sowjetischen Dissidententums." *Osteuropa* (November 1979), 29(11):923–935.

Lubin, Nancy. *Labour and Nationality in Soviet Central Asia*. London: Macmillan, 1984.

Lustick, Ian. "Stability in Deeply Divided Societies: Consociationalism versus Control." *World Politics* (April 1979), 32(3):324–344.

Mace, James E. *Communism and the Dilemmas of National Liberation: National Communism in Soviet Ukraine, 1918–1933*. Cambridge: Harvard Ukrainian Research Institute, 1983.

Mace, James E. "Famine and Nationalism in Soviet Ukraine." *Problems of Communism* (May–June 1984), 33(3):37–50.

Majstrenko, Iwan. *Borot'bism: A Chapter in the History of Ukrainian Communism*. New York: Research Program on the USSR, 1954.

Mannheim, Karl. *Ideology and Utopia*. New York: Harcourt, Brace & World, 1936.

Marczewski, Jan. *Crisis in Socialist Planning*. New York: Praeger, 1976.

Marighella, Carlos. "Minimanual of the Urban Guerrilla." In James Kohl and John Litt, eds., *Urban Guerrilla Warfare in Latin America*, pp. 87–135. Cambridge: MIT Press, 1974.

Marples, David R. "The Soviet Collectivization of Western Ukraine, 1948–1949." *Nationalities Papers* (Spring 1985), 13(1):25–44.

Marples, David R. "Western Ukraine and Western Belorussia Under Soviet Occupation: The Development of Socialist Farming, 1939–1941." *Canadian Slavonic Papers* (June 1985), 27(2):156–177.

Selected Bibliography

Marx, Karl and Friedrich Engels. *Ireland and the Irish Question*. Moscow: Progress, 1978.

Matossian, Mary Kilbourne. "Communist Rule and the Changing Armenian Cultural Pattern." In Erich Goldhagen, ed., *Ethnic Minorities in the Soviet Union*, pp. 185–197. New York: Praeger, 1968.

Mawdsley, Evan. *The Russian Civil War*. Boston: Allen & Unwin, 1987.

Mayer, Arno J. *Dynamics of Counterrevolution in Europe, 1870–1956*. New York: Harper & Row, 1971.

Mayer, Lawrence C. *Redefining Comparative Politics: Promise Versus Performance*. Newbury Park, Calif.: Sage, 1989.

Mazlakh, Serhii and Vasyl' Shakhrai. *On the Current Situation in the Ukraine*. Ann Arbor: University of Michigan Press, 1970.

McAuley, Mary. "Nationalism and the Soviet Multi-ethnic State." In Neil Harding, ed., *The State in Socialist Society*, pp. 179–210. Albany: State University of New York Press, 1984.

McAuley, Mary. "Soviet Political Reform in a Comparative Context." *Harriman Institute Forum* (October 1989), 2(10):1–8.

Meadwell, Hudson. "Ethnic Nationalism and Collective Choice Theory." *Comparative Political Studies* (July 1989), 22(2):139–154.

Medish, Vadim. "Special Status of the RSFSR." In Edward Allworth, ed., *Ethnic Russia in the USSR*, pp. 188–196. New York: Pergamon Press, 1980.

Merton, Thomas. *The Seven Storey Mountain*. New York: Harcourt Brace Jovanovich, 1948.

Merton, Thomas. *The Sign of Jonas*. New York: Harcourt Brace Jovanovich, 1953.

Meyer, Alfred G. "Coming to Terms with the Past . . . And with One's Older Colleagues." *The Russian Review* (October 1986), 45(4):401–408.

Meyer, Alfred G. *The Soviet Political System*. New York: Random House, 1965.

Migdal, Joel S. *Peasants, Politics, and Revolution*. Princeton: Princeton University Press, 1974.

Migranian, A. M. "Vzaimootnoshenie individa, obshchestva i gosudarstva v politicheskoi teorii marksizma i problemy demokratizatsii sotsialisticheskogo obshchestva." *Voprosy filozofii* (1987), no. 8, pp. 75–91.

Migranyan, A. "The Long Road to the European Home." *Current Digest of the Soviet Press* (November 15, 1980), 41(42):6–9, 32.

Mihajlov, Mihajlo. "Mystical Experiences of the Labor Camps." *Kontinent*, no. 2, pp. 103–132. Garden City, N.Y.: Anchor Books, 1977.

Millar, James R., ed. *Politics, Work, and Daily Life in the USSR*. Cambridge: Cambridge University Press, 1987.

Millar, James R. *The ABC's of Soviet Socialism*. Urbana: University of Illinois Press, 1981.

Mills, C. Wright. *The Sociological Imagination*. London: Oxford University Press, 1959.

Selected Bibliography

Minogue, K. R. *Nationalism*. London: Batsford, 1967.

Misiunas, Romuald J. and Rein Taagepera. *The Baltic States: Years of Dependence, 1940–1980*. Berkeley: University of California Press, 1983.

Mockunas, Liutas. "The Dynamics of Lithuanian Émigré-Homeland Relations." *Baltic Forum* (Spring 1985), 2(1):50–69.

Montias, J. M. "Modernization in Communist Countries: Some Questions of Methodology." *Studies in Comparative Communism* (Winter 1972), 5(4):413–427.

Moore, Barrington, Jr. *Injustice: The Social Bases of Obedience and Revolt*. White Plains, N.Y.: M.E. Sharpe, 1978.

Moroz, Valentyn. *Report from the Beria Reserve*. Chicago: Cataract Press, 1974.

Moskovs'ki vbyvtsi Bandery pered sudom. Munich: Ukrains'ke vydavnytstvo, 1965.

Motyl, Alexander J. "Policing Perestroika: The Indispensable KGB." *Harriman Institute Forum* (August 1989), 2(8):1–8.

Motyl, Alexander J. "Reassessing the Soviet Crisis: Big Problems, Muddling Through, Business as Usual." *Political Science Quarterly* (Summer 1989), 104(2):269–280.

Motyl, Alcxander J. "'Sovietology in One Country' or Comparative Nationality Studies?" *Slavic Review* (Spring 1989), 48(1):83–88.

Motyl, Alexander J. "The Foreign Relations of the Ukrainian SSR." *Harvard Ukrainian Studies* (March 1982), 6(1):62–78.

Motyl, Alexander J. "The Rural Origins of the Communist and Nationalist Movements in Wolyn Wojewodztwo, 1921–1939." *Slavic Review* (September 1978), 37(3):412–420.

Motyl, Alexander J. "The Sobering of Gorbachev: Nationality, Restructuring, and the West." In Seweryn Bialer, ed., *Politics, Society, and Nationality Inside Gorbachev's Russia*, pp. 149–174. Boulder, Colo.: Westview, 1989.

Motyl, Alexander J. *The Turn to the Right: The Ideological Origins and Development of Ukrainian Nationalism, 1919–1929*. Boulder, Colo.: East European Monographs, 1980.

Motyl, Alexander J. "Ukrainian Nationalist Political Violence in Inter-War Poland, 1921–1939." *East European Quarterly* (Spring 1985), 19(1):45–55.

Motyl, Alexander J. *Will the Non-Russians Rebel? State, Ethnicity, and Stability in the USSR*. Ithaca, N.Y.: Cornell University Press, 1987.

Muller, Edward M. and Karl-Dieter Opp. "Rational Choice and Rebellious Collective Action." *American Political Science Review* (June 1986), 80(2):471–488.

Nagel, Ernst. *The Structure of Science: Problems in the Logic of Scientific Explanation*. 2d ed. Indianapolis: Hackett, 1977.

Narizhnyi, Symon. *Ukrains'ka emigratsiia*. Prague: Musei vyzvol'noi borot'by Ukrainy, 1942.

Selected Bibliography

"Natsional'naia politika partii v sovremennykh usloviiakh (platforma KPSS). Priniata Plenumom TsK KPSS 20 sentiabria 1989 goda." *Pravda,* September 24, 1989, pp. 1–2.

Nielsen, Francois. "Toward a Theory of Ethnic Solidarity in Modern Societies." *American Sociological Review* (April 1985), 50(2):133–149.

Nietzsche, Friedrich. *On the Genealogy of Morals and Ecce Homo.* New York: Vintage, 1969.

Nissman, David B. *The Soviet Union and Iranian Azerbaijan.* Boulder, Colo.: Westview, 1987.

North, Douglass. "A Neoclassical Theory of the State." In Jon Elster, ed., *Rational Choice,* pp. 248–260. New York: New York University Press, 1986.

Nove, Alec. *Political Economy and Soviet Socialism.* London: Allen & Unwin, 1979.

Nove, Alec. *Stalinism and After: The Road to Gorbachev.* 3rd ed. Boston: Unwin Hyman, 1989.

Oberschall, Anthony. *Social Conflict and Social Movements.* Englewood Cliffs, N.J.: Prentice-Hall, 1973.

O'Connor, James. *The Meaning of Crisis.* Oxford: Basil Blackwell, 1987.

Olcott, Martha B. "The Basmachi or Freemen's Revolt in Turkestan, 1918–24." *Soviet Studies* (July 1981), 33(3):352–369.

Olcott, Martha Brill. *The Kazakhs.* Stanford: Hoover Institution Press, 1987.

Olson, Mancur. *The Logic of Collective Action.* Cambridge: Harvard University Press, 1965.

Olson, Mancur. *The Rise and Decline of Nations.* New Haven: Yale University Press, 1982.

Olzak, Susan. "Ethnicity and Theories of Ethnic Collective Behavior." *Research in Social Movements, Conflicts and Change,* vol. 8, pp. 64–85. Greenwich, Conn.: JAI Press, 1985.

Osadchy, Mykhailo. *Cataract.* New York: Harcourt Brace Jovanovich, 1976.

Outhwaite, William. *Concept Formation in Social Science.* London: Routledge & Kegan Paul, 1983.

Page, Bruce, et al. *The Philby Conspiracy.* New York: Ballantine, 1981.

Parming, Tönu and Elmar Jarvesoo, eds. *A Case Study of a Soviet Republic: The Estonian SSR.* Boulder, Colo.: Westview, 1978.

Parming, Tönu. "The Soviet Union and the Émigré Communities: A Case Study in Active Measures and Disinformation." *Contemporary Soviet Propaganda and Disinformation,* pp. 309–328. Washington, D.C.: Department of State, 1987.

Patterson, Orlando. *Ethnic Chauvinism.* New York: Stein and Day, 1977.

Penikis, Janis. "Activism in Latvia 1988." *Occasional Papers on Baltic Political Action* (September 1988), no. 2/3, pp. 24–31.

Pierce, Richard A. *Russian Central Asia, 1867–1917.* Berkeley: University of California Press, 1960.

Pipes, Richard. *The Formation of the Soviet Union*. New York: Atheneum, 1974.

Piven, Frances Fox and Richard A. Cloward. *Poor People's Movements: Why They Succeed, How They Fail*. New York: Vintage, 1979.

Plyushch, Leonid. *History's Carnival*. New York: Harcourt Brace Jovanovich, 1979.

Poltava, P. "Preparatory Steps Toward the Third World War and the Tasks of the Ukrainian People." In Peter J. Potichnyj and Yevhen Shtendera, eds., *Political Thought of the Ukrainian Underground, 1943–1951*, pp. 263–282. Edmonton, Alta.: Canadian Institute of Ukrainian Studies, 1986.

Pomerants, G. "Pluralism or Empire?" *Glasnost* (1987), no. 12, pp. 4–7.

Pond, Elizabeth. *From the Yaroslavsky Station*. New York: Universe Books, 1988.

Popkin, Samuel. *The Rational Peasant: The Political Economy of Revolution in Vietnam*. Berkeley: University of California Press, 1979.

Popper, Karl. *The Logic of Scientific Discovery*. New York: Harper & Row, 1965.

Popper, Karl. *The Poverty of Historicism*. New York: Harper & Row, 1961.

Potichnyj, Peter J. and Yevhen Shtendera, eds. *Political Thought of the Ukrainian Underground, 1943–1951*. Edmonton, Alta.: Canadian Institute of Ukrainian Studies, 1986.

Potichnyj, Peter J., ed. *The Soviet Union: Party and Society*. Cambridge: Cambridge University Press, 1988.

Potichnyj, Peter J. "Ukrainians in World War II Military Formations: An Overview." In Yury Boshyk, ed., *Ukraine During World War II*, pp. 61–88. Edmonton, Alta.: Canadian Institute of Ukrainian Studies, 1986.

Present-Day Ethnic Processes in the USSR. Moscow: Progress, 1982.

Przeworski, Adam. "Marxism and Rational Choice." *Politics and Society* (1985), 14(4):379–409.

Quattrone, George A. and Amos Tversky. "Contrasting Rational and Psychological Analyses of Political Choice." *American Political Science Review* (September 1988), 82(3):719–736.

Quine, W. V. *From a Logical Point of View*. Cambridge: Harvard University Press, 1953.

Quine, W. V. *Quiddities: An Intermittently Philosophical Dictionary*. Cambridge: Belknap Press, 1987.

Quine, W. V. *Theories and Things*. Cambridge: Belknap Press, 1981.

Rabinowitch, Alexander. *The Bolsheviks Come to Power*. New York: Norton, 1976.

Raeff, Marc. "Patterns of Russian Imperial Policy Toward the Nationalities." In Edward Allworth, ed., *Soviet Nationality Problems*, pp. 22–42. New York: Columbia University Press, 1971.

Rakowska-Harmstone, Teresa. "Islam and Nationalism: Central Asia and

Kazakhstan Under Soviet Rule." *Central Asian Survey* (September 1983), 2(2):7–87.

Rasiak, Ruslan O. "'The Soviet People': Multiethnic Alternative or Ruse?" In Edward Allworth, ed., *Ethnic Russia in the USSR*, pp. 159–171. New York: Pergamon Press, 1980.

Raun, Toivo U. *Estonia and the Estonians*. Stanford: Hoover Institution Press, 1987.

Reddaway, Peter. "Is the Soviet Union Drifting Towards Anarchy?" *Report on the USSR* (August 25, 1989), pp. 1–5.

Reddaway, Peter. "Policy Towards Dissent Since Khrushchev." In T. H. Rigby et al., eds., *Authority, Power and Policy in the USSR*, pp. 158–192. London: Macmillan, 1983.

Reddaway, Peter. "Soviet Policies on Dissent and Emigration: The Radical Change of Course Since 1979." *Occasional Paper*, No. 192. Washington, D.C.: Kennan Institute, August 28, 1984.

Rejai, Mostafa with Kay Phillips. *Leaders of Revolution*. Beverly Hills, Calif.: Sage, 1979.

Remeikis, Thomas and Bronius Nainys, eds. *The Violations of Human Rights in Soviet Occupied Lithuania: A Report for 1978*. Glenside, Penn.: Lithuanian American Community, 1979.

Reshetar, John. *The Ukrainian Revolution, 1917–1920*. Princeton: Princeton University Press, 1952.

Ricci, David M. *The Tragedy of Political Science: Politics, Scholarship, and Democracy*. New Haven: Yale University Press, 1984.

Rice, Condoleeza. "Gorbachev and the Military: A Revolution in Security Policy, Too?" *Harriman Institute Forum* (April 1989), 2(4):1–8.

Rigby, T. H. et al., eds. *Authority, Power and Policy in the USSR*. London: Macmillan, 1983.

Ritter, William S. "The Final Phase in the Liquidation of Anti-Soviet Resistance in Tadzhikistan: Ibrahim Bek and the *Basmachi*, 1924–31." *Soviet Studies* (October 1985), 37(4):484–493.

Rokeach, Milton, ed. *Understanding Human Values*. New York: Free Press, 1979.

Roos, Aarand, ed. *Estonia: A Nation Unconquered*. Baltimore: Estonian World Council, 1985.

Rorlich, Azade-Ayse. *The Volga Tatars: A Profile in National Resilience*. Stanford: Hoover Institution Press, 1986.

Rosenberg, Alexander. *Philosophy of Social Science*. Boulder, Colo.: Westview, 1988.

Ross, Jeffrey A. et al., eds. *The Mobilization of Collective Identity: Comparative Perspectives*. Lanham, Maryland: University Press of America, 1980.

Roth, Paul A. *Meaning and Method in the Social Sciences*. Ithaca., N.Y.: Cornell University Press, 1987.

Selected Bibliography

Rothschild, Joseph. *East Central Europe Between the Two World Wars*. Seattle: University of Washington Press, 1974.

Rothschild, Joseph. *Ethnopolitics*. New York: Columbia University Press, 1981.

Rothschild, Joseph. *Return to Diversity: A Political History of East Central Europe Since World War II*. Oxford: Oxford University Press, 1989.

Rumer, Boris Z. *Soviet Central Asia*. Boston: Unwin Hyman, 1989.

Russian Nationalism Today. Radio Liberty Research Bulletin, Special Edition, December 19, 1988.

Rybalka, L. "The Russian Social Democrats and the National Question." *Journal of Ukrainian Studies* (Spring 1982), 7(1):52–78.

Rywkin, Michael, ed. *Russian Colonial Expansion to 1917*. London: Mansell, 1988.

Rywkin, Michael. *Moscow's Muslim Challenge*. Armonk, N.Y.: M.E. Sharpe, 1982.

Salert, Barbara. *Revolutions and Revolutionaries*. New York: Elsevier, 1976.

Salitan, Laurie. "Soviet Emigration Policy: The Case of Jews and Germans." Unpublished paper, n.d.

Sartori, Giovanni, ed. *Social Science Concepts*. Beverly Hills, Calif.: Sage, 1984.

Sartori, Giovanni. "Soviet Studies: A Scheme for Analysis." Unpublished paper, February 1988.

Sautman, Barry. "Retreat from Revolution: Why Communist Systems Deradicalize." Ph.D. dissertation, Columbia University, 1989.

Sawczuk, Konstantyn. *The Ukraine in the United Nations Organization*. Boulder, Colo.: East European Quarterly, 1975.

Schapiro, Leonard. *Russian Studies*. New York: Penguin Books, 1988.

Schapiro, Leonard. *Totalitarianism*. New York: Praeger, 1972.

Schlesinger, Rudolf. *The Nationality Problem and Soviet Administration*. London: Routledge & Kegan Paul, 1956.

Schroeder, Gertrude E. "The State-run Economy: Stability or Ossification? An Essay on the Soviet Production System." In Terry L. Thompson and Richard Sheldon, eds., *Soviet Society and Culture*, pp. 239–253. Boulder, Colo.: Westview, 1988.

Schulte, Theo. *The German Army and Nazi Policies in Occupied Russia*. Oxford: Berg, 1989.

Schurmann, Franz. "Politics and Economics in Russia and China." In Donald W. Treadgold, ed., *Soviet and Chinese Communism: Similarities and Differences*, pp. 297–326. Seattle: University of Washington Press, 1967.

Schweder, Richard A. and Robert A. LeVine, eds. *Culture Theory*. Cambridge: Cambridge University Press, 1981.

Schweder, Richard A. "Divergent Rationalities." In Donald W. Fiske and

Selected Bibliography

Richard A. Schweder, eds., *Metatheory in Social Science*, pp. 163–196. Chicago: University of Chicago Press, 1986.

Scott, James C. *The Moral Economy of the Peasant*. New Haven: Yale University Press, 1979.

Selucky, Radoslav. *Economic Reforms in Eastern Europe*. New York: Praeger, 1972.

Shafarevich, Igor. "Separation or Reconciliation? The Nationalities Question in the USSR." In Alexander Solzhenitsyn et al., *From under the Rubble*, pp. 88–104. Boston: Little, Brown, 1975.

Shapiro, Michael J. "Rational Political Man: A Synthesis of Economic and Social-Psychological Perspectives." *American Political Science Review* (December 1969), 63(4):1106–1119.

Sheremet, Yevhen. *Ukrainians by Profession*. Kiev: Ukraina Society, 1981.

Sherlock, Thomas. "Politics and History Under Gorbachev." *Problems of Communism* (May–August 1988), 37(3–4):16–42.

Shtromas, Aleksandras. "On the Current Situation in Lithuania." *Occasional Papers on Baltic Political Action* (September 1988), no. 2/3, pp. 16–23.

Shtromas, Alexander. "How the End of the Soviet System May Come About: Historical Precedents and Possible Scenarios." In Alexander Shtromas and Morton A. Kaplan, eds., *The Soviet Union and the Challenge of the Future*, vol. 1, pp. 201–300. New York: Paragon House, 1988.

Shumuk, Danylo. *Life Sentence*. Edmonton, Alta.: Canadian Institute of Ukrainian Studies, 1984

Silver, Brian D. "Social Mobilization and the Russification of Soviet Nationalities." *American Political Science Review* (March 1974), 68(1):45–66.

Simon, Herbert A. "Human Nature in Politics: The Dialogue of Psychology with Political Science." *American Political Science Review* (June 1985), 79(2): 293–303.

Skilling, H. Gordon and Franklyn Griffiths, eds. *Interest Groups in Soviet Politics*. Princeton: Princeton University Press, 1971.

Skocpol, Theda. "Rentier State and Shi'a Islam in the Iranian Revolution." *Theory and Society* (May 1982), 11(3):265–83.

Skocpol, Theda. *States and Social Revolutions*. Cambridge: Cambridge University Press, 1979.

Skocpol, Theda. "What Makes Peasants Revolutionary?" *Comparative Politics* (April 1982), 14(3):351–375.

Smith, Anthony D., ed. *Nationalist Movements*. London: Macmillan, 1976.

Smith, Anthony D. "Nationalism, Ethnic Separatism and the Intelligentsia." In Colin H. Williams, ed., *National Separatism*, pp. 17–41. Cardiff: University of Wales Press, 1982.

Smith, Anthony D. *The Ethnic Origins of Nations*. Oxford: Basil Blackwell, 1986.

Selected Bibliography

Smith, Anthony D. *Theories of Nationalism*. London: Duckworth, 1971.

Smith, Hedrick. *The Russians*. New York: Quadrangle, 1976.

Snyder, Jack. "Richness, Rigor, and Relevance in the Study of Soviet Foreign Policy." *International Security* (Winter 1984/1985), 9(3):89–108.

Snyder, Jack. "Science and Sovietology: Bridging the Methods Gap in Soviet Foreign Policy Studies." *World Politics* (January 1988), 40(2):169–193.

Solomon, Susan Gross, ed. *Pluralism in the Soviet Union*. New York: St. Martin's Press, 1983.

Solzhenitsyn, Aleksandr. "Misconceptions about Russia Are a Threat to America." *Foreign Affairs* (Spring 1980), 58(4):797–834.

Solzhenitsyn, Aleksandr. *Pis'mo vozhdiam Sovetskogo Soiuza*. Paris: YMCA Press, 1974.

Solzhenitsyn, Alexander et al. *From Under the Rubble*. Boston: Little, Brown, 1975.

Sosnovs'kyi, Mykhailo. *Mizh optymizmom i pesymizmom*. New York: Trident International, 1979.

Spragens, Thomas A., Jr. *The Dilemma of Contemporary Political Theory*. New York: Dunellen, 1973.

Stashkevich, N. S. *Prigovor revoliutsii: Krushenie antisovetskogo dvizheniia v Belorussii 1917–1925*. Minsk: Universitetskoe, 1985.

Steiner, George. *Real Presences*. Chicago: University of Chicago Press, 1989.

Stinchcombe, Arthur L. *Constructing Social Theories*. Chicago: University of Chicago Press, 1968.

Stokes, Gail. "The Undeveloped Theory of Nationalism." *World Politics* (October 1978), 31(1):150–160.

Styrkul, Valery. *Up a Blind Alley*. Kiev: Dnipro, 1986.

Styrkul, V. *The SS Werewolves*. L'viv: Kamenyar, 1982.

Subtelny, Orest. *Ukraine: A History*. University of Toronto Press, 1988.

Sullivant, Robert S. *Soviet Politics and the Ukraine, 1917–1957*. New York: Columbia University Press, 1962.

Sultan-Galiev, M. S. *Stat'i*. Oxford: Society for Central Asian Studies, n.d.

Suny, Ronald Grigor, ed. *Transcaucasia: Nationalism and Social Change*. Ann Arbor: University of Michigan Press, 1983.

Suny, Ronald Grigor. *The Making of the Georgian Nation*. Bloomington: Indiana University Press, 1988.

Swietochowski, Tadeusz. "Soviet Azerbaijan Today: The Problems of Group Identity." *Occasional Paper*, No. 211. Washington, D.C.: Kennan Institute, July 1986.

Symmons-Symonolewicz, Konstantin. *Modern Nationalism: Towards a Consensus in Theory*. New York: Polish Institute of Arts and Sciences in America, 1968.

Symmons-Symonolewicz, Konstantin. "The Concept of Nationhood: Toward a Theoretical Clarification." *Canadian Review of Studies in Nationalism* (1985), 11(2):215–222.

Szporluk, Roman, ed. *The Influence of East Europe and the Soviet West on the USSR*. New York: Praeger, 1976.

Szporluk, Roman. *Nationalism and Communism*. Oxford: Oxford University Press, 1988.

Szporluk, Roman. "West Ukraine and West Belorussia." *Soviet Studies* (January 1979), 31(1):76–98.

Taagepera, Rein. "Estonia under Gorbachev: Stalinists, Autonomists, and Nationalists." *Occasional Papers on Baltic Political Action* (September 1988), no. 2/3, pp. 2–15.

Taagepera, Rein. *Softening Without Liberalization in the Soviet Union: The Case of Juri Kukk*. Lanham, Maryland: University Press of America, 1984.

Taagepera, Rein. "Soviet Collectivization of Estonian Agriculture: The Deportation Phase." *Soviet Studies* (July 1980), 32(3):379–397.

Taagepera, Rein. "Soviet Collectivization of Estonian Agriculture: The Taxation Phase." *Journal of Baltic Studies* (1979), 10(3):263–282.

Taagepera, Rein. "Soviet Documentation on the Estonian Pro-Independence Guerrilla Movement, 1945–1952." *Journal of Baltic Studies* (1979), 10(2):91–106.

Tauras, K. V. *Guerrilla Warfare on the Amber Coast*. New York: Voyager Press, 1962.

Thaden, Edward C., ed. *Russification in the Baltic Provinces and Finland, 1855–1914*. Princeton: Princeton University Press, 1981.

Thaden, Edward C. *Russia's Western Borderlands, 1710–1870*. Princeton: Princeton University Press, 1984.

Thompson, Dennis L. and Dov Ronen, eds. *Ethnicity, Politics, and Development*. Boulder, Colo.: Lynne Rienner, 1986.

Thompson, Terry L. and Richard Sheldon, eds. *Soviet Society and Culture*. Boulder, Colo.: Westview, 1988.

Thurston, Robert W. "Fear and Belief in the USSR's 'Great Terror': Response to Arrest, 1935–1939." *Slavic Review* (Summer 1986), 45(2):213–234.

Tillett, Lowell R. *The Great Friendship: Soviet Historians on the Non-Russian Nationalities*. Chapel Hill: University of North Carolina Press, 1969.

Tilly, Charles. "Does Modernization Breed Revolution?" *Comparative Politics* (April 1973), 5(3):425–447.

Tilly, Charles, ed. *The Formation of National States in Western Europe*. Princeton: Princeton University Press, 1975.

Tilly, Charles. *From Mobilization to Revolution*. New York: Random House, 1978.

Tiryakian, Edward A. and Ronald Rogowski, eds. *New Nationalisms of the Developed West*. Boston: Allen & Unwin, 1985.

Tishkov, V. "Narody i gosudarstvo." *Kommunist* (January 1989), no. 1, pp. 49–59.

Selected Bibliography

Tökés, Rudolf L., ed. *Dissent in the USSR: Politics, Ideology, and People.* Baltimore: Johns Hopkins University Press, 1975.

Tökés, Rudolf L. "Introduction: Comparative Communism: The Elusive Target." *Studies in Comparative Communism* (Autumn 1975), 8(3):211–229.

Trotsky, Leon. *The Russian Revolution.* Garden City, N.Y.: Doubleday, 1959.

Tucker, Robert C. "Communist Revolutions, National Cultures, and the Divided Nation." *Studies in Comparative Communism* (Autumn 1974), 7(3):235–245.

Tucker, Robert C., ed. *The Lenin Anthology.* New York: Norton, 1975.

Tucker, Robert C., ed. *The Marx-Engels Reader.* 2d ed. New York: Norton, 1972.

Tucker, Robert C. *Political Culture and Leadership in the Soviet Union: From Lenin to Gorbachev.* New York: Norton, 1987.

Tys-Krokhmaliuk, Yuriy. *UPA Warfare in Ukraine.* New York: Vantage Press, 1972.

UHVR v svitli postanov Velykoho Zboru ta inshykh dokumentiv z diial'nosty 1944–1951 rr. Munich: Zakordonni Chastyny OUN, 1956.

Ukraina: Suchasne i maibutnie: Zbirnyk stattei. New York: Proloh, 1959.

Ukraine: A Concise Encyclopedia. Toronto: University of Toronto Press, 1963.

Urban, Michael E. "Political Language and Political Change in the USSR: Notes on the Gorbachev Leadership." In Peter J. Potichnyj, ed., *The Soviet Union: Party and Society,* pp. 87–106. Cambridge: Cambridge University Press, 1988.

Vakar, Nicholas. *Belorussia: The Making of a Nation.* Cambridge: Harvard University Press, 1956.

Van Dyke, Vernon. *Political Science. A Philosophical Analysis.* Stanford: Stanford University Press, 1960.

Van Dyke, Vernon. "The Individual, the State, and Ethnic Communities in Political Theory." *World Politics* (April 1977), 29(3):343–369.

Vardys, V. Stanley and Romuald J. Misiunas, eds. *The Baltic States in Peace and War, 1917–1945.* University Park: Pennsylvania State University Press, 1978.

Vardys, V. Stanley, ed. *Lithuania Under the Soviets.* New York: Praeger, 1965.

Vardys, V. Stanley. *The Catholic Church, Dissent and Nationality in Soviet Lithuania.* Boulder, Colo.: East European Quarterly, 1978.

Varvartsev, Nikolai N. *Ukrainian History in the Distorting Mirror of Sovietology.* Kiev: Naukova Dumka, 1987.

V. I. Lenin, KPSS o sovetskom mnogonatsional'nom gosudarstve. Moscow: Izdatel'stvo politicheskoi literatury, 1981.

von Borcke, Astrid. *Unsichtbare Macht KGB.* Neuhausen-Stuttgart: Hänssler Verlag, 1987.

Selected Bibliography

von Hagen, Mark. "History and Politics Under Gorbachev: Professional Autonomy and Democratization." *Harriman Institute Forum* (November 1988), 1(11):1–8.

von Rauch, Georg. *The Baltic States: The Years of Independence. Estonia, Latvia, Lithuania, 1917–1940*. London: C. Hurst, 1974.

Walker, Edward W. "Totalitarianism, Comparative Politics, and Sovietology." Unpublished paper, March 1988.

Walker, Rachel. "Marxism-Leninism as Discourse: The Politics of the Empty Signifier and the Double Bind." *British Journal of Political Science* (April 1989), 19(2):161–189.

Walton, John. *Reluctant Rebels*. New York: Columbia University Press, 1984.

Waltz, Kenneth N. *Theory of International Politics*. New York: Random House, 1979.

Webb, Sidney and Beatrice Webb. *Soviet Communism: A New Civilization*. New York: Scribner's, 1936.

White, Stephen. *Political Culture and Soviet Politics*. London: Macmillan, 1979.

Wilkinson, Paul. *Social Movement*. New York: Praeger, 1971.

Williams, Colin H., ed. *National Separatism*. Cardiff: University of Wales Press, 1982.

Williams, Robert C. *Culture in Exile: Russian Émigrés in Germany, 1881–1941*. Ithaca, N.Y.: Cornell University Press, 1972.

Williams, Robin M., Jr. "Change and Stability in Values and Value Systems: A Sociological Perspective." In Milton Rokeach, ed., *Understanding Human Values*, pp. 15–46. New York: Free Press, 1979.

Wimbush, S. Enders, ed. *Soviet Nationalities in Strategic Perspective*. London: Croom Helm, 1985.

Wolf, Eric R. *Peasant Wars of the Twentieth Century*. New York: Harper & Row, 1969.

Wrong, Dennis H. *Skeptical Sociology*. New York: Columbia University Press, 1976.

Wuorinen, John H. *A History of Finland*. New York: Columbia University Press, 1965.

Young, Crawford. *The Politics of Cultural Pluralism*. Madison: University of Wisconsin Press, 1976.

Yurkevych, Myroslav. "Galician Ukrainians in German Military Formations and in the German Administration." In Yury Boshyk, ed., *Ukraine During World War II*, pp. 67–88. Edmonton, Alta.: Canadian Institute of Ukrainian Studies, 1986.

"Zaiavlenie po ukrainskomu voprosu." *Kontinent* (1977), no. 12, pp. 210–211; no. 14 (1977), p. 332.

Ziedonis, Arvids et al., eds. *Problems of Mininations: Baltic Perspectives*. San Jose, Calif.: Association for the Advancement of Baltic Studies, 1973.

Selected Bibliography

Zotov, V. "Natsional'nyi vopros: deformatsii proshlogo." *Kommunist* (February 1989), no. 3, pp. 79–89.

Z. "To the Stalin Mausoleum." *Daedalus* (Winter 1990), 119(1):295–344.

Zwick, Peter. *National Communism*. Boulder, Colo.: Westview, 1983.

Index

Index

Index

February Revolution, 134
Federalism: Austro-Marxism, 77-79, 179; constraint, 58; system breakdown, 99; in USSR, 84-85, 96, 170
Fergana Valley, 176
Feudalization, political, 65
Finland, 105-19
First Five-Year Plan, 95
Fleron, Frederic J., Jr., 3
Fragmentation, horizontal, 64
France, 120, 134, 168
Franz Josef, Emperor, 99, 160
Freedom House, 138
Free-rider problem, 36-38, 51; mobilization, 95; Slavic movements, 184; effect of solidarity, 66; influence of state, 42

Galich, A., 163
Galicia, 82, 107
Galiev, Sultan, 83
Galtung, Johan, 18, 20-21
Gaukroger, Stephen, 18-19, 34
Geertz, Clifford, 32, 40, 56, 149
Gellner, Ernest, 54-56, 79, 118, 157
Genetic fallacy, 55, 57
Georgia, 79, 97, 157; statehood, 105-19
Georgians, 96, 154, 156, 185
German Ideology, The, 73
Germans, 127, 135
Germany: Baltics, 112-13, 122; Belorussians, 113; collaboration, 128; expansion, 111; Lithuania and Ukraine, 126; occupations, 120; pre-World War I, 114; Soviet immigration, 134, 138; secret service, 126
Ghandi, Mohandas, 58
Glasnost: 71; bureaucracy, 177; consequences, 188, 191-92; dissent, 159; émigrés, 140; opposition, 144; political liberalization, 98; Sakharov, 147; Sovietology, 9
Glazunov, Ilia, 172
Gorbachev, Mikhail S.: ascension to power, 187; crisis, 188; dissent, 159; émigrés, 135, 141-42, 144-45; human

rights, 140; mafias, 179; mobilization, 190; national Communism, 88, 95, 98; political reform, 176; popular activism, 172; Russia, 172-73; Sakharov, 147; state, 178; Ukraine, 183
Gorbanevskaia, N., 163
Gorskii, V., 164
GPU, 5. *See also* KGB, NKVD
Great Britain, 74, 117; secret service, 126, 136; Soviet immigration, 135, 138
Great Leap Forward (China), 84
Great Terror, 136
Greece, 82, 120
Guevara, Che, 131
Gurr, Ted Robert, 188-89, 191

Habsburg Empire, 76-78, 107, 114, 160
Hagopian, Mark, 52
Hayes, Carlton J. H., 54
Hechter, Michael, 75
Hegemony, 55
Heller, Michael, 133
Helsingfors, 106, 112
Helsinki Groups, 135, 157
Helsinki Watch, 138
Hirschman, Albert O., 133
Hitler, Adolf, 164
Hohenzollern Germany, 114
Holism, 20-22, 34
Homans, George Caspar, 18
Hrushevs'kyi, Mykhailo, 110
Hume, David, 32, 36
Hungarians, 77
Huntington, Samuel P., 188-91
Hypercentralization, 62

Ibragimov, Galimdzhan, 88
Ibragimov, Veli, 88
Ideals: in collective action, 38-41, 44; concept, 161; nationalism, 52-53
Ideas, 46
Ideology: in collective action, 38-41, 44; nationalism, 52-53, guerrillas, 121; Soviet, 128
Imperialism, 162, 166, 169; Russian, 167, 173

Index

Index

Index

Index

Index